Never Known Questions
Five Decades Of The Residents

Never Known Questions
Five Decades Of The Residents

Ian Shirley

First published in Great Britain in 2015 by Cherry Red Books
(a division of Cherry Red Records), Power Road Studios, 114 Power Road,
London W4 5PY.

A CIP Catalogue record for this book is available from the British Library.

ISBN: 978-1-909454-26-2

Design/Layout: Nathan Eighty (nathan.eighty@gmail.com)
Edited by: Belvedere Sacremento

With thanks to Homer Flynn for photographs and The Residents' logo.
Back cover photograph courtesy of Dawid Laskowski

Contents

Author's Note

The original edition of this of this book was published in 1994, and it was subsequently updated in 1996. The word processor it was written upon – and the floppy discs used – are now museum pieces, so this new edition was written from scratch. In updating the book I have not only brought the story up to the present day, re-examined research materials and interviews conducted between 1992 and 1996, rewritten and revised but also interviewed or re-interviewed the following people, who were gracious enough to meet me, exchange emails or conduct interviews over the phone, and even on Facebook. The only way I did not conduct an interview was by text! So thanks to:

Homer Flynn, Don Hardy, Roland Sheehan, Bill Reinhardt, Pamela Zeiback, Brian Poole, Dave McKean, David Janssen, Nolan Cook, Molly Harvey, Hein Fokker, the legendary Paulie, Lorrie Murray, Maarten Postma, Chris Cutler, Andy Partridge, Peter Whitehead, Guido Randizo, Carla Fabrizio, Andreas Mathews, Toby Dammit, Robert Schilling, Matt Howarth, Grace Ellen Barkey, Daniel Miller, Laurie Amat, Joshua Raoul Brody, Dawid Laskowski and Tom Timony. There were a few cats that were, for one reason or other, not available for a stroke but such is life. Finally, special thanks to the John Peel family for archive access, Zoe Miller for access to Daniel Miller and Richard Anderson at Cherry Red for commissioning this book.

Finally, all errors and omissions are down to me - there are still some questions to which the answers are known by the eyeballs but withheld from us literary opticians.

Introduction

"You really have to accept that you are being removed. It got quite difficult for me towards the end. We were starting to play to ten thousand people from behind a screen and it was odd. I found it very difficult not to get out there in front of the audience. Occasionally the odd leg would come out from behind the screen because I wanted to be out there performing, as it is a very compelling feeling."

This quote is from an interview I conducted with Damon Albarn in 2004, in his role as the mastermind behind Gorillaz. At that time, Gorillaz had only recorded one album but already scored massive hits. Albarn was discussing his frustration at having to remain anonymous and in the background when the band undertook their first tour and, as the singer, he had to perform behind a screen, out of sight of the audience whilst his vocals were semi-synched to the graphics of the fictional band being projected on the other side. Ironically, when he conceived the idea of an imaginary band, Albarn and his co-conspirator Jamie Hewlett wanted their involvement to be secret and Gorillaz to be judged on its own musical and visual merits. Despite enjoying massive UK success with Blur, Albarn's record company just could not see the point. "Originally, originally, originally it was meant to be a total mystery who was behind it,' he told me, "but it just proved impossible to do that, so to get it off the ground Jamie and I had to do quite a lot of press and stuff, which was okay, but slightly compromised the original idea."

When it comes to The Residents, there has been no compromise. The band has operated under a self-imposed rule wherein they do not reveal their identities, and have held fast to that for the last forty years or more.

Of course, in this digital age that bubble is permeable, but the most thrilling thing about The Residents is not to wonder who is behind the mask or under the eyeballs but to buy into the mystery and mythology they've spun around themselves like candy-floss around a stick, from the intellectual concept of The Theory Of Obscurity to the cast of characters and collaborators that inhabit the domus of their work. To say that The Residents were pioneers would be an understatement. True, they were not the first band in the word to build their own recording studio, as they did in the early '70s, but they were certainly the first to do so and persevere when there was initially no interest in the music on the records they pressed. But they kept at it, and although they gained recognition it did not lead to untold riches but simply the ability to sustain a creative continuum that persists today. The Residents were one of the first bands to explore promotional films and videos, and one of the first to grasp the march of technology from tape recorders to samplers, where the most fundamental sonic tools could be used for personal musical expression. They were not afraid to put in long hours to learn how create sonic symphonies on two, four, eight and sixteen-track magnetic tape, or how to get the best two seconds out of an early sampler for use on albums or in live performance. At their most extreme in the early '80s, they were proto Pet Shop Boys when Neil Tennant was still earning a crust working at *Smash Hits* rather than experimental avant-garde pranksters working on the margins of the music business. The Residents even rode the roller coaster upwards to a level of commercial success in the late '70s that allowed them to sign like-minded artists to their own record label, then experienced the downward side when they were short circuited by the bursting of the dot com bubble when CD-ROM's proved not to be the next step forward in interactive media. Later on, Apple ruined their dream of strong revenues generated by podcasts.

Remaining anonymous behind an array of disguises and image changes has shifted attention onto the music and the visual element of their output. Away from the eyeballs, over the last forty four years The Residents have been just like any of us, marrying wives and husbands, having children and dealing with the attendant joys and worries that go with such emotional and financial responsibilities. Separating their personal lives from their work has seen the triumph of imagination, and has also allowed the band to remain seemingly ageless to old and new fans. The Residents have created their own audio and visual worlds, allowing hardcore fans and curious Millennials to either sample or immerse themselves in this creative *Weltanschauung*.

Comparing The Residents to other bands is pointless. There is, as you will come to understand, simply no other band like them. Comparisons with The Rolling Stones, Wire, Sun Ra, Devo, Laibach, The Beatles or Slipknot are fruitless as most of these artists enjoyed commercial and creative peaks before falling into formula or turning longevity into a winning globe touring package. Of course, in their decades of existence The Residents have had a few creative stumbles and released a few turkeys out of the Christmas season, but as a creative audio and visual force they continue to plough forward come what may, betraying a restless nature that will not stay still. I might admire Radiohead for their musical creativity and willingness to sell their music direct to their fans, but they did so from a citadel of financial well being with a worldwide fan base to sustain them. But, as experimental and wonderful as their music grew, they have not embraced the possibility of multi-media quite like Randy Rose, the Residents lead singer. Only he would undertake a one hundred and forty three part series of short video brocades that range from the fascinating to the truly bizarre.

The story of The Residents is about the fulfillment of artistic expression. Whilst the recent documentary *The Theory Of Obscurity* presents their history in visual form and serves as an entry point into their world, this book does so in the written form, although more people will probably see the film than read this book, just as more people will listen to the latest U2, Green Day or Muse album than listen to anything The Residents care to release. Those with a short attention span might listen to a few Residents songs on YouTube and then move onto something else, and in doing so ignore one of the most creative artists since Sun Ra. Musically they are poles apart but what they have in common with Sun Ra is this: The Residents have never let a lack of acceptance or sales prevent them from spending a lifetime of doing what they wanted. In doing that they have created a body of work that, due to its striking visual, audio and engaging nature, will never fade away.

Ian Shirley

The Obscurity Of Theory

"There is no true story of The Residents. You should know that right off. The secrets of The Residents will never be revealed by anyone but The Residents themselves, and so far they aren't saying much." - Matt Groening, 1979.

As a music journalist I have interviewed hundreds of musicians, written hundreds of features and knocked out a few books. Thus, tales of how bands got together fall into a number of categories. These range from school friends who shared a passion for music to those inspired by the shared epiphany of witnessing a live performance and wanting to get up on stage themselves. Then there is boredom, or meeting like-minded people through accident, design, an advert in a music paper or plain chance. Other artists have been through several bands before finding the right chemistry or chemicals to bind their atomic parts together. Some, like Orbital, The National and Oasis, even found an inbuilt advantage as membership included brothers, for whom it became a natural thing to work together.

When dealing with the formation of The Residents, though, everything hangs on a mixture of facts, disinformation and conjecture. After all, we are dealing with a band that, to the public at large, have traded on keeping their identities secret for over four decades since the appearance of the *Santa Dog* EP in 1972. Thus, during their subsequent career there has been more disinformation than truth. Even the garrulous Randy Rose, who *revealed* himself as the lead singer of The Residents in 2010, bends fact into fiction. The most effective purveyor of counterfactual early Residents history was *The Simpsons* creator Matt Groening, who, back in 1979, penned *The Official W.E.I.R.D Book of The Residents* as part of the band's early fan club. This slim book blended fact, fiction, myth and red herrings, and worked with many of the central tenets under which The Residents worked, such as The Theory Of Obscurity, which laid down the mantra that The Residents would conceal their identities so that people could focus on the music, art and visual presentation they created.

To be frank, when dealing with the self-styled most well-known obscure band in the world it's only right and proper that there remains a veil of secrecy over their origins. If this were a biography of Barack Obama, Bill Gates or Bono from U2, I would invest time and pages writing about ancestors or school days and looking for the seeds of what turned them towards success in politics, business or megalomania tempered by irony. Maybe one of The Residents wrote an essay at school about how they wanted to be a film director when they grew up, or another dreamed of making records or becoming the new Andy Warhol. Who knows? So, there are no dates of birth here, no records of High Schools or Colleges attended. No first kisses or mystical moments when a first guitar or tape-recorder was handed down by a hip older brother or found in a junk shop. As Hardy Fox of The Cryptic Corporation told a journalist in New Zealand in 1987, "I've heard mother say they can't brag – they seem to get over it."

What *is* documented is that they hailed from the Shreveport area of the American South, and once they got through College and worked for a short time they decided to head West. As Homer Flynn, also of The Cryptic Corporation, once stated, "The South in the '60s... was not a pleasant place for anybody who had any kind of offbeat point of view about life at all. So it's not particularly hard for me to see why they were glad to get out of the South." They went to San Francisco because one of them, or a friend, was already living out there. According to legend, their truck broke down in the residential San Francisco suburb of San Mateo. Life is too short to challenge this fact or wheedle the precise information out of Fox and Flynn. The key fundamental is that they settled here, eventually taking a low rent apartment en-masse.

They did not immediately begin making music. At this time in the late '60s, despite San Francisco being at the centre of the flower power and hippie movement, bearing witness to bands like Frank Zappa And The Mothers Of Invention or Captain Beefheart required money, and so to finance their lifestyle they got jobs. One of them, at one time, unloaded luggage from continental airliners and was a source of amusement to the others, because in order to retain his job he had to keep his hair short. Randy Rose once related a story at a Residents show about a coffin being unloaded from an aircraft which was dropped, causing the body to fall out. Was that a true story or disinformation based on fact? Apparently the others had jobs that ranged from selling insurance to working in a medical facility. According to Roland Sheehan, who actually lived with them in San Mateo during one summer, "Two of them worked as clerks in the filing room of a big hospital out there. Obviously they weren't getting rich but rent and all that at that time was much lower than it is now."

Sheehan had first met one of The Residents down South. "I grew up in a little town in the North of Louisiana, Dubach of all places, and me and my brother and a few other local guys were playing in a band. I met (one of them) at a mutual friend's house and we just clicked right off. He was three or four years older than me but age didn't make a difference, and he became the band's manager and did all of the artwork." The Resident concerned was studying art and was soon designing flyers to promote the band, as well as helping with mail-shots sent out in order to secure bookings for Sheehan's band. And, it is *not* the one you think....

The band were called The Alliance, and after a number of personnel changes and the passing of time they became reasonably well-accomplished, playing British invasion music and, as Sheehan played keyboards, even songs by The Doors at proms and other dates as far afield as Arkansas. The Alliance ended up breaking in a new studio in Ruston, Louisiana, and recorded a single – *Somewhere They Can't Find Me/(I'm Not Your) Stepping Stone* - whose sleeve design was the first manifestation of a Resident on a record. "We paid for it and made it locally, and needless to say it was not a *mean* seller," laughs Sheehan today. He also met The Residents' other creative friends at this time, and thus when Sheehan signed up for a three-month course to study recording techniques at San Francisco University he came out to stay with them in San Mateo.

By this time The Residents were already expressing their artistic natures. This ranged from making silkscreens, painting and even taking photos of themselves posing naked in boxcars on the railway sidings next to their apartment. I actually saw these photos when conducting research for the first edition of this book, and these particular Delta Nudes were full frontal. Maybe The Residents will release them one day – with strategically placed eyeballs to cover their modesty. According to Sheehan, music was just one string to their bows, "They were working regular jobs, and after work or at the weekends they would work on their art. By art I mean movies, music, painting whatever. In other words, they were working to pay the bills but what they really wanted to do was be in film and music."

Early musical activities were probably a natural extension of their interest in the progressive and chart music of this time, inspired by the bands they saw at venues like the Fillmore West, films like *2001 A Space Odyssey,* in which the soundtrack meshed perfectly with the visuals Stanley Kubrick put on screen, and the records they were buying. "We would go to Tower Records, which at that time was the biggest record shop out there, and we would spend hours there," recalls Sheehan. "They were buying things like world music, Beefheart, Zappa and Sun Ra, but they would also listen to The Grateful Dead, Janis Joplin and Neil Young. So it was a wide range, not just one or two genres. I would also buy world music - I remember buying Olatunji - but I didn't buy Captain Beefheart or the Mothers. But they were buying all that kind of stuff. They bought albums I had never heard of in a place that was like Walmart with thousands and thousands of records, and a lot of them were promo copies. We would walk out with armloads – literally armloads of records. If you paid ninety nine cents for an album and it is not very good, so what?"

Perhaps at this time they considered forming a band in the traditional sense – guitar, drums, bass, keyboards and vocals – and writing songs. What needs to be stressed is that even at this point some of The Residents could play musical instruments. You see, some of them had been in bands during their days at College in the South and, whilst not technically proficient, must have scratched or honked their way through a number of garage songs, chart hits and maybe a James Brown number or two - Randy once gushed on stage about briefly meeting the Godfather Of Soul when he performed a show at Lafayette, Louisiana in 1965.

Thus, when they turned their minds to making music there was some competence there. And ideas. *Lots and lots of ideas.*

Santa Dog

"There were always girls. Back then a drawl was a great way to attract a girl if you were from Louisiana out there in California." - Roland Sheehan.

They were not a band, they did not have a name but they began making music together for their own amusement around 1969. Crucially, at this stage they were less interested in performing live than in recording. An alleged Resident once related that "The tape recorders were more important than the instruments" and Cryptic Corporation spokesman Jay Clem told *Keyboard* magazine in 1982 that, "...they had something like a two-track and a single track and they just mixed down and mixed down." Not that The Residents would agree with Clem's statement, as one of them later commented on this comment, "The information is technically embarrassing. That's what happens when accountants are allowed to talk to the press."

The way their music was played and recorded at this time was informal. Due to the constraints of day jobs and social commitments, they only jammed on some evenings and at weekends. Sometimes these sessions were highly structured, and they might try to cover a song or work out an original idea that someone had brought along, just like any other band. At other times they would just jam and see if anything came out of it, even experimenting with not allowing musicians to play their default instrument as, "It would stimulate new ideas you would not have had otherwise."

Of course, who these musicians were remains a moot point. Although the core of the group who would go on to become The Residents was present there would be also be a number of other people involved, as Roland Sheehan confirms, "There would be parties and there would be musicians. I first met Snakefinger at one of these and we jammed together. The Residents would pick up a drum or whatever was laying around or basically make their own (instruments). There were other folks around who were able to play the guitar, bass or drums. As I remember I was the only one playing the keyboard back in those days as most folks wanted to be rock and roll guitar players for some reason." Another person who got involved with the proto-Residents around this time was Pamela Zeiback, "I was the girlfriend of one of their roommates. I remember the place was near the railroad tracks, and one of them had white sheets hanging from the ceiling breaking up the rooms into small spaces. It was really cool. I used to jam and sing with them in that place a lot."

There was, however, a definite decision at some point to start recording on a reel-to-reel recorder, and parts of these jam sessions were taped - the fact that Sheehan spent three months studying recording techniques in an eight-track studio at the University of San Francisco may have helped them with this. The *Rusty Coathangers For The Doctor* tape was recorded around June 1970, and *The Ballad Of Stuffed Trigger* in August of the same year (with Sheehan present). Both tapes have since taken on legendary status amongst Residents fans and collectors as they document some of their earliest recordings. Of course, this was not The Residents but a group of friends having fun, and it sounds like it – a segment of the song *Rusty Coathangers* – acoustic guitar and vocals - has seen the light of day, and Roland Sheehan played a crucial part in its genesis. "So, I was there with those guys one hot afternoon," he told me, "and looked out of the window and there was an old pickup truck. It was a 1953 or 1954 pickup, real rusty. But what caught my eye was that there had to be thousands of rusty coathangers in that truck, so I called over other guys and said, "You all got to see this." We were bored and did not have anything better to do, so I picked up my guitar and there was a two-track reel-to-reel tape recorder there - as I recall we had one microphone – and we began to write a song about rusty coathangers. That evolved into *Rusty Coathangers For The Doctor*."

The Ballad Of Stuffed Trigger is another early track that has seen the light of day, and Sheehan also had a hand in this song, "It may have been that same afternoon, or a day or two later, and we got talking about Roy Rogers' horse that had died. Roy had taken the horse to a taxidermist and had Trigger stuffed! So there again it was one of those things, a fluke really, and we wrote a song called *The Ballad Of Stuffed Trigger*." Jay Clem later said of these tapes, "The first two are highly documentary in nature. Most of them consisted of conversations, but there *was* some actual music." Actually, there was a lot of music on both tapes, which document many jam sessions where the players were drunk, stoned or just having an exceedingly good time. You can hear that the tape recorder was usually switched on just as songs were about to be performed or when everyone was working up to play something, although on some occasions a track just starts.

Both tapes run for around thirty minutes and the conversations are usually playful banter between several people. They include some great lines like, "Play something with some rhythm to it" or "Who wants some dope?" which give a great feel for the time. Musically there are spaced out jams and cover versions of songs like *Let It Be*, *Satisfaction*, *Bringing In The Sheaves* and *House Of The Rising Sun* woven into other tracks.

Considering that The Residents have been very thorough in releasing most of their music recorded over the last forty four years, after hearing these tapes it's quite understandable that they've kept them under physical and digital lock and key. It's not bad music – hell, it is great to listen to! – but it is Pre-Residential, and as their technical and professional prowess improved over the following years this music was seen as part of their musical adolescence and, for them, best forgotten.

Probably also best forgotten are some of the antics the group got up to at this point, which range from the bizarre to the downright hilarious. Even today, Roland Sheehan recalls some very weird scenes from inside the goldmine, "I remember one girl, I walked by this room one night and she was laying on the bed, she did not have a stitch of clothes on but she was wrapped up with a big snake. Now look, I'm from Louisiana – that's stuff you don't see every day. It was just wrapped around her and (one of them) was fully clothed on the edge of the bed talking to her as if it was no big deal. So, I walked by trying to be cool and said, "How you doing? My name is Roland." And all of the time I'm looking at that big snake."

On another occasion, Sheehan got the opportunity to look at another snake – of the trouser variety. "I tagged along with a few of the guys and their girlfriends and we pulled over in the woods somewhere. They were going to make a porn movie! You have to understand this was not a professional deal, they just decided, "What the hell, we'll make a porn movie." I tag along and they throw a blanket on the ground and one of them has an eight or sixteen millimeter film camera and this guy and girl get out of their clothes and start getting after it! I'm standing there thinking, "Yeah, now I can tell everybody I've been involved in making a porn movie." It was real short and the processing of the film was not very good because they probably did it themselves - they did not want to take it down to the local Walmart to have the film processed for obvious reasons. They never did anything with it, but that is the kind of stuff they did just for the hell of it. They had nothing to do, the girl was ready and willing and so off we went."

Despite their primitive recording apparatus, when they were not jamming with friends the proto-Residents were taking their music very seriously and beginning to write and record songs. Whatever disinformation was subsequently put out as a smokescreen in later years, this collective of musicians began to actively pursue a recording contract.

It's important to remember that these were not eighteen year old boys but young men in their early to mid-twenties who began to focus their energies, resources and finances into various forms of artistic expression. Thus their next tape, completed around September 1970, was deemed good enough and displayed enough interesting ideas and songs to send to Warner Brothers Records, complete with silkscreened cover art, a track listing and liner notes – this was aptly entitled *The Warner Bros. Album.*

Crucially, they sent a copy to Hal Halverstadt who, as Marketing Director at Warner Brothers subsidiary Reprise, promoted Captain Beefheart – someone who they greatly admired. Indeed, later in 1971 Halverstadt booked Beefheart's groundbreaking Dada-esque *Lick My Decals Off, Baby* commercial onto American TV, who refused to show it as it was simply too weird. Although he was not a talent scout, The Residents thought that Halverstadt would, at least, lend a sympathetic ear. Halverstadt mailed the tape back a few months later with a rejection as well as a brief note "AXPp – A for ariginality (sic); X for Xecution: P for Presentation and p for Potential." Whether he told them to keep at it or tighten their grip on their day jobs is not documented.

But the most significant consequence of this encounter came on the return envelope. According to legend, they'd sent in the tape anonymously with a return address, so Halverstadt returned the tape to "The Residents". They'd been toying with the idea of a name for some time – New Beatles being one of many – and would later decide to function under the "collective" name, The Residents.

For years *The Warner Brothers Album* was the Holy Grail for Residents fans. That The Residents and The Cryptic Corporation let fans know it existed in the late '70s and refused to release the tapes made it even worse. But, although it has not been officially released in its original form, in the 1970s copies of the tapes were made for radio specials and subsequently the music has been bootlegged. You can understand why Halverstadt rejected it - it makes Captain Beefheart, and even Frank Zappa, sound like the Everly Brothers. *The Warner Bros. Album* reveals a wide range of styles, with some tracks lasting a couple of minutes whereas others are mere fragments of ideas and musical interludes. It is, however, the nascent sound of The Residents, from a skewed version of The Beatles' *Strawberry Fields Forever* to the bonkers but beautiful *Baby Skeletons And Dogs*. The deliciously named *Jimi Hendrix Dildo* is pert, and *Oh Yeah Uhh Cop Shu Bop* is a wonderful doo-wop parody. *Love Theme From A Major Motion Picture* is very short but, along with other tracks on the LP, introduces the world to the 'famous' Residents piano, and demonstrates that at least one of them had some classical chops. It's interesting to imagine what would have happened if Warner Brothers had taken the plunge - if released as it was the album would have been the most extreme and un-commercial recording the label had ever released.

By this this time, Philip Lithman and the mysterious N. Senada had appeared on the scene. Lithman was a guitar player and singer from England, influenced by American blues music, who had played in various London club bands like Juniors Blues Band and Smiley with little success. He'd met Pamela Zeiback and her friend Margaret Smik when they were travelling in Europe and came to San Francisco to experience the counter culture. As for Nigel Senada, Lithman had apparently met him in the forests of Bavaria recording bird songs, and brought him to San Francisco with him. Here, Lithman met and became friends with The Residents, and was soon jamming with them.

At one of these jam sessions, Lithman was told to play the trombone, an instrument he'd never played in his life. That there was a trombone at the session shows how diverse the sonic palette was, and Lithman later related in an interview in 1986 what it was like to play with The Residents at this time.

"When we first met we were living in this place which was divided into cubicles with bits of plastic. After we'd jammed all day, I'd climb into my little black lagoon and they would still be at it. It was an exploratory time when we were feeling the possibilities of what we could do. We put ourselves in all sorts of mental conditions – feeling fresh, tired, using drugs – to see what the outcome would be under those conditions."

As for Nigel Senada...

What is important about Senada is not whether he exists or not but that The Residents used him to expound some philosophical views on their music and how it was put together. Because of a convenient inability to speak or write English, there is no record on tape or in writing of Senada explaining his concept of music. There was, however, a recording made on 30th October 1970 of a hilarious Lithman radio interview with KHSC-FM Arcata, California, where the only thing that seems to be keeping him not laughing as he relates his colleague's theory of Phonetic Organisation is the tongue in his cheek (Senada was allegedly sitting next to Lithman in the studio). There follows a 'demonstration' by the duo, a furious performance of a piece entitled *Cantata fur der Saxophonen Un Violinen*, a free form improvisation that starts nowhere, goes nowhere and ends nowhere. Perhaps most fascinating about this is not the music or the interview but how they actually got on the radio in the first place!

Whether Senada existed or not is a matter of speculation. However, when dealing with The Residents there is no escaping his Theory

Of Phonetic Organisation. Over the next ten years it was presented as the cornerstone of how they approached and produced their music, and as the band were faceless and did not do interviews it became a fundamental part of The Residents' mythos. Although Senada never appeared, this did not stop the members of The Cryptic Corporation speaking on his behalf.

The best explanation, to my mind, appeared early on in *Vacation* magazine, when one of them stated, "Phonetic organisation was developed at that time. The theory actually applied itself to lyric writing more than it did to the music. It was a point of view by which the contents of the words were made subordinate to the sound of the words as they put themselves together. This applied itself to the music sometimes because The Residents would write the words first, then try to create music to follow the lyrics."

When you listen to the early Residents records this actually makes sense. One of the key elements is the intricate vocal arrangements, which range from deranged to sophisticated wordplay and forms of vocal expression. It's easy to imagine tracks like *Never Known Questions* and *Laughing Song* starting off as vocal ideas to which music was added. This is speculation on my part, and in most instances things may have worked in the usual musical fashion, with pieces of music being composed first and then lyrics being added later, but the ability to lay down music on tape and experiment was a key factor. "To their mind anything was music," recalls Roland Sheehan, "it did not matter if it had melody or no melody. In fact one of them told me early on that the whole point is to prove that you don't need to be able to play music in order to play music. That always hung with me."

The first documented live performance of this San Mateo collective was on October 1971, an audition night at the Boarding House in San Francisco when anyone could get up on stage and perform. Thankfully, even at this stage there was a pathological desire to document everything, so this appearance was not only recorded but also partially filmed on very rudimentary black and white videotape. The introduction by the singer/sax player sets the scene to perfection...

"Hello everybody, how y'all doing tonight? Well, here we are again. Got a nice little show all worked up for ya. Well, I think you're gonna like it. We got all kind of little songs for ya, gonna have a few nice dances for ya, it's just going to be a wonderful, wonderful show. Yes, yes, yes you're going to be crazy about it. Well, we're going to start now with a little song all about evil and wicked spirits. You think you gonna like that? Eh? Eh? EEEEHHHHHH?"

The song itself sounds like a group exorcism, full of screams and petrified vocals, and the only musical accompaniment is what sounds like wind or rudimentary white noise. The piece progresses into a wildly improvised saxophone solo accompanied by some circus thumping of a big bass drum, and ends to complete and utter silence from an obviously stunned audience. The ice is only broken by one of the people on stage – future Cryptic Official Jay Clem - starting off some cheerleading around the theme of "N Senada! N Senada!" The performance continues with chants, more saxophone, Phil Lithman on violin and a song by close friend and collaborator Peggy Honeydew (aka Margaret Smik).

Clocking in at less than twenty-five minutes, the performance ends to wild applause from an audience of what sounds like forty people. Photographs and video footage show a tiny stage crammed full of people, with performers sporting long hair, sunglasses and beards. One significant photo was taken of Lithman playing his violin - in this picture one of his fingers seems boneless, wriggling in the air like a demented snake. One of The Residents commented upon this 'Snakefinger' and Lithman, believing that any decent guitar player had to have a good nickname, accepted this baptism with good grace. Thus a legend really was born.

This live performance formed part of their next demo tape, which was also, I assume, rejected by record companies. Entitled *Baby Sex*, the cover art was a rather unfortunate picture taken from a Danish porn magazine of a woman fellating a baby. As with *The Warner Bros. Album*, this tape has not been officially released but has been bootlegged online, and it pulls aside the curtain to reveal what The Residents were producing in their San Mateo studio at the time. Led Zeppelin's *Whole Lotta Love* becomes *Whole Lotta Dick* and features some Page-like guitar pyrotechnics, whilst Frank Zappa's *King Kong* is given a great rendition by Snakefinger. Elsewhere, *Eloise* and *Kamikaze Lady* reveal that what was to later become The Residents' early trademark sound was already coming together. *Eloise* revolves around a fantastic multi-tracked trombone and saxophone riff over which a gruff, hysterical voice delivers a lyrical poem that had been performed without music a year previously at a private party, whilst *Kamikaze Lady* is carried by another guttural Beefheartish vocal, heartbeat bass drum and tape effects. On another track a classical record is 'sampled' as a backing track. To my mind, *Baby Sex* is less focused than the Warner Bros. tape but equally compelling.

Around this time, Snakefinger returned to England. The exact circumstances concerning his departure are vague, although there exists a tasteful silkscreened poster announcing his wedding at 3pm on the 31st October 1970 (Halloween). According to sources close to the band the ceremony did take place but, in keeping with the relaxed attitude of the time, nobody thought about going up to City Hall and formally notifying the relevant authorities of the union. This may account for Snakefinger's sudden departure - his visa may have expired. He returned to England to form Chilli Willi And The Red Hot Peppers and tour like a demon. As for the mysterious N Senada, according to legend he simply vanished into the thin arctic air of Greenland. Which would be of great convenience later on...

In 1972 The Residents moved into the heart of San Francisco. They rented an extremely long, rectangular two-storey building in Sycamore Street, in the run down Mission District, which had previously been the offices of a magazine called *Western Kennel World*. "When The Residents took over that building," states Homer Flynn, "the whole front of the building contained a massive printing press." This was sold for scrap, although as the press was so large it took one man several weeks to remove all of the machinery and metal with a sledgehammer. "So what you had was two floors, and the top floor for this printing magazine had been the offices and dark room for photography and making printing plates and stuff like that," Flynn continues, "The Residents made it almost like a commune situation, and put bedrooms, a living room and a kitchen all upstairs, built their studio downstairs and had like a warehouse space at the front once the printing press was torn out." They looked at Sycamore Street as somewhere they could fully express themselves.

Around this time Sheehan moved back down South. It would be wrong to say that he left the band as, at this time, there really was not a band to speak of. He simply moved away from their artistic grouping. He recalls that, "I left when they moved into San Francisco. It was a two-storey building, and they lived on the top floor and the bottom was where the business used to be. They had lots and lots of room, which later became the movie and recording area. I left right about the time they were beginning to get into that in a really big way. It was partly emotional problems and partly I was not really into what they were doing. I told them that I did not have the vision that they did. I never really understood at the time that it was not music they were after, it was more the art – not the painting type – but more towards theatrics and film." As for his musical contribution, Sheehan is very modest, "I was up there in the formative period and they have given me a lot of credit for getting them off the ground, but I don't know if I deserve any - I was just there and knew how to play," he reflects today. Although he returned to the South, Sheehan would, for the next few years, still come out to visit his friends as they evolved into The Residents, and as late as 1977 recalls going to see David Lynch's *Eraserhead* with them in San Francisco.

At this point, the proto-Residents decided to record and produce a record. Their attempts to secure a recording contract had floundered, and so they decided that if nobody else was going to release their music then they would do it themselves. A statement of artistic independence, *Santa Dog* was a double pack 7" single that also served as a Christmas card and a tool to promote the music that they were recording. It was, in effect, an early marketing move – a play for attention and something physically tangible to show for two years of musical activity. The gatefold, hand-printed cover was a silkscreen of an original photograph of a dog in Christmas clothing, complete with beard. According to Homer Flynn, "The original *Santa Dog* image came from a photo that The Residents found in that building." The innards featured a very George Cruickshank-like drawing illustrating the track titles, and the message 'Seasons Greetings – Residents Uninc.' The record label was named Ralph Records, the name stemming from an in-joke – going outside to call Ralph meant to vomit. Ralph was also a reference to a pet dog. Indeed, The Residents always regarded Ralph Records as their 'pet' label.

The four tracks – *Fire*, *Explosion*, *Lightning* and *Aircraft Damage* – were given random names taken from an insurance policy (remember, one of the group is alleged to have sold insurance) and attributed to four different bands, namely Ivory And The Braineaters, Delta Nudes, The College Walkers and Arf & Omega (featuring The Singing Lawn Chairs). It should be stressed that The Residents did not exist at this time, but each person had their own group for the record and the membership of each band was the same.

Around five hundred sets of *Santa Dog* were manufactured, although damage to some of the sleeves meant that only four hundred complete sets could be made up. Even then they were hardly perfect. Many of the records were packed and shrink-wrapped before the varnish that was applied to seal the ink and give the sleeves a high gloss finish had dried. Consequently, most of the gatefold sleeves were stuck together. Three hundred sets were mailed out - "special fourth class rate sound recordings" - to friends, record companies, radio stations and people whom The Residents admired, such as Frank Zappa. President Nixon's copy was returned – he had moved - and his personalised copy was later given away in a competition.

The response to *Santa Dog* was hardly enthusiastic - it generated no record company interest and friends and family either enjoyed the music or thought it was a seasonal joke. No wonder - the music on *Santa Dog* is very experimental. *Fire* – the beginning of the *Santa Dog* series of recordings - is the only track that utilises what can be considered a song structure, and even this is twisted into disconnect. The other three tracks are a series of tape splices collaged into short sonic suites. *Explosion* is an instrumental which starts with the melody of *Jingle Bells* before getting really interesting, whilst *Lightning* opens with almost a soul jazz organ prowl before moving on – like *Aircraft Damage* – to include vocal orchestration, chants, conversation, screams and scraps of poetry. There is also a beautiful lyrical madness of a kind you just don't find anywhere else, notably the "Kick a cat! Kick a cat? Kick a cat today!" line, which develops into an insane chorus, screamed and crooned.

None of these tracks could have been realised without the overdubbing techniques allowed by the tape recorder. Even at this stage there was someone in the group who was not only growing technically proficient in recording and overdubbing but in arrangement and understanding how music - even music this experimental – could hang together so beautifully. The final product is musically disturbing, unsettling, and avant-garde, yet strangely compelling. Even at this stage it sounded unlike anything else being recorded.

Thus the recording career of the proto-Residents commenced. They would not release another record on Ralph Records for two years, and in the meantime would devote their energies to a project advertised on the perimeter of the gatefold sleeve of *Santa Dog*: a full-length feature film.

Vileness Fats

"They did not have the technical expertise about lighting or anything. When I would say they needed more key light or more fill lighting they thought that I was getting too bossy. They did not like being told what to do so I just went back to smoking dope." - Bill Reindhardt.

Once they got settled in at Sycamore Street, The Residents started work on a very ambitious project – a full-length film shot on video. That they knew literally nothing about the complex world of film production was a minor detail, and, as with their music, attempting to make a physical reality of their ideas was the driving force. The fact that they were not advanced musicians or studio engineers had not stopped them recording and releasing music – similarly they were not filmmakers, but they would attempt their own feature length production. The area where the printing press had one been was converted into a film set, and working within the limitations of that space meant that they had to develop a plot to fit in with their surroundings. As the ceilings were eleven to twelve feet high, and in order to give the illusion of space, they decided to base their story in a kingdom of one-armed midgets. The kingdom was originally to be called Vileness Flats, but it was decided to remove the L and call the film *Vileness Fats.*

Initially, at least, the group decided to meet all the production costs themselves. Exercising full creative control over all aspects of the project, they also designed and constructed the sets and made or hired the costumes. Although they owned a 16mm film camera (and, as we saw earlier, had shot some footage with it), a decision was made to film everything on half-inch black and white videotape as they'd bought video cameras and recorders second-hand from a local TV station. They also bought lights from a friend in Los Angeles for $1000.

Videotape, as they saw it, was the coming medium, and also served another important function - as none of the group knew anything about film production, videotape would allow them to see the results of what they had filmed straight away, like rewinding and playing back musical tape. Thus lighting and camera angles could be adjusted and retakes done immediately. The only downside was that the sets and costumes were vibrant and colourful but the playback on tape, and the final film, would be in black and white. Perhaps they had the great films of Fritz Lang in mind.

Although *Vileness Fats* was produced by the group, other people were involved, including friends and girlfriends. Indeed, one actress played such a major role that she was at one time promised 5% of any gross profits arising from the film – in writing! Friends, and even casual acquaintances, were roped in to help out as extras. Even though he didn't know them at the time, musician Joshua Raoul Brody recalls a chance telephone conversation leading to an invitation to "...come down to the studio this weekend. We'll put you in the movie." That was the sort of offer nobody could refuse, and he describes the set up at Sycamore Street at that time, "It was a small room that had most of their electronic gear and some instruments, acoustically tiled, and next to that... the rest of the garage was their storage for props and stuff, and also the film set of *Vileness Fats*. The upstairs was living quarters, which again is another thing that attracted me to their work. It was just more heavily decorated than anything I have ever seen in my life. I felt, these guys know what they're doing... I was just a struggling musician at the time who didn't really think about the bigger picture, these guys not only thought about the bigger picture but had an idea of the bigger picture they wanted to put out."

Brody ended up playing a waiter, serving huge broccoli heads to the Mayor of Vileness Fats during the banquet scene, and was later to assist The Residents on some of their recording projects, as well as establishing a successful career as a musician, composer and arranger.

Another insight into *Vileness Fats* comes from William Reinhardt, program director at the Portland radio station KBOO. "I had the job of going through all of the music that came into the station and decided what was to get played or thrown out. The Residents sent in *Santa Dog* and I really noticed it as we usually got sent LPs rather than EPs." Amazingly, one of the mailed out copies of *Santa Dog* had hit the right person, and Reinhardt played it on a weekend show he helmed called *The Radio Lab*, becoming the first person to play a Residents record on the radio. This led to communication with the group and the development of a friendship, and Reinhardt visited them in San Francisco every year from 1972. "They were really jazzed because I was the only person they knew who had played their record on the radio, so they welcomed me in and treated me like family. I hung with them that summer when I was visiting San Francisco, and I went back every year to hang out with them."

Thus Reinhardt got a peek into the world of the production of *Vileness Fats* that he can still recall today. "The time I remember most was the first year I was there and they were just building sets mostly," he says. "They used a lot of Mylar and cardboard, and I used to love to get stoned and play on the set. I was younger then and pretty immature, frankly." Reinhardt also knew how to use a camera and took some photos of the sets when he visited in 1972 and 1973 (which were posted on YouTube in 2008) that offer a fascinating peek behind the curtain of the production of the film. This small batch showed the vibrancy and colour of the sets and costumes, and that the video cameras were wheel mounted. Reinhardt would also socialise with future Cryptic Corporation members Jay Clem, Hardy Fox, Homer Flynn and John Kennedy, "John Kennedy was never around. He was always on some trek," Reinhardt laughs, "he was a real outdoorsman. I remember when they showed me the Sycamore Street studio there was a huge kayak talking up the *Vileness Fats* set because John was such an avid watersports guy."

It was around this time that Graeme Whifler also came into The Residents' orbit. In 1971 he was studying film at San Francisco State University and living in a small apartment in the Fillmore District when an old friend from High School contacted him out of the blue as he needed a place to stay for a few days. "Around the second day (he) suggested I go with him to visit some pals of his who had a sort of four guy art commune over in the Mission District. He told me that I'd probably really like these guys, that we had a lot in common and, who knew, I might end up collaborating with them on something someday."

One reason Whifler's friend was such a frequent visitor to The Residents' address was because he was also a drug dealer, and, "He had secretly hidden his one pound stash (of cocaine) in their sprawling warehouse; a fact none of us knew at the time." Whilst his friend went off to check up on his investment portfolio, Whifler got on well with The Residents, who, at that time, also needed help painting their ceiling black. As Whifler knew "How to swing a paint brush" he got involved. Not only did he become a firm friend but he gained a real insight into how driven the group were, "At the time they were toiling even harder than I was, doing the lowest level jobs at a San Francisco teaching hospital. I mean, they were all making just a few bucks an hour, but every two weeks all their pay checks were pooled to support this communal thing they were envisioning. There was a lot of sharing; ideas, dreams, food, chores, intoxicants and lovers."

As The Residents had day jobs, filming took some time. As with their music, they could only work on *Vileness Fats* during evenings and weekends, and rotas were drawn up so that one person would cook each night of the week whilst the others worked downstairs, making sets and props or filming scenes. Pooled income was allocated to buy food, equipment, props and tape for the video machines, and one of them actually made the ultimate sacrifice and sold his sports car to help with the finances, photographing the $1,200 cash received. They even produced *Vileness Fats* stationary.

As the film was made on a shoestring, one set had to be taken down before another one could be built, meaning production was spread across a few years, which shows the intense devotion the collective invested in the project. Bear in mind, the group were also working and recording music in their studio, so were fully deployed in an artistic capacity. Roland Sheehan vaguely recalls that he came to visit at one point and, "I did see part of the early cut of it, but it was made when I was not there and I was not involved in that."

Fortunately, Graeme Whifler saw much more, "*Vileness Fats* was sort of like a scene out of the movie/play *The Music Man,* where group hypnosis convinced everybody a movie was being made. They pooled hours over weeks creating elaborate sets and costumes, and then on a given weekend all their friends from the hospital where they worked would come over to play a part and the taping would begin. So much time, so much effort. Each shoot was like a celebration; a party where guests worked hard to make the dream of *Vileness Fats* come true. And then the sweet payoff after a shoot, we would retire to the carpet room to watch the video. And that was the problem, all that work was recorded onto the most primitive black and white home video, awful stuff really. Fun to have instant playback of sorts after a day's work, but sad to think it was for naught."

Eventually, after four years, the film was abandoned. What went wrong? For one thing, it became increasingly obvious that the format was obsolete, and that there was no way that black and white videotape could be transferred onto 35mm film stock as originally envisioned. In fact, the only 35mm images were stills taken by Graeme Whifler as, "I tried to document the entire process on 35mm color slide stock. That's one reason I helped light the sets, so they could be recorded on film, albeit still and silent." In addition, despite all the painstaking efforts the film was nowhere near being finished. Only 60% of the script had been filmed, and that had taken up at least fourteen hours of videotape. The fact that there had never been a completed script no doubt hampered filming - apparently dialogue would usually be written shortly before or during shooting to keep things spontaneous.

The small studio was also restrictive, and, with each hand-painted set having to be totally removed before another could be erected, progress was slow. The nightclub scene, for example, took an entire year to construct and film. Functioning as a commune had not helped - direction was general rather than specific, and no-one was in overall control in the sense that a director would be on a normal feature film. Thus, as John Kennedy told me, "Progress was slowed and denuded by the number of discussions over what should be done, what was desired and what was to be accomplished."

The group would also not take kindly to outside input from opinionated visitors like Reinhardt, "They were doing *Vileness Fats* and I would sit there laughing at them for being so clumsy. I used to sit there getting stoned and watching them try to operate a video camera. Frankly, it was pretty amateurish, and I used to tell them "God damn, man! Use some *close ups!*" They were shooting everything in wide angle on a muddy one inch recorder." The film was officially abandoned in February 1976, after *The Third Reich and Roll* was released.

In later years, as the success and artistic reputation of The Residents grew, the failure of *Vileness Fats* became woven into the rich tapestry of myth and legend surrounding the band. Photographs adorned album sleeves, and promotional material gave fans tantalising glimpses of what might or might not have existed. Ironically, the very technology that led to the abandonment of the project later allowed it to twitch back to life when, in 1984, video enhancement technology first allowed some of the better footage to see the light of day. What was released on videotape that year as *Whatever Happened To Vileness Fats?* was hardly representative of the entire film, but it did allow us a glimpse of what went on in that studio during those four years. The half hour video focuses upon Arf and Omega, a Siamese twins tag wrestling team, from their arrival in *Vileness Fats* until their death in the nightclub. There is no audible dialogue on the revised version - which is now on YouTube - only The Residents' soundtrack, which makes any attempt to follow it great fun.

However, as a visual spectacle, and even in black and white, the footage is overwhelming. The sets and costumes are stunning, particularly the interior of The Cave, which is a womb of black balloons. Whatever the technical shortcomings on show – and there are many – there is no doubting the amount of effort that went into creating this strange and compelling surrealistic world, and no opportunity is wasted to fill the camera with strong and arresting visual imagery. Perhaps the highlight is the nightclub scene, which opens with a band playing an original piece from the *Baby Sex* tapes entitled *Eloise*. Trombones, trumpets and an accordion are played by three men in silver masks and black tuxedos, and there is a stunning and visually arresting performance from the lead singer, who plays saxophone before singing and ending the song with an extreme close up. This sets the scene for the arrival of Arf and Omega, who then enjoy the warbled vocals of the following act – Penny Honeydew – so much that they invite her to sit at their table. Much the worse for wear from drink, the twins fall into quarreling over their affections. After much arm wrestling, Honeydew produces two swords and they fight to the death, watched by the nightclub crowd. Arf kills Omega and therefore himself.

The film was intended to be a musical parody.

Meet The Residents

"We heard that George or Ringo had a copy of 'Meet The Residents' but who the fuck knows?" - Jay Clem.

Although *Vileness Fats* took up a lot of time and energy, The Residents still made time to record music in the studio they'd put together in Sycamore Street and aptly named El Rapho, in deference, perhaps, to the iconoclastic Jazz/Free/Space music composer Sun Ra, who called his own studio El Saturn. They had a reel-to-reel tape recorder, instruments and a tremendous amount of ideas. Jay Clem, who was resident at Sycamore Street at this time, later stated that, "They worked on the tapes which later became the record just to take breaks from the filming. They never thought it would become a record. Later when they realised that it was going to be released they added some extra material."

Thus, on 1st April 1974, The Residents issued their first long-playing record, aptly entitled *Meet The Residents*, on their own Ralph Records label.

Meet The Residents was the group's first real full-length musical statement. It should be stressed that the *Warner Bros.* and *Baby Sex* tapes, despite their album length, were demos recorded with a mind to securing a record deal. *Meet The Residents*, on the other hand, was a full length LP and sequenced as such. Despite the poor audio quality – the record was poorly mastered and in mono – it laid the firm foundations of what was to become The Residents' trademark sound - textured music, multi-tracked organic progression, punchy horns and a wide range of instrumentation and percussive orchestral effects, as well as a gumbo of vocal styles. Unlike *Santa Dog*, the music on *Meet The Residents* was confident in both structure and composition.

"None of that stuff was done in a real recording studio," states Homer Flynn today, "they were taking and adapting developing technology (tape-recorders) as fast as it was growing. So their first four-track recording was recorded on four channels, but it was two stereo pairs, so you could not record the four channels separately. What you had to do was record two and then you could record two more and then you could mix those together and then you could record two more and mix those together, so that process of mixing down and recording more, mixing down and recording more... that is a very integral part of the sound of that album, and if I'm not mistaken that (a four-track) is what that album was started on."

The first side of *Meet The Residents* is constructed of short songs, and is compelling from the opening deconstruction of *These Boots Are Made For Walking* to the piano texture of the neo-classical instrumental *Rest Aria*. *Smelly Tongues* is all frantic guitar and a chorus that, once heard, never leaves you and would probably defy exorcism, whilst the dominant horn refrain and spoken word narrative of *Skratz* is hypnotic and an early classic. *Spotted Pinto Bean* closes the side with a mini operatic aria, featuring Pamela Zeiback, "I was in College at the time studying music, and yes I am a classically trained singer. I don't remember doing retakes at all. At that time it was just first takes." Although some were to find the music The Residents were making bizarre, she had no problems with it, "Well I viewed it as Avant Garde, and since I was working with a group at University who only wrote *new music* I was very open to it."

Side two of the LP opens with *Infant Tango*, a James Brown mixture of wah wah guitar, bass and drums, punctuated by what was to become trademark horns. These, and subsequent brass arrangements, were inspired by a number of influences that both showed the wide musical tastes of The Residents and their respect and understanding of arrangers like Stan Kenton, Henry Mancini, Perez Prado and Sun Ra. *Seasoned Greetings* follows, relaxed, confident and stately with a slight tinge of jazz, before *Nobody But Me* by The Human Beinz is 'sampled' and then stuck in a groove to finally become an experiment in music concrete on *N-R-Gee (Crisis Blues)*, a driving, forceful musical and guttural vocal rant, again powered by brass blows. The album closes with a slow fading chorus of "Go home America, fifty five'll do," a direct commentary upon the thousands of American casualties during the Vietnam War.

As with *Santa Dog*, tremendous effort went into the packaging of the LP. The Residents wanted to make a statement upon contemporary music, and present a strong, arresting image that might invite random purchase. They settled upon the most iconoclastic thing they could think of - an artistic defacing of the world famous *Meet The Beatles* LP cover, which lent itself to becoming *Meet The Residents - The First Album By North Louisiana's Phenomenal Pop Combo*. The liner notes on the back of the LP were pure hype and self-promotion that already deployed veils to disguise the mysterious Residents and invited the reader into the realms of Phonetic Organisation, "Unknown Britishman, 'Snakefinger' Lithman", N Senada and "The Residents' first full-length film *Vileness Fats*, which is to be a musical comedy based upon the same theories set forth in this album."

As they had done with *Vileness Fats*, the group put up their own money to master and manufacture a thousand and fifty copies of the LP, although one or two hundred were deemed unusable due to warping. But selling the album was a different proposition. At this time Ralph Records was not a proper record company with any sort of distribution, and thus The Residents had no mechanism for nationwide distribution, or even getting the album accepted into record shops in California. Also, as The Residents had no interest in promoting their music through live performance or touring (not that this music could have been replicated on stage), there wasn't even the option to sell records at gigs. They were, in essence like many of the artists and bands captured in that magnificent book edited by Johan Kugelberg, Michael P. Daley and Paul Major titled *Enjoy The Experience* (Sinecure USA 2012) - people who had made a record because they felt compelled to do so, but who had a hard time getting anyone to listen to it let alone buy it. Obviously, The Residents sent copies out to friends like Roland Sheehan, who played it straight away, "I listened to it and it was not what I would do, but then again I am not a Resident. But in its own way I liked it because it was different." They were, in essence, people who had made a record only because they felt compelled to do so, but they soon found they had a hard time getting anyone to listen to it, let alone buy it.

Even at this stage, however, The Residents showed an inventive approach to marketing. They decided to try and stir interest with the novel idea of manufacturing four thousand 8" flexi-discs containing an abbreviated seven minutes of music from the album. These samplers would be given away free and hopefully encourage sales. Subsequently, a full-page advertisement was taken out in the February 1974 issue of the Canadian art publication *File*, which also included a free copy of the flexi disc and offered the LP for a bargain price of $1.99....

"Yeah, that's right hippies and squirrels, the first one is almost free. Do you have any idea why we would have 1000 records pressed to sell for $1.99 each while losing eighty-five cents on each one? Well, I'll tell you why – It's so that you'll know our name when you freak out over this groovy, outasite disc."

That this ad appeared two months before the LP was released showed forward planning, but when it appeared there was a general belief that, as the advert featured the defaced Beatles cover, it was an elaborate artistic joke. Also, anybody who actually played the flexi disc may have been put off by the music. There was, it is believed, not one single response.

They also advertised in *Friday* (17th May 1974), a free magazine distributed amongst San Francisco's Colleges. Again the LP sleeve was prominently displayed, and the advertisement offered 'free samples' of the record, and even a contact telephone number. Free copies were also given away in the magazine's competition, but again the response was not overwhelming. In fact, in the first year of release it is believed that only forty people bought the album of their own free will. This is not mythology but hard fact. When a record store (Rather Ripped in Berkeley) took a few copies, The Residents were so overjoyed that they went down and took photographs of a copy prominently displayed in the racks. William Reinhardt, who had played *Santa Dog* on his radio show, also helped out in his native Portland, "I put twenty or thirty copies of *Meet The Residents* in Music Millennium (a local record store) and they sat there for almost a year - only one or two copies got sold. Eventually they sold half of them and (one of The Residents) actually came to Portland to get the cheque for sales."

That *Meet The Residents* hardly sold upon release is not surprising. In 1974, ear-friendly bands like Abba, Chicago, Grand Funk, The Osmonds and The Jackson Five were dominating the airwaves, and whilst there was a vibrant left-field scene, even fans of Van Der Graaf Generator, Frank Zappa, Captain Beefheart and the Krautrock movement would have found *Meet The Residents* unpalatable. It was more experimental than anything Zappa, Pink Floyd or even the like-minded German collective Faust had produced. The sound simply defied niche at a time when music – soul, funk, classical, rock, blues, country, opera and so on - was sold and marketed in specific boxes. *Meet The Residents* was not rock, not classical, not blues and not jazz, although there were elements of all of these strands in the music. Of course, some who heard it would have argued that it was *not music at all.*

Meet The Residents was a new sound and an entirely new approach to music. This was not a 'band' writing songs, playing them live and then recording them. Instead, The Residents were interested in the possibilities offered by the recording process itself, and constructed their music piece by piece on tape. They were not just learning to master a wide array of instruments but also the sonic possibilities available to those prepared to invest time and energy into the workings of their own rudimentary studio. "When I was there all they had was a little two track, but I do know that as soon as an affordable four-track was out they bought one... and had their own recording studio," Roland Sheehan stated with some insight, "It was less money. There was no hourly fee so they had all the time in the world to play around. If it worked, fine, and if it didn't work you can just back up the tape and do it over. I don't know if they had other people involved who knew more about it than they did or if it was trial and error, but they used it a lot and put in a lot of effort and learned as they did it. They were always wanting to push the envelope further."

The idea of a promotional flexi disc was a good one, but perhaps a double-edged sword. Those who did take the trouble to play it probably didn't take too kindly to the atonal explosion that leapt out of their speakers. The flexi, rather than gaining sales, probably lost them, but at least those few brave souls who may have bought the LP based on the flexi knew what they were letting themselves in for.

However, for a few the music resonated, and once they got into it they would play it again and again and again. They heard something that was new and it connected. One of these was Tom Timony, later to work for Ralph Records and run the TEC Tones mail order business, "I got turned on to The Residents in 1975 in France. Someone had a *Meet The Residents* Record and hated it. I was into progressive music and they said I might like it. It was so minimal. I hated it... I thought they were so primitive. They didn't know anything about music. But as a musician you could tell that they had something that most musicians never have, which is that savvy for timbres and things... all these exotic sounds and different time signatures that, in traditional music, are not supposed to happen."

Of course, nothing did happen. Apart from a few 'dedicated fools' the world was not yet ready to embrace the music of The Residents.

The Third Reich And Roll

"The two things they really enjoy doing are creating music that nobody has ever heard before and then taking other peoples' music and making it sound like music that nobody has ever heard before." - Homer Flynn, 1978.

When *Meet The Residents* failed to sell and gained minimal traction, The Residents carried on throwing their energies and financial resources into *Vileness Fats*, and also developed their Theory Of Obscurity. To be frank, they did not have to work too hard at it - they *were* obscure. Worse than that, they were not even seen by many to exist. They had released a double 7" single and an entire LP's worth of material to the worst kind of response - indifference. Therefore, why not take their obscurity as far as possible and record an entire LP and then announce that it was *Not Available?* This is precisely what The Residents apparently did in 1974, stating that the record could only be released once they had forgotten about its existence. Of course, this didn't stop them stirring up interest in the music by mentioning that the LP was *Not Available* in the liner notes to their *third* LP *The Third Reich And Roll.*

Unlike *Meet The Residents*, which was – *Boots* aside – a low fidelity realisation of their own music, *The Third Reich And Roll* was a concept album. The Resident were interested in what the American and British music press termed the *Krautrock* phenomenon; progressive German bands like Can, Neu!, Tangerine Dream, Amon Duul II, Kraftwerk and Faust and the adventurous and cosmic music that they were making. Jay Clem told the *Berkeley Barb* in 1978 that "*Third Reich And Roll* was an attempt to treat top forty rock and roll from the '60s as if it were avant-garde material as performed by early '70s progressive German bands." Sometimes even *accountants* speaking to the music press get something right.

The LP was recorded in a year between October 1974 and October 1975, and the reason for their taking this length of time was simple - The Residents could still only take vacation time from their day jobs to work on the project, and they were simultaneously working on *Vileness Fats*.

There's no doubting that they spent a considerable amount of time working on the tapes before the LP was released, and also upgraded during the project from a four to eight track reel-to-reel recorder. When it came to recording the music, large parts of the album were laid down by taping the original version of the song to be covered on one track and The Residents building up overdubs of themselves playing along with it on the rest. Finally, the original version was erased from the tape leaving only The Residents' *new* interpretation.

When their own musicianship was not up to playing the parts they would rope in people competent enough to create the music they required. People like Gary Philips, who later told the UK music magazine *Sounds*, "I was working one night at Rather Ripped (Records)... somebody called and asked if there was a guitar player who could add a part to their record... I walked into this big warehouse and somebody asked me did I know *Hey Jude*. I said, "Sure", and he asked me if I knew *Sympathy For The Devil*. I said "Sure" again, and he said that was all they wanted me to play on the end of their record. I got my portable tape recorder and plugged into that. I didn't even use an amplifier. All I can remember is these enormous sponge rubber broccolis lying around everywhere. They looked exactly like the real thing – right shape, right colour and everything – only they were bigger than me."

Released in February 1976, *The Third Reich And Roll* is one of the cornerstones upon which The Residents' reputation is based, a dense collage of sound totally alien yet familiar. The music is divided into two suites, *Hitler Was A Vegetarian* and *Swastikas On Parade*, but, this is no *Springtime For Hitler* Broadway production. Each side is a tapestry made up of a number of '60s hits, including *Land Of A Thousand Dances*, *Telstar*, *Psychotic Reaction*, *I Want Candy*, *Yummy Yummy Yummy*, *Gloria*, *Light My Fire*, *It's My Party*, *Pushin' Too Hard*, *Good Lovin'* and *The Letter*, all of which are gutted, deconstructed and given 'Residential' interpretation. Chubby Checker's *Let's Twist Again* and James Brown's *Papas Got A Brand New Bag* are even plundered for what everyone now knows as 'samples'.

There is a phenomenal amount of playful iconoclasm about the music - for example, the short version of *Let's Twist Again* is augmented by German lyrics before dissolving into a mutation of *Land of A Thousand Dances* – and a considerable breadth of instrumentation is used, including saxophones, trombones, guitar, bass, koto, accordion, oud, pipe organ and xylophone, to name a few. The album also boasts the first use of synthesisers on a Residents record – an Arp Odyssey, which was introduced into the American market in 1972 and which one of The Residents had bought, and a rented Arp String Ensemble –

both of which bubble and scratch accompaniment on both sides, perhaps to best effect on *Good Lovin'*.

Of course, the main instrument on show is The Residents' mastery of their recently acquired Tascam eight track recording equipment and a battery of effects – reverb, echo and distortion – demonstrated in the skilled construction and mixing of the music, which enables the songs to either bleed or bend into each other. In one fantastic sequence helicopters buzz between the speakers, cars crash, gunfire breaks out and music rises out of the mix like the creature from the black lagoon.

The cover art was as shocking as the music. Taking the German connection to its logical conclusion, a smiling, cartoon-like Dick Clark, host of *American Bandstand - the* programme on '60s American TV– is pictured in full Nazi uniform, holding a hand coloured carrot and surrounded by dancing teenage Hitlers. The design, with its black, red and grey colours, is totally arresting and, as with *Meet The Residents*, served up a visually engaging sleeve for the record racks. The back cover of the first pressing also featured a large Germanic emblem with a swastika inside, and liner notes were folded around the record's sleeve.

As with *Meet The Residents*, a thousand copies were pressed and released, and the band invested a lot of time and energy in taking promotional photos featuring The Residents wearing huge swastikas on their heads - pictures that were banned when hung in a window display in Rather Ripped Records in Berkeley, one of the few shops that were now stocking and selling – in small quantities – their records. Even so, The Residents found there was a market for *The Third Reich And Roll*, not a floodgate but a definite interest in the product. *Meet The Residents* also begun to sell, and they were beginning to acquire a small, cultish following.

To promote themselves and the new album, the group even went as far as appearing live on 7th June 1976, at Rather Ripped's fifth birthday party at the Longbranch Saloon. It was a performance event more than a concert, and entitled *Oh Mommy! Oh Daddy! Can't You See That It's True: What The Beatles Did To Me. "I Love Lucy" Did To You.* The promoter recalled, "It was rather difficult, we didn't know who these people were... I don't think audiences were ready for this sort of thing... we hold ourselves to be pretty progressive here in Berkeley but I really don't think that could be called entertaining... they arrived with a lot of scaffolding, and by the time they'd finished you could hardly see anything. And as for the music – well, I'm not sure there was any music... I like to see who I'm dealing with and these people were all wearing fencing masks..."

The performance was meticulously planned. 16mm segments from *Vileness Fats* and what would later become the *Third Reich And Roll* promotional video were shown, and the set list gave precise running times for the songs as well as stage direction, due mainly to the fact that some of the music was not played live and some backing vocals, by the Pointless Sisters, were pre-recorded onto backing tapes. "I think the songs we (I think I did sing on these) worked on included *Numb Erone* and *Kick A Cat*" recalls Joshua Raoul Brody. There were also a number of other collaborators involved, including Pamela Zeiback and Peggy Honeydew, who'd also contributed vocals to *Third Reich And Roll*.

"I do remember a concert we did and we all wore costumes," recalls Zeiback, "Yes, they wore bandages and Margaret was Penny Honeydew. I think I was Sheena of the jungle or something. I don't remember any rehearsals, but because I was used to performing, and as it was The Residents, it wasn't a problem for me. Anyway, I came out on stage when they told me to and ad libbed an operatic riff. I'd been studying voice for some time and that was the style that I was comfortable with. I think it was quite shocking to the audience. Anyway, it was so much fun." Of greater significance, the concert also featured the recently returned Snakefinger on guitar, dressed as an artichoke of course. Brody recalls, "I remember Snakefinger played guitar wearing boots that were screwed down into a wooden board that was raised and lowered and tilted so he was at a very sharp angle to the floor." Arf and Omega from *Vileness Fats* also appeared, performing the infectious *Kick A Cat* segment from *Santa Dog*.

Lithman had not been idle during his time in England (1972-76). He'd formed Chilli Willi And The Red Hot Peppers with friend Martin Stone and recorded and released two LPs of mellow country blues, *Kings Of The Robot Rhythm* (1974) and *Bongos Over Balham* (1975). A Third was supposed to be released on Stiff Records around 1976 (label co-founder Jake Riviera used to be their manager) but it never happened. Both sound as if they were recorded in America rather than England and are highly recommended.

The Residents also performed a truncated version of a new work, *Six Things To A Cycle*, from behind a net curtain, swathed from head to toe in surgical bandages. It looked fantastic but, as you might imagine, made playing *something* of a challenge. As one of them later wrote in *Future* fanzine, "We did a science fiction and horror show and were dressed as mummies throughout the performance... Unfortunately, we had not tried playing while wearing the costumes in advance... we're still trying to figure out what we did. Marvelous... just marvelous."

Also featured in the *Oh Mommy!* performance was a short, abbreviated version of what was to become their next single. The

Residents had contemplated releasing something from the *The Third Reich And Roll*, but finally decided to cover one final song and invest it with *everything* that had gone into the making of that album. The chosen stalking horse was The Rolling Stones' classic *Satisfaction*, and Snakefinger and The Pointless Sisters were again drafted in. Joshua Raoul Brody, who arranged and sometimes performed with the Sisters, told me, "They needed extra singers for *Satisfaction*, which they were just about to record, and asked (us) to do the back-up vocals."

The resulting single was later described by a critic from *Trouser Press* magazine as "The most determinedly repellant music I have ever heard, guaranteed to empty a room inside ten or fifteen seconds," and is without doubt the most *extreme* of all The Residents' recordings. Whilst the songs on *Third Reich And Roll* are covered with humour, or at least spiteful amusement, *Satisfaction* is gunned down and murdered. Eviscerated. Everything is totally overloaded, the vocals are screamed and rendered almost incoherent into feedback by electronic treatment and Snakefinger brings what was to become his sonic trademark guitar to bear. As for the Pointless Sisters' back-up vocals, legend is that they were so bad they were edited out of the final mix. *Satisfaction* is raw, bleeding music, challenging the listener to respond by either enduring or turning it off. The best description I've have read of the song came in the first Ralph Records mail order catalogue, back in 1977, and was, I suspect, penned by a Resident;

"Over-equalised bass and configurations, etc... while still delivering the emotional punch which makes rock and roll that thing which drives adults up the wall while thrilling the masochistic fringes of teenagehood."

The *Satisfaction/Loser=Weed* single was to become a Residents sleeper, although the first pressing was limited to two hundred copies shrink-wrapped in hand-coloured sleeves and marketed as a collectors item. There was even a card inside to be returned to Ralph Records so that the purchaser could be kept informed of the subsequent increase in value.

Schwump's *Aphids In The Hall* single, released on Ralph at the same time as *Satisfaction*, is a real oddity and now one of the rarest of all Residents related records. Schwump was Barry Schwam, and William Reinhardt was the go-between. "Barry was hired by me to do a show on KBOO," Reinhardt recalls today, "I hooked him up with The Residents. He was a one-man band on drums when I met him and thought he was a perfect match for the Rez. We sent him to SF and they hit it off and recorded his song *Aphids*." According to legend there were plans to record a full-length album for Ralph, but Schwump was worried that people might rip off his original material. At first, he liked the idea of a single being released and limited to two hundred copies, then his position shifted 180 degrees and he suggested to The Residents that they were not pressing enough records to give his genius the attention it deserved! As for the recording, Schwump later told Residents fan Paulie, "The basic tracks were made by only one of The Residents and myself. Everything else was added later. We made the three songs for the *Aphids* single in one afternoon."

Compared to *Satisfaction*, *Aphids In The Hall*, *You're A Martian* and *Home* are very straight. Indeed, *Aphids* sounds like a few guys having fun and swings like an old Broadway show tune. *You're A Martian* is more of the same with a nicely whistled opening, whilst *Home*, is the only track that might be considered 'Residential. ' In 1993, Schwump re-established contact with The Residents by completing and returning his collector's card inside his personal copy of *Aphids* and mailing it back to their address at that time. Today, he can be found online performing his music and has released his own CDs, although, to date, none of them contain the additional material intended to grace his mythical Ralph Records LP.

The Cryptic Corporation

"The bureaucracy is there because it's necessary in the music business at present – which is not to say it doesn't have some symbolic significance."- Jay Clem, 1978.

The two hundred hand-printed *Satisfaction* singles were all numbered and signed 'Goodbye Residents Uninc'. This did not refer to the demise of the band and record label but to a radical change in its business structure. Henceforth, there would no longer just be The Residents and Ralph Records, there would also be The Cryptic Corporation.

The Cryptic Corporation were four friends who wanted to manage and promote The Residents. "Our relationships go way back," Homer Flynn told me, "John and I went to the same elementary school together, we were not friends at that time but I knew who he was. Jay and I were friends at High School and College. Hardy and I met in College, so our relationships went way back."

Significantly, one of the Corporation – John Kennedy – had just inherited a substantial amount of money and was prepared to sink some of it into supporting and promoting The Residents. The other three put some equity into the venture, but The Cryptic Corporation was formed mainly to protect his financial stake. If the business had been a partnership any creditors could legally target the individual with the most money, i.e. Kennedy.

When I interviewed Kennedy back in 1994, he was an athletic looking man of around fifty years old, and, as Don Hardy's recent film *The Theory Of Obscurity* has shown, he is now an athletic looking man around seventy years old. "I wasn't a Resident," Kennedy told me, "The Residents did the recordings." Kennedy simply bankrolled the entire affair, and the four officers of The Cryptic Corporation each assumed roles - Kennedy became President Kennedy (which was probably also a bit of a pun) with special responsibility for production and administration, whilst business school graduate Jay Clem became the business manager and publicist. Homer Flynn assumed responsibility for graphic design and Hardy Fox used his knowledge of sound engineering to assist The Residents in realising their musical projects.

After incorporation, the next act of The Cryptic Corporation was to buy a building, the famous 444 Grove Street. Back in 1976 the area was low rent and run down - the motel across the street was a favourite place for prostitutes to entertain clients, and when The Cryptic Corporation first arrived to inspect the property with a view to purchase, the first thing they saw was a fresh bullet-hole in the door. Inside, there were holes in the roof, but none of this deterred them as the building was ideal for their needs, being double fronted with a large warehouse to one side and offices on the other. There was also a house included in the price. The important thing, Kennedy stated to me, was "We could afford it. It was cheap. We bought the building." The cost was $100,000.

The Residents gleefully moved into their new business premises, although they never lived there. Even though *Vileness Fats* had been abandoned they still brought along the sets and costumes, all of their musical equipment and a huge record collection that the band often rifled through for ideas. Chris Cutler argued in the excellent chapter on The Residents in his book *File Under Popular* (ReR Megacorp 1991) that The Residents sound developed "not from a knowledge of the various musical (rules) of construction, but from a highly developed listening familiarity." This theory certainly holds water in the early part of their career. Indeed, one source close to the band and interviewed for this book recalls them listening intently as late as 1981 to the music of soundtrack composer Ennio Morricone, eager to work out just how he put his music together so that they could appropriate his style in their own music. Cutler was also on the money when he stated that, "The Residents were, above all, a group born, educated and nourished in the recording studio. And not unconsciously; it was because they realised what a studio *was* and how it could be used to compose, construct and carry from conception to completion soundworks that had little or nothing to do with played music that, at the first opportunity, they *built their own.*" Today many musicians set up their own studio and construct music from samples of other artists' work. The Residents were simply ahead of the game.

The Grove Street building was soon redesigned, as Graeme Whifler recalls, "They moved from a rented space on Sycamore to 444 Grove Street, a huge old brick building, a former stable they had purchased. The place looked pretty shabby on the outside so I was asked if I could give it a coat of paint - I had a painting company at that time. But instead of paint I proposed an exterior makeover involving sandblasting the building, moving a doorway, covering over windows with sculptured stucco and reflective glass mosaic and an entranceway of cut and welded steel sculpture with a dash of blue plexiglass woven in. They said "OK" so I spent several months creating the new exterior. That turned out so good they invited me inside. First thing I did was build myself an office and figure out what to do next."

As for the inside decoration, a journalist from the *San Jose Mercury* later wrote "...one passes through a hallway lined in blue plastic, past the Mickey Mouse statue, stacks of record boxes and a gigantic version of the RCA dog, up a circular stairway adorned with mummified baby dolls hung from the banister with hangmen's nooses and into the corporate loft..."

Now they had their own defined space to work from and business support, The Residents all gave up their various day jobs to concentrate full-time upon their music and related activities. Whether day-to-day living expenses were paid by The Cryptic Corporation is a grey area that I cannot add colour to, but if there *were* eight people working at Grove Street they could certainly not live on the money generated by record sales alone. At this time The Residents were still a cult band, and although they were picking up a review here and there – "And if *Meet The Beatles* started it all, *Meet The Residents* ends it" - as late as February 1977 they were still offering copies of *Satisfaction* and *Aphids In The Hall* for sale, both of which, as you may recall, had been limited to pressings of two hundred singles each. Sales were *not* strong. What The Cryptic Corporation expected to get for their investment in what Kennedy deliciously told me was "a far corner of the art world" is a matter for speculation. The Residents were not a McDonald's franchise.

Crucially, there was now much more of a business attitude to everything that happened. William Reinhardt, who was beginning to fall out of The Residents' orbit around this time, certainly saw a difference, "When I came to visit them Jay had to spend a lot of time doing office work. After five years I think they got fed up with me coming to party. They were so involved in creating The Cryptic Corporation at that time that they did not have time to party."

There was a flurry of activity around this time. Whereas the previous Residents art commune had marketed themselves in a limited way, The Cryptic Corporation intended to sell The Residents as if they *were* McDonald's hamburgers, and in February 1977 the first Ralph Records mail order catalogue was printed. This not only offered all of The Residents' records for sale but even a T-shirt featuring the iconic *Meet The Residents* LP cover:

"When one walks down the street wearing this defiled Beatle cover, an unusual amount of attention is received. They come in the usual sizes, and mean instant friendship when you spot another one."

There was even a special limited edition *Third Reich and Roll* collector's boxed set, as well as the inducement of a new LP, *Fingerprince.*

Fingerprince is, in my opinion, a seminal release, and revealed the true depth of the musical divergence of the band, and a growing mastery of the studio. The second side was taken up by *Six Things To A Cycle*, a piece inspired by Indonesian Gamelan music and the challenging, compelling and repetitive music of minimalist composters like Phillip Glass, Steve Reich and Terry Riley. The main influence, though, was the obscure maverick composer Harry Partch (born Oakland California, June 1901) who, like The Residents themselves, developed his career outside of the mainstream. Rejecting Western scales and classical techniques, Partch looked to Africa and the Far East for inspiration, and therefore his music is extremely rhythmic in nature.

Partch developed his own forty three note scale and modified existing instruments, as well as building his own and giving them fantastic names like the Harmonic Canon III, Cloud Chamber Bowls and the Whang-gun (which made a Whang sound). He then recruited and trained his own Gate 5 Ensemble to play these instruments and perform and record his compositions. In one instance, Partch recorded a film score himself by multi-tracking all the instruments, so he really was a man after The Residents' own hearts. He ploughed his unique furrow in obscurity, funding his existence by live performance and various short-lived teaching and research posts, and also through his own Gate 5 record label. Recognition only came in his final years.

On *Six Things To A Cycle* The Residents play normal, found and self-constructed instruments, and, according to Homer Flynn, the recordings straddled locations, "I know that *Six Things To A Cycle*, a lot of that was recorded live in the studio, and I know that was done at Sycamore Street as I have a strong memory of that recording session, but I think it was completed at 444 Grove." As the sleevenotes state, the long, rhythmic suite tells a story in which "Man, represented by a primitive humanoid, is consumed by his self-created environment only to be replaced by a new creature, still primitive, still faulty, but destined to rule the world just as poorly." The piece is beautifully realised, from the opening jungle sounds to the screamed birth of man and the subsequent unraveling of the music over a fifteen-minute period. There is humour too, including a long, rhythmic chorus of "Chew chew gum, chew gum gum."

The entire piece is life-affirming music, and another string in the Residential bow, revealing deep interest in the cutting edge of American contemporary classical music as well as a willingness to experiment with non-western forms, structure and instrumentation. It appears that some orchestral percussion was hired specifically for this project, and some additional players were also drafted in in addition to Snakefinger and Pamela Zeiback. Reference was also made in the sleevenotes to the fact that *Six Things To A Cycle* had been commissioned as a ballet to be performed at the Museum Of Modern Art in San Francisco, but was never performed. In fact, this was part of a planned collaboration with the art-architecture group Ant Farm – famous for their Cadillac desert art structure titled *Cadillac Ranch* – whom The Residents were very close to. Homer Flynn and Hardy Fox (along with Graeme Whifler) had acted as FBI agents during their performance piece *Media Burn* at the Cow Palace on 4th July 1975, wherein a customised Cadillac was driven through a wall of burning TV sets.

"Ant Farm and The Residents shared social connections," recalls Graeme Whifler, "so when the Media Burn project came up a phone call invite was made. I remember a bad feeling of dread as the car readied to smash into the flaming wall of TVs. I really thought there was a good likelihood somebody was going to die that day." There was a compelling documentary made of this art piece which is now available on YouTube. And yes, I also wonder why John Kennedy didn't play the President.

Of course, *Six Things To A Cycle* was only the second side of *Fingerprince.* The first side was a collection of short, more typical Residents pieces. All are excellent, especially the two fantastic versions of *You Yesyesyes* that open and close the side. *Godsong*, with its memorable refrain, "All that God wanted to be was just a normal deity", is great fun and sung by the second Resident rather than the main vocalist, whilst *Tourniquet Of Roses* features a *classic* opening with parps of brass, Snakefinger slide guitar and a vocal that sounds like a man calling the moves of a country hoe-down on acid. For me, the best element is the witty coda, when multi-tracked vocals deliver the lines, "Is no more to say now/is no more to say". The fifty eight second *March De La Winni* was composed as the soundtrack for the opening credits of the soon to be completed *Third Reich And Roll* promotional film and is equally memorable.

Fingerprince was intended to be a three-sided LP, and was originally going to be entitled *Tourniquet of Roses,* as the cover suggests, before a last minute change of mind. But the idea was abandoned due to the cost of pressing a 2-LP set, which shows that The Cryptic Corporation had to count the cents as well as the dollars. It was decided to include the missing side of music as a 7" EP in a limited edition *Fingerprince* boxed set advertised in the first mail order catalogue. This product was later abandoned, but the EPs were pressed and sent out to the dedicated few who had paid $50 for them, along with a full refund. Now that was customer service! *The Babyfingers EP* was finally released as a parting shot by The Residents' first fan club, W.E.I.R.D., in 1981, and featured a track named *Death In Barstow*, a reference to the death of Harry Partch on the 3rd September 1976.

The *Fingerprince* album was evidence again that The Residents defied categorisation, and that they were making innovative music solely to satisfy themselves rather than market forces. Like Partch before them, they stayed true to their art despite struggling in obscurity, but it did not pay the bills. So, with a view to generating some much needed cash flow from other sources, The Cryptic Corporation began exploring the possibility of opening their own movie theatre.

"The Cryptic Corporation wanted to be able to ensure that there was some kind of income there," recalls Homer Flynn, "and it was obvious that there was not enough income from the music to do it strictly from that, so (they had) the whole idea of creating this movie theatre as a source of income that would also be a place where The Residents and other people could perform for special events." Indeed, they even "procured property" at 11th and Howard. The idea behind this Science Fiction and Fantasy Theatre was, according, to the first Ralph Records mail order catalogue...

"For the institution of entertainment facilities for both film and live show attractions. The design and format of the operation are to express a heavily fantasy-orientated point of view. Besides plans for Science Fiction and Horror film festivals, The Residents are said to be writing a show for the facility to be presented in late 1977."

The Cryptic Corporation began remodeling the building, but before this could all get off the ground there was a small matter of civil law to attend to. Movie theatres had to provide sufficient parking space for patrons and, if this was not possible, potential owners had to demonstrate that there was enough off street parking in the surrounding area to cope with patrons and obtain a variance in this law. The Cryptic Corporation thought this wouldn't be a problem as the surrounding area was mainly industrial and there was plenty of free parking space. Therefore they assumed all they had to do was turn up on the day of the hearing to obtain the variance.

However, when local residents heard of the plans they believed that, as The Cryptic Corporation had been so secretive about the whole thing, they were intending to open a hardcore gay porno cinema. The local community, from the Catholic Church to local Day Care Centres, mobilised and raised petitions and objections. The Cryptic Corporation attempted to explain their real purpose – splatter movies and aliens with two heads – but nobody believed them. "We learned a huge lesson at that point about PR and promotion," recalls Homer Flynn," because we were not ready (prior to the hearing) to announce what we were doing there, so we were just doing all of this work and people could tell that something was happening, but no-one knew what it was." The Cryptic Corporation actually hired a lawyer to fight their case on appeal.

Back at Ralph, the first mail order catalogue was sent to all those who had sent back names and addresses when buying *Meet The Residents* and other Residents records, and proved to be such a success that, to cope with demand, it was reprinted in April 1977. The Residents also contributed a track, *Whoopy Snorp*, to a compilation album featuring cover art by Captain Beefheart and called *Blorp Essette*, which was released by the Los Angeles Free Music Society. Word was slowly spreading, assisted by features in the various fanzines that sprang up in the wake of the slowly emerging punk and new wave scenes in New York and San Francisco.

At this point, The Residents even allowed themselves to be interviewed, providing written answers to questions posed by a New York based fanzine called *Future* and a sympathetic journalist from *Friday* magazine. These 'interviews' are, in retrospect, hilarious. This from *Friday:*

> *A RESIDENT:* "I will say that our music tends to polarise people."
> *ANOTHER RESIDENT:* (Chuckle) "Yeah, they love it or they hate it. But that's all to the good. At least they're reacting, even if they send us threatening letters. You can sleep your way through most of the records on the market today."

And this from *Future*

> *RESIDENT 1:* "We do not hate The Beatles."
> *RESIDENT 2:* "The Beatles are merely symbols of culture which we are forced to eat, drink and breathe."

Evidently, despite The Theory Of Obscurity, The Residents were, at this point in time, keen to engage the press directly in an attempt to sell records. Obscurity was not its own reward. That interest was growing was shown by the fact that *Meet The Residents* was re-mastered in stereo, losing seven minutes of music in the process as The Residents tidied up the sound for repressing. As well as playing their records on his radio show, William Reinhardt was also something of a critic, "*Meet The Residents*, when I heard the original pressing it had *Godawful* technical quality. I said "What the hell is wrong with the quality, why are you recording so badly?" (One of them) told me once that they were aggravated and annoyed that I was criticising them. He said, "We built that in because we don't want to sound like professionals." So I showed them how to set up the audio gain on their mixer and when they released the second version they got the signal to noise ratio better and cleaned it up."

Indeed they did, and the recording of *Third Reich And Roll* and *Fingerprince* had also given them much more production and engineering experience. The re-released version of *Meet The Residents* also featured a new 'crawfish' sleeve, allegedly due to legal representation from Capitol Records, The Beatles' American label, over the original cover art. Was this truth or hype? The defaced cover still appeared on the rear of the sleeve, and if Capitol had objected surely they would have objected to the image being printed in any form. Also, the second mail order catalogue, from August 1977, was still selling original copies of *Meet The Residents,* but at a higher price of $10 whilst the new pressing was for sale for $4....

"It has attracted so much attention on the speculators' market (including Beatles collectors), that the price on the remaining stock of the original edition of 1,000 has been elevated to the same level it is drawing on the Open Market – expensive of course."

In the *Future* interview, one of The Residents stated, "We all love The Beatles, and will soon prove it!" And prove it they did, with a limited edition of five hundred seven inch singles offered for sale in the second Ralph catalogue and appropriately entitled *The Beatles Play The Residents and The Residents Play The Beatles.*

This 7" is, in many respects, one of the most perfect of all Residents releases. It encapsulates everything they were about at this point in time in that it is witty, spiteful, irreverent and totally original. The A side – *Beyond the Valley Of A Day In The Life* – is a Frankenstein-like composition consisting of portions of various Beatles recordings. It's an absolutely wicked pastiche, jarringly unmusical yet compelling to listen to, and the effort involved in recording, treating, splicing and sequencing the parts together must have been tremendous. The result is a classic. As Jon savage called it in a review in *Sounds,* "A terrifying, dehumanised/eerie/hallucinary collage." The B-side, The Residents' version of *Flying*, is equally as good. Here they hijacked a snippet of a Paul McCartney speech heard on the A-side (and taken from a Beatles fanclub flexi) – "Please, everybody, if we haven't done what we could have done we've tried" – and screamed it with stoned, scornful glee.

The packaging was again exemplary. The graphics arm of The Cryptic Corporation – known as Poreknowgraphics or punning variations - was mostly handled by Homer Flynn, who had worked on sleeve design from *Meet The Residents* onwards, although Hardy Fox, who had an art background, also played a significant part. For this release the band conducted a photo shoot that saw The Residents pose naked, arms aloft, their faces hidden by fake John, Paul, George and Ringo masks and only their pubic hair visible (an effect obtained not by airbrushing out their genitals but by pulling them back between their legs and keeping them out of sight by a judicious use of string). Meanwhile, five fan-like hands reach out and attempt to touch them.

And by this time more and more people *were* beginning to reach out to touch the music of The Residents.

Duck Stab

"We like to keep barriers between us and our audience," explained one Resident in an anonymous phone interview. "Our fans expect us to be the weirdest people in the world, so whatever we are, it would be a disappointment to them." – Interviewed in Melody Maker, July 1978.

"You could not find such a group in Britain but only in one of the Latin countries where they drink WINE rather than BEER, read SATRE rather than Dennis Wheatley & get worked up about their EXISTENTIAL CONDITIONS rather than having their PHOTOGRAPHS taken." - Chris Cutler on Art Zoyd.

The catalyst for the growth in interest in The Residents around this time was not their own marketing strategies but the English music press, who discovered them with a vengeance in late 1977 and 1978. By then, The Residents had built a small following in America, which had grown slowly through word of mouth and a couple of sympathetic journalists and radio stations. Bill Reinhardt not only staged a six hour Residents marathon on his show in early 1977 but the band actually gave him, and allowed him to broadcast, copies of the *Warner Brothers* and *Baby Sex* demo albums on reel-to-reel tape, as well as all of their other releases to date. This was hardly the Theory Of Obscurity in action. *Meet The Residents*, *Third Reich And Roll* and *Fingerprince* were selling very slowly and in quantities that only generated a small cash flow, but the establishment of The Cryptic Corporation, the acquisition of 444 Grove Street and the fancy headed stationary gave the impression of health and vitality where, in reality, there was little more than the hyperbole of the first two Ralph Records mail order catalogues (of February and August 1977) to suggest a financially bright future. In fact, not only were limited editions like *Schwump* and *Satisfaction* still available in these catalogues, but Ralph were so desperate for sales that, for $7 each, they were even offering copies of the first three albums on hand-dubbed cassettes, "Using a first generation copy of the actual master tape... these are not mass-produced, so no graphic work is included."

However, a musical revolution was taking place, and although it had its American counterpart the most significant manifestation of punk rock was to be found in England. Early adopters like the Ramones aside, the heyday of the punk movement was encapsulated in the recording career of the Sex Pistols, which may have been short lived but was a touch-paper that inspired an explosion of punk and new wave of bands, and a new attitude to music and the music business. As well as leading to the formation of hundreds of groups, the new wave also threw up all manner of new forms of music, from the industrial sound of Throbbing Gristle to the sub-Roxy punk electronica of the first incarnation of Ultravox! More importantly, punk inspired a whole new attitude and a rejection of society, including the established musical landscape; bands like Pink Floyd, Yes and Genesis became boring old farts overnight (although they kept breaking musical wind for some time to come), and rock was no longer the preserve of highly trained musicians - now everybody could take part, form a band, write a fanzine, even put out a record on their own. It really was a whole new ball game.

At first the English music press attempted to ignore this new phenomenon and clung dearly to the established musical order. Slowly, however, resistance crumbled and publications like *Sounds* and the *New Musical Express* began to cover this new explosion, until its energy and diversity dominated their pages. The other two English weeklies at the time, *Record Mirror* and *Melody Maker*, also rather grudgingly and half-heartedly covered the new music and, as a result, a new generation of journalists who listened with their ears and guts and critical faculties emerged. They were open minded and went out of their way to seek out and hear the new bands and new forms of musical expression that seemed to be crawling out of the woodwork, always on the lookout for the next big thing or something different to bring to the attention and turntables of their eager weekly readership. It was time for new talent to flourish, and The Residents were soon caught in the net. True, they were not a young new wave band – to reference The Sex Pistols' song *Seventeen*, they were all around 29 years old in 1977, "with a lot to learn" – but after years of trading in obscurity they were grateful for an opportunity to market and sell their particular sound.

The first mention of The Residents in the English rock press was penned by Jon Savage, who'd read an article on the band in the short lived, punk inspired, San Francisco fanzine *Search And Destroy*. Intrigued, he found out more about them and included them in a *Sounds* survey of New Music in November 1977, along with Brian Eno, Devo, Throbbing Gristle and Kraftwerk. He described the music thus:

"Mixture surprisingly attractive. Afterwards, most rock 'n' roll ridiculously 1D (dimensional) and straightforward. Vague air of undefinable menace, deeper subversion."

A month later, Savage enthusiastically reviewed *Meet The Residents, Third Reich and Roll* and *Fingerprince*: "What they offer is so radically different that effort is needed to break out of your/my box before you/I can fully enjoy... There is a deep design behind The Residents' sound - what they want they do know. But they're not telling. And why should they? This leaves room for your free-association, using Residents records as soundtrack. Often they are like walking dreams. Elements rearranged (deliberately) in such a way as to strike at the subconsciousness. Yes - that powerful. Think I'm trying to say that they're like nothing you/I have heard before."

The exposure heralded a breakthrough, and The Cryptic Corporation were so grateful for Savage's five star endorsements of their releases (***** equated with 'Very Important Platter'), and the fact that he even included their address at the end of the review, that they sent him a telegram with five stars on it. Jay Clem was quick to correspond with Savage and to keep him in the loop about future plans and releases. Even today, Homer Flynn warmly recalls the fillip in sales that Savage's review generated, "Up until that point there had been zero attention towards The Residents at all, if anything. The sales were so abysmal that when *Meet The Residents* was created a thousand were pressed, when *Third Reich And Roll* was created a thousand were pressed and when *Fingerprince* was created only five hundred were pressed because The Residents had rooms in their warehouse full of all these records that they could not sell and they did not want to get a thousand more to put in. Then those reviews came out and suddenly those records were flying out of the door, so it was a huge shock when that happened."

More pleasant shocks were to follow. Andy Gill, writing for the *New Musical Express*, began to add his own enthusiastic endorsements, and suddenly The Residents had two partisans in the very heart of the most influential British music magazines of the day. According to Homer Flynn, this change put paid to The Cryptic Corporation's plans to appeal over the decision not to grant their movie theatre a license, "At that point the whole plan was rethought and it was ultimately decided that, if the music was selling, why did we want to open a movie theatre, especially in the face of all this protest? That whole plan was dropped. But it went far enough that a business plan was created and we had hired Ant Farm as architects to design the interior of the whole thing. The plan had got pretty advanced, but the music started selling so the plan got dropped."

The Residents' mail order catalogue at the time stated, "When questioned about the project's demise, Cryptic President John Kennedy explained that superficially the project cost had exceeded its earning potential... Something had to go, so obviously it had to be the theatre."

One assumes that if the building had been bought it was now sold.

Next came the important patronage of the late John Peel, at that time, without doubt, the most influential DJ on the air in England. Like The Residents, he was weaned on The Beatles and the progressive and outsider music of the '60s and early '70s, and he was open-minded enough to allow his ears to dictate what he played. Despite initial reservations, he had fallen under the spell of punk and the new wave and turned his nightly 10-12pm nationwide radio show over to that music (with a heavy slice of reggae thrown in for good measure). At the time, he was the only DJ playing new wave music on a regular basis and, importantly, he did not simply play releases by established artists but personally took great trouble to listen to anything and everything sent to him, from bedroom demo tapes to newly pressed singles on obscure-one-shot labels. If he liked something he played it. And if he really liked it, he played it a lot. This helped sell records, from the major label release of the first Ramones album to the self-pressed debut EP single by a band like The Cybermen in 1978.

Peel was sent copies of *The Third Reich And Roll* and *Fingerprince* through a source at Virgin records, found The Residents' music, "Fresh, innovative and exciting," and may have first played the medley of *96 Tears/It's My Party/Light My Fire* from *Third Reich And Roll*, as well as material from *Fingerprince*. Peel had his own three star system for rating good music but also took the time to personally time each track that he played so that he knew exactly how long they would run for when he played them on his show (thus the three tracks listed above were timed at 3.35). He did not trust running times printed on record labels and sleeves.

Clem was quick to put him on the Ralph Records mailing list and send over an original copy of *Meet The Residents*, as well as *The Residents Play The Beatles and The Beatles Play The Residents*, which Peel soon dropped the needle on (his handwritten timings were 3.50 and 2.10). With Peel playing The Residents' music, his large and devoted audience took note.

One of those turned on to The Residents in this manner was the illustrator Edwin Pouncey, aka Savage Pencil, who recalls hearing their take on *Flying,* "I thought what the hell is *this?*" He resolved to find out, but, it was hard work. No-one seemed to stock this record or any of The Residents' albums, or knew how to get their hands on them. Finally, he got in touch with Ralph Records directly and began to buy the records via mail order. He, "loved the music, but also important were the graphics and artwork... I thought they were real artistic statements."

Pouncey had a weekly strip in *Sounds* called *Rock and Roll Zoo* – a satirical animalistic view of the music business – and quickly did a cartoon strip on The Residents. This was so appreciated by Cryptic publicist Jay Clem that Pouncey was told that he would never have to buy a Residents record again. Pouncey also did a *Santa Dog* collage which he sent to The Cryptic Corporation and was later reproduced and given away as a limited edition print to members of W.E.I.R.D. The Residents first short-lived fan club (1978-81). Another crucial convert was Chris Cutler, drummer in the art-rock band Henry Cow, who heard The Residents through Jumbo Van Rennen, who performed A&R duties for Virgin records, - Henry Cow's record label. Van Rennen (who I suspect also sent the records to John Peel) told Cutler that the music was great, but that Virgin would never touch them. Cutler took the records, listened to them, found some kindred spirits and started to correspond with The Cryptic Corporation, and then the band, directly. As Henry Cow were in the process of splitting up, he was starting his own company with his partner Nick Hobbs, called Recommended Records. The plan was to distribute the music of bands he found particularly interesting but who were totally unknown outside of a devoted but limited circle, such as Art Zoyd, Univers Zero, Magma and Sun Ra. Cutler offered to distribute Ralph Records in England and Europe, and the offer was gratefully received.

"We were the first people to bring the records in, and we held onto our monopoly effectively when other people started to bring them in," Cutler told me. "So, for a very long time we were the main distributor." Unlike Sun Ra, who had initially exchanged money for records on a street corner in America, The Cryptic Corporation shipped records to Recommended, and they appeared in its first catalogue, with a strong personal recommendation:

"Take over where (F. Zappa &) Faust failed to tread. Their music is unique & represents the furthest point yet reached in the use of the studio as a compositional instrument. Start with *Third Reich 'n' Roll*, which tears pop music into PIECES & then <sort of> RECONSTRUCTS it again – exposing it's contradictions – does for music what Berlin photomontage did for photography. Crucial."

After a write-up like this many people put in orders, and press reviews of the albums also attracted sales that Recommended fulfilled. "I can't recall how many of each we ordered," Cutler recently told me when I asked how many copies were shipped over, "but we sold hundreds in a fairly short time." Under this agreement Residents records began appearing in English shops as imports, slightly more expensive than other albums but at least John Peel listeners and those who were reading reviews in the music press could now go out and buy the records.

At 444 Grove Street this attention saw an increase in activity, most notably in the mail order department. Whereas previously The Cryptic Corporation had literally not been able to give the records away, they were now inundated with orders, and demand even began to outstrip supply, so that the first pressing of a thousand copies of *Third Reich And Roll* and the first five hundred copies of *Fingerprince* had sold out by December 1977 – "Due to a delightfully surprising increase in demand this album is temporarily out of stock." But The Cryptic Corporation were not slow in re-pressing or issuing new product.

Although The Residents were reported to have been working on their next LP – "They are being extremely secretive, other than occasionally shouting "ESKEYMOW"" - this did not stop them swiftly recording and releasing an EP, *Duck Stab,* in February 1978. "It was done with a lot of energy and enthusiasm," recalls Homer Flynn, "At that time Snakefinger was in and out again... he was trying to become a studio musician - this is before he started his own band - and he was living in Los Angeles a lot, so he would be around then he would be back in LA then he would be around then back in LA. He was definitely in the Bay area for a while when *Duck Stab* was being recorded, so he brought a lot of life and energy to that. Also, they were in the process of recording *Eskimo* at that point, a very big long-term conceptual project, and they were not unhappy with the way that *Eskimo* was going but it was slow, so they wanted to do something fresher and more of the moment. That was a lot of the motivation for doing *Duck Stab*."

Knowing that there was a market for the product, The Cryptic Corporation initially produced two and a half thousand copies and quickly got one out to John Peel, (who again wrote down his own precise timings – 2.05, 3.05, 2.20, 1.05, 3.25, 1.10 and 2.35 – on the copy be began to play), Andy Gill, Jon Savage and other reviewers. "*Duck Stab* is not a limited edition," Clem feverishly wrote to Jon Savage, "and they're selling so fast I can't believe it"" So fast, in fact, that a further twelve and a half thousand were eventually pressed up.

Duck Stab remains a seminal Residents record. It received gushing reviews – "dazzling breadth and diversity," (Jon Savage in *Sounds),* and "It's like Eno mated with Zappa, Yoko Ono and the computer in Solaris" (Ian Birch in *Melody Maker*) - and even Paul Morley stated "The obtuse fed by Lewis Carroll, the curious eased by rock culture," in the *NME*. Each of the seven tracks were distinctly Residential but imbibed with the nagging beauty of nursery rhymes. The breathless vocal run of *Constantinople*, the slow balladry of *Blue Rosebuds* sliced open with a falsetto knife, and *Bach Is Dead, Elvis And His Boss* and the compelling *Laughing Song* all shone. That *Sinister Exaggerator* showcased Snakefinger's guitar was the icing on the cake.

As ever, the packaging was superb and stood out from the cut and paste of the DIY new wave *and* the slick major label packaging of bands like The Stranglers or Generation X. The surreal black and red cover featuring a Resident stabbing a duck commanded attention. For the first time the lyrics were also printed on the back sleeve, and with an eye on the collector's market Ralph issued a limited edition package containing the EP, a T-shirt and a colour poster. The only downside was the record's poor sound quality, due, in part, to the fact that nearly sixteen minutes of music had been crammed onto two sides of a 7" record. Later in 1978, *Duck Stab* was re-released on *Duck Stab/Buster And Glen,* an LP featuring another batch of songs that were intended for a second EP. The music on the *Buster And Glen* side was every bit as good and accessible as *Duck Stab*, with tracks like *Semolina*, *Hello Skinny*, *Lizard Lady* and *The Electrocutioner* becoming instant classics. The LP sold strongly through Recommended and, crucially, a new independent distribution network established by Rough Trade's Geoff Travis also began handling copies. It appears that Jon Savage was instrumental in opening up this avenue, Jay Clem having written to him in late December 1977 to thank him for this and tell him that "*Fingerprince* is delayed daily (for nitshit reasons that infuriate me) but we'll ship the first day and wire them regarding arrival time." This was, of course, the first repressing.

Hot on the heels of *Duck Stab/Buster And Glen* came a re-release of *Satisfaction*. The Residents had been keen to keep the original version, which had now sold out, as a limited edition art piece and not re-release it in any form, but such was the demand for product that they finally bowed to commercial demand – and The Cryptic Corporation – and allowed its reissue. They would have been foolhardy not to - although not typical of their output, the screamed vocals and manic delivery of the song fitted perfectly into the new wave musical bag. It was hard and fast music, painful to listen to and totally irreverent to The Rolling Stones' original. Its ferocity matched anything being produced by punk rock's market leaders and new wave stallholders.

Remarkably, Devo's cover version of *Satisfaction* was released in England just two weeks before The Residents' released their re-issue. Whereas The Residents overloaded the song, Devo had stripped it down in a version that worked just as well. According to William Reinhardt, The Residents were not happy at the timing, particularly as the record was issued in America around the same time, "I was there the night *Saturday Night Live* presented the first appearance of Devo. We were all sitting in front of the TV in their den, and I remember the palpable envy they had that Devo had become successful. They were very jealous of Devo. I remember them being extremely envious because they thought they were doing stuff that should get more recognition."

Maybe The Residents were worried that they had just paid to have thirty thousand copies of their own version of the song pressed on translucent yellow vinyl, but they need not have worried as *Satisfaction* quickly began flying out of shops in England and America, as well as through The Cryptic Corporation's mail order operation. It became, at that time, the biggest selling Residents record, netting the band some $20,000.

Flushed with growing success, Ralph Records also released the first solo single by longtime collaborator Snakefinger. Not that, according to Joshua Raoul Brody, he intended to record it. "He was working on a pop demo tape because he really wanted to score a major label deal, so he came to The Residents studio... and his deal with The Residents was, in exchange for them letting him use the studio and their production time to make these quirky little pop demos – which, I believe turned The Residents' stomachs – Philip would agree to work with them on a Residents sounding song. That was *The Spot*."

Released on blue vinyl, with a new version of *Smelly Tongues* on the B-side, this single launched Snakefinger's solo career. The Cryptic Corporation strongly promoted the single in the UK, taking out an advert in the music press that managed to play every card they knew, from his association with The Residents to his time with Chilli Willi And The Red Hot Peppers; "Nick Lowe played bass on Chilli Willi's first LP. The Willis' drummer now plays with Elvis Costello. And their manager founded Stiff Records. And the list goes on..."

Unlike Devo, Talking Heads, Blondie and Pere Ubu, who were all breaking in England at this time, The Residents could not follow up the growing media attention with a series of live concerts to promote the band or their new releases. Also, as they were now fully adhering to the Theory Of Obscurity, they would do *no more* interviews, although publicist Jay Clem was quick to make himself available and baste the self-created myths surrounding the band. The Theory Of Phonetic Organisation, the mysterious N Senada, The Theory Of Obscurity, the lengths to which The Residents went to keep their identities secret and the abandoned *Vileness Fats* project were all trotted out time after time like a team of highly trained circus horses, but the fact that The Residents sounded and acted unlike any other band could not generate anything other than the occasional feature as a supplement to record reviews. Photos purporting to reveal who The Residents really were (Homer Flynn and John Kennedy at a Pere Ubu concert) even began to appear. As 1978 came to a close something else was required to keep The Residents in the public eye.

"We no longer have The Residents. They're missing," stated Jay Clem to Michael Goldberg of the *Berkeley Barb* on 8th September 1978.

According to Clem, the day before they were due to deliver the completed tapes of their next album, *Eskimo*, to The Cryptic Corporation, The Residents vanished in a puff of smoke and magically re-appeared in London with Chris Cutler. They left the LP master tapes with him and then flew off to Japan. "They weren't pleased with some of our marketing techniques," Clem was quick to relate to the *New Musical Express*, "they felt we were promoting them too fast, and endangering the anonymity that they feel is vital to their creative process."

The Cryptic Corporation's response to this decampment was to release "Some old tapes they left lying around the studio," which contained, rather conveniently, the *Not Available* album from 1974. This was, of course, a pre-planned release - the *Not Available* tapes had been on the master shelf and clearly marked, and great care and attention was also given to the mastering and the finished artwork. Also, a full-page advert was strategically placed in the English music press on 4th November 1978 to publicise the release of the LP, stating that, "And now, for reasons known only to Ralph Records, the long suppressed story can now be sold".

The following week Jay Clem and John Kennedy arrived in London to retrieve the missing *Eskimo* master tapes and used the time to hold fruitful conversations with Radar and Virgin records, who had both expressed an interest in signing The Residents or licensing their records for release. The *Eskimo* tapes were handed back to John Kennedy by a smiling Chris Cutler outside the National Safe Deposit Box Company in the City of London, where they had – allegedly – been stored. Was the *Eskimo* master really inside the box or back in San Francisco? Even today, Chris Cutler is wonderfully cryptic, "Whatever was on those fifteen inch masters, I wrote the title on the box in runes and I sealed them with wax." For all we know, they could have been Henry Cow out-takes. The whole event was, of course, photographed and reported by attendant music journalists, and the icing on the cake was the reappearance of The Residents back in San Francisco, which generated another press release and more coverage.

It was promotion, and it worked. As the understated Chris Cutler told me, "The media paid a lot of attention to it. Made them come and take photographs." In addition, it not only increased interest in the upcoming *Eskimo* LP but allowed Ralph Records to channel *Not Available* into a market eager for new Residents product. "They violated their agreement by not delivering *Eskimo*," stated Clem back in 1978 with his tongue firmly in his cheek "so we have released *Not Available* – because we have to have something to ensure the future viability of our company." It was clever game theory, managing to maintain The Residents' artistic integrity, sell a new album, promote the next one, generate a nice sheath of press clippings and garner record sales.

As for The Residents? Well, according to the Ralph press release they just got on with exploring their new sixteen-track studio, installed under the watchful eyes of sound engineer Hardy Fox and graphic designer Homer Flynn, who had stayed in San Francisco. Maybe they witnessed The Residents laying down a new version of *Fire* from *Santa Dog*, which, paired with the original version on a 7", was given away free as a Christmas gift to everyone on Ralph Records' mailing list, along with an official explanation as to why The Residents had disappeared.

And as for *Not Available,* "According to the theory of obscurity the LP cannot be released until its makers literally forget it exists," and we are led to believe that it was, sequentially, The Residents' second album, recorded in 1974. If so, the difference between this and *Meet The Residents* is astounding. Not only in sound quality – there is much more space in the mix – but in compositional strength. *Meet The Residents* was very rudimentary music, roughly recorded and roughly played but totally beguiling. *Not Available* is much more assured, both in execution and studio technique. If it was recorded in 1974, there was obviously some fine-tuning and re-recording done in the four years before release.

Another reason The Residents might have wanted to forget about the LP was the very personal nature of the tracks. "There was a period right around there when it almost felt like everything was breaking up," recalls Homer Flynn, "and like so much mythology there is truth and there is embellished truth, and there were definitely parts of it recorded in the time slots when it was allegedly done according to the mythology. But then it was finished having survived this period of almost having broken up, it was recorded almost like a reinforcing project of things coming back together again. A lot of the story in it is about the break up, or near break up, but told in an abstract way."

Not Available is a surreal opera divided into four suites. The music is haunting and darkly compelling, and the plot is literally unfathomable as much of the poetic lyricism is elusive and somewhat unintelligible due to extensive vocal multi tracking and delightfully inventive wordplay. The details of what contributed to the near break-up around the mid-Seventies, whether it was related to strained relationships inside the group or to relationships with people outside of the group that impacted upon it, remain unknown, but the lyrics *are* allusive and hint at all manner of things, from sex and marriage – "'It's opening was known to need a token diamond ring" - to honesty and revelation - "I've got some questions that are guaranteed to shake you up" - as well as some form of reconciliation after crisis - "Now who is gone and who is right and who is left to see for who is left is just a few and two be more than… three."

Whatever the lyrics relate to, combined with the hypnotic music they have a powerful effect. Synthesisers and pianos carry the recurring thematic motifs, along with all manner of other instruments and extensive use of percussion. All of The Residents' trademarks are in evidence – multi-tracked horns and vocals that pine, groan, mewl, cry and convulse and are full of spell-like invocations, either solitary or multi-tracked, and studio trickery and techniques that have been mastered to serve the dynamics of the four suites of music. Conceptually, one might be tempted to compare *Not Available* to something like *Dark Side Of The Moon* by Pink Floyd, but this would be misleading. For all of its groundbreaking innovation *Dark Side Of the Moon* is still a collection of rock songs, albeit well arranged and recorded, whereas *Not Available* is all concept and sound, and conveys emotional heft that is mostly absent from Pink Floyd's music, apart from *Wish You Were Here*, on which Roger Waters took off his armour to sing about Syd Barrett. There are no songs on *Not Available*, only semi-operatic suites that Andy Gill was correct in describing as "…a shifting collage effect of recurring, interwoven themes, amongst which languish some of the most haunting music The Residents have ever produced…"

Not Available is one of The Residents' greatest albums, and can also be touted as one of the greatest concept albums of all time, with an ability to appeal to a broad spectrum of listeners, from those who enjoy the progressive music of the early '70s to those who revel in avant-garde and post punk music. That the curtain has never been drawn back to reveal the details of how it was recorded, or even where (it was probably started at Sycamore Street and finished in Grove Street), allows it to retain an element of mystery made even more fascinating by the fact that it was also a very personal album, and one which saw The Residents musically and vocally express issues they were personally working through at that time. They probably eventually allowed it to be released as the strong emotions at play during its recording were in the past.

After the sheer dissonance of *Satisfaction* and the quirky accessibility of *Duck Stab/Buster And Glen,* The Residents had revealed, in the space of twelve months, the breadth of their studio based musical explorations and a restless refusal to settle into one particular musical niche.

Eskimo would confirm this.

First vinyl record sleeve designed by a Resident
(Courtesy of Roland Sheehan)

Inside 444 Grove Street (Courtesy of The Cryptic
Corporation)

Sycamore Street before the printing press was removed (Courtesy of The Cryptic Corporation)

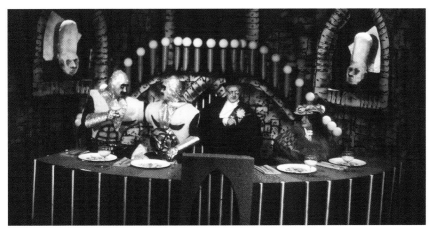

Arf and Omega dine in *Vileness Fats* (Courtesy of Graeme Whifler)

Gorgeous atmospheric image from *Vileness Fats* (Courtesy of Graeme Whifler)

The moment that gave us Snakefinger (Courtesy of The Cryptic Corporation)

The Residents meet… the meat (Courtesy of The Cryptic Corporation)

First T-shirt modelled by the original Mr. Skull (Courtesy of The Cryptic Corporation)

THE RESIDENTS ARE ON RALPH RECORDS!

FOR RESIDENTS INFORMATION WRITE: 444 GROVE STREET,
SAN FRANCISCO, CA. 94102

© 1977 THE CRYPTIC CORPORATION

Early Residents publicity photo (Courtesy of The Cryptic Corporation)

Early *Buy Or Die* catalogue (Courtesy of The Cryptic Corporation)

Original photo for *Chewing Hides The Sound* LP cover (Courtesy of The Cryptic Corporation)

Chris Cutler hands the *Eskimo* tapes to John Kennedy (Courtesy of The Cryptic Corporation)

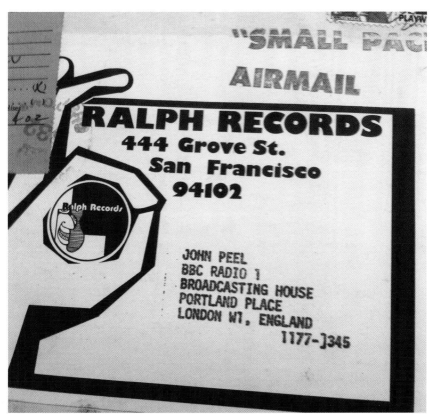

Urgent delivery for John Peel! (Courtesy of Ian Shirley)

Grove Street 1981: Doug Kroll, Helen Hall, Brian Poole, Homer Flynn, Hardy Fox, Tom Timony, Jay Clem and Graeme Whifler (Courtesy of Brian Poole)

Those now famous eyeballs (Courtesy of The Cryptic Corporation)

Eskimo

FUTURE: *Let me back up for a moment. You mentioned N. Senada, and I'm aware that he is often mentioned as a major influence.*
RESIDENT 4: *If you wanted to get right down to it, all that we are, we owe to him. He is possibly the last remaining unique individual. Our entire musical concept stems directly from his Bavarian works.*
RESIDENT 3: *With a fear of being premature, I'll venture to comment that we received a cassette from N. about a year ago which he recorded at the North Pole with the Eskimos. We have been reinterpreting this tape for our fifth album. It is perhaps the hardest thing we've attempted yet. (To other Residents)... Y'all think it's OK to say that, don't you? (Others shrug their shoulders).*
RESIDENT 2: *You see, the thing is that the album is so unique in its structure that we are hesitant to discuss it until it is further along.*
FUTURE: *And when is that to be?*
RESIDENTS: *(all laugh) Eskymow! Eskymow! Eskymow!*

The one truth that lay behind the *Eskimo* tapes publicity saga was that the album was not finished. Like *Vileness Fats* before it, it was an ambitious, mammoth undertaking, and even The Residents themselves were unsure if they could complete it. In 1982 Hardy Fox, speaking to *Keyboard* magazine, was quite frank about the challenges the band had faced, "Music had to be written that was reasonably true to Eskimo life. It had to be written using a limited scale and with a very simplistic primitive sound. So the music was being recorded just on its own, and simultaneously sound effects were being collected for the stories. Gradually the whole thing was being assembled. It was started on an eight-track, but it was discovered that it was impossible to do on an eight-track. The mixing was incredible, even on a sixteen-track, because everything was squeezed in so tightly that there was just no space between one thing and another. Something was always going out and something else coming in because they had to share tracks. All the way through it was like a giant puzzle. And there was very much a concern that it might not make a very interesting record because there was just no way of telling until it was finished."

The Residents' embarking upon this ambitiously esoteric project – an attempt to document Inuit life and culture on record – was the result of an alleged re-establishment of contact with the mysterious N. Senada. He had, rather conveniently, spent most of his time since 1972 studying Inuit culture, and had sent cassette tapes of his research to The Residents. According to the delicious mythology related by a Resident through the prism of a 1978 article by Chris Cutler, he even turned up at the studio, "In the middle of the night with a thermos flask full of Arctic air. He was very excited. "Get this on tape," he kept saying. He thought that we should all live in a refrigerator for a year."

The real reason for this attempt at an aural documentary was more to do with The Residents' fascination with sound and musical restlessness, rather than a slavish devotion to a mythical guru who managed to be more mysterious than they themselves. Successive releases had shown that they had no interest in simply regurgitating what they'd already done, and that their music was only limited by the endless possibilities of their imagination, musical competence and studio technique. After growing recognition and sales, *Eskimo* was an attempt to take their mastery further that it had ever been taken before, and to create an audio documentary.

Recorded by a core of two members, *Eskimo* was greatly assisted by a studio upgrade. "With *Eskimo* they got their first sixteen-track," recalls Homer Flynn, "So it was started on eight and then made the transition to sixteen-track in the middle of the project." As you might imagine, even then this was not enough, and The Residents had to push the technology hard to enable them to record the instruments and voices *and* add effects to arrive at the soundscape they wanted. "I think back to when The Residents were doing stuff like *Meet The Residents,* or *Third Reich And Roll* or *Eskimo* and how difficult it was for them to create some of the effects that they did," muses Flynn today, "They would do gigantic tape loops and have tape streaming all around the room."

As well as The Residents slaving away day after day in the studio, there were guest musicians on the project. In fact, every Residents project from *Meet The Residents* onwards had featured the necessary talents of additional players, who might contribute anything from a guitar solo to a compelling violin part. Despite the outward marketing ploy of anonymity, The Residents were highly collaborative. Or, as a Cryptic spokesman told a magazine in 1978, "The Residents are record producers; if they have to hire studio musicians, they do."

As well as Snakefinger, they employed Don Preston, ex keyboard player with Frank Zappa's Mothers Of Invention, who had been introduced to The Residents by famed jazz composer Carla Bley (although how they actually met Carla Bley is unknown). The Cryptic Corporation were not shy in sharing Preston's appearance on the LP, and even issued a press release that was sent out to journalists to publicise the fact.

Chris Cutler, who was distributing Residents records in the UK and Europe, had flown out to meet and record with them in April 1978. In an article for *Sounds* magazine a month later he set the scene:

"It was with interest, therefore, and a certain excitement that I approached the windowless warehouse on 444 Grove Street where The Cryptic Corporation had their offices... Here I found a genuine recording company with studios, conference rooms, a graphics studio, photographic darkrooms, shipping and receiving offices and, still under construction, filming and live performance facilities."

As for the recording sessions, Cutler told me in 1992 that, "There were finished pieces, half-finished pieces and blank tape and I played along with some stuff that was half-finished, almost finished... I put stuff on tape for them to use as they wanted later... It was professional, straight ahead, fairly creative and inventive, but a lot of studio work is." Working with anonymous musicians was no big deal - there was no curtain in the studio or adjoining percussion room, no disguises or darkened rooms. Sometimes all of The Residents would be there and sometimes he might only be working with the core. "On a musical level, as far as I could see, there were really two..."

During that period, Cutler gained a unique insight into the way The Residents worked at this time, "They would clock in every day just like going to work. Nine o'clock in the morning. Get there, open the doors, look at the mail, have a cup of coffee and discuss what they were going to do for the day. Work on their various projects. Five, half past five, go home. Every day. If you want to be romantic, it was like Andy Warhol's factory. It you want to be unromantic it was like a day job. A bit of a weird day job, but the product they were producing was a weird product."

Eskimo was unleashed onto the world in October 1979, and sold more copies in the first five weeks than every other previous Ralph release combined. Everything about the record was perfect, with the usual superb packaging. The first ten thousand copies were pressed on "arctic white" vinyl, and the sleeve was their first gatefold, with various Inuit stories printed inside to be read in conjunction with the music. But the most striking aspect of the packaging was the front cover. The Residents had always taken great trouble to present an image in promotional photographs that conformed to the accepted format of there being four members in a band. Previous publicity shots included the band wearing newspaper suits whilst standing behind a drum upon which was perched a skull, arrayed on the set of *Vileness Fats* inside four atomic shopping carts and wearing radiation suits in a supermarket. The front cover of *Eskimo*, though, saw The Residents decked out in top hats and tails - white dress shirts, bow ties and canes - against an arctic background. But that was not what grabbed the attention. Now, four huge, head-sized eyeballs disguised their faces. The effect of this image was quite stunning, and it became an instant trademark.

Interestingly, the eyeballs were not originally going to be used at all. Homer Flynn, The Cryptic officer mostly responsible for graphic design, initially wanted to have silver heads reflecting Arctic mist, but he abandoned the idea when he discovered that the silver heads were virtually impossible to manufacture to his specifications. The eyeballs were his *second* choice. Fortunately, they were easy to manufacture and reasonably cheap at a total cost of $1,800. They were fabricated by Mark Siegel, of a company called Dinosaur Productions who specialised in theatrical props and effects for feature films. Considering how iconic they were to become over the next three decades, it was exceedingly good value for money.

As for the music on *Eskimo,* it met with critical acclaim. Andy Gill of the *New Musical Express* panted, "It's without doubt one of the most important albums ever made, if not the most important. Quite simply, The Residents are halfway up the ladder while the rest are still trying to find a place to put it so it won't fall over when they step onto the bottom rung."

The album went on to sell over a hundred thousand copies worldwide upon release, which was a fantastic amount for an independent record, especially considering the content. *Eskimo* was hardly easy listening, and really was, as one review described it, "A moody collection of abstract melodies, punctuated by primitive vocals and rhythms that tell the legends of the Eskimo people entirely through the use of sound." Musically, it shares kinship with the experimental ambient music that was being issued by Brian Eno, as well as the embryonic move towards what would come to be known as world music. But, despite its abstract concept, *Eskimo* was, and is, a highly listenable album, an immersive soundtrack to a movie that can easily be generated in the listener's head. Each part glides effortlessly into the next, from the memorable opening melody of *The Walrus Hunt* through to the finale, *Festival Of Death*. It's a rich tapestry of sound, and The Residents must have spent a tremendous amount of time recording it. They read everything they could about Inuit culture, built their own ceremonial Inuit instruments and even spent time working out the phonetics of the language. As Hardy Fox told *Keyboard* magazine, "Most of the lyrics are English words that approximate the sound of an actual Eskimo word. That's the only thing that was really worked with. You'll have a whole series of English words that, when strung together, sound vaguely like Eskimo. Authentic Eskimo at that."

Some of these chanted English words were recognisable as TV adverts from that time. Phrases like "You deserve a break today", "Coca Cola adds life" and "We are driven!" lead some cynics to suggest that the entire LP was another practical joke rather than a serious work of art. Fox was very keen to set the record straight, "Some of the people who have noticed that have started assuming that's what the lyrics are throughout the record. That's not the case. It's only in the one section, and it relates to the fact that, at that point in the story, the Eskimos are being subjected more and more to Western civilisation and culture. As a result, their native chants start changing into commercial slogans."

Eskimo has not aged at all, and even today retains the power to draw the listener into the Arctic world that The Residents sculptured. This certainly pleases Homer Flynn, "You have to open up to it. You have to understand what it is about. If you go at it from the point of view of hearing rock music, you're going to go "What the fuck is this?" but, if you open up to what it is and what it is trying to do, it is great and successful."

The *Eskimo* project had been a long, arduous job of work, but to show they did not take themselves too seriously, in April 1980 The Residents released a disco version called *Diskomo,* wherein the entire LP was condensed into eight minutes and propelled by a disco beat. The other side of this 12" single, *Goosebumps*, featured a number of songs played on children's instruments bought from a local Toys R Us store and treated with studio effects and multi-tracking. Basically, The Residents having a little fun at their own expense.

And why not? At this time they were America's most successful independent band with their own devoted fan club, formed in June 1978. The aptly named W.E.I.R.D. (We Endorse Immediate Resident Deification) was formed by Residents devotees Phil Culp and Mimi King. Naturally, The Residents remained aloof from their cheerleaders, although The Cryptic Corporation did allow their distinctive membership application cards, which were headed "Ignorance of your culture is not considered cool" – to be placed inside LP covers to attract membership.

Culp and King received an overwhelming response, and soon had over five hundred paid up members. The membership package took a long time to appear, but when it did arrive it was superb. Not only was there a membership card, but also *The Unofficial W.E.I.R.D. Book Of The Residents*, which gave an excellent, if somewhat mythological, history of the band. The book was written by music journalist and Residents fan

Matt Groening, best known today for his iconic TV programme *The Simpsons,* and the cover art was by artist Gary Panter, who had also designed an eye-catching Rozz-tox icon on the inner sleeves of the *Eskimo* LP, which was soon replicated onto a T-shirt.

W.E.I.R.D. only lasted for three years, and membership peaked at around a thousand. It experienced tremendous administrative problems, but I, like many, can vouch for the fact that it did deliver on what it promised, including limited edition fine art prints by Gary Panter and Savage Pencil, snips of the *Eskimo* master tape and the occasional newsletter – usually several months late. It finally closed down in 1981 after releasing the *Babyfingers* EP, the missing side of the *Fingerprince* album.

Ralph Records - Buy Or Die

"Here we are again, trying to tempt you with more Ralph LPs. Obviously we are totally unsatisfied that you just bought this one in your hands and haven't even heard it good yet. But when you've got really exciting records like Ralph, it is hard to stay just calm." - 'Buy Or Die' inner sleeve, 1980

Eskimo marked the high watermark of interest in The Residents, and became their biggest selling record to date, even charting in Greece! But, with an eye on the future, there was another significant release at that time. *Subterranean Modern*, released a month after *Eskimo*, was Ralph Records' first tentative foray into releasing music by other like-minded artists (Snakefinger and Schwump had been friends). The album was a sampler that featured the cream of San Francisco's avant-garde scene - Chrome, Tuxedomoon and MX-80 Sound were all given one fourth of an LP and artistic license to record whatever they pleased. The only rule laid down by The Residents was that each band had to contribute a version of Tony Bennett's classic *I Left My Heart In San Francisco*.

Chrome, whose core consisted of Damian Edge and Helios Creed, were established studio explorers who had already released three LPs on Edge's own Siren label. The first, *The Visitation* (1976), did not feature Creed and sounded like the Blue Oyster Cult jamming with Jimi Hendrix, but with 1977's *Alien Soundtracks* they transformed their world into a collision of Stooges-like rock, sci-fi lyricism and Dadaist cut-up techniques to produce totally original, effective and powerful music. As Edge was agoraphobic they'd never performed live, but, like The Residents, Chrome had stirred interest in the UK and John Peel played music from *Alien Soundtracks* on his radio show. This, in turn, sparked interest from major record labels, and Edge, whose stationary included the hand-stamped title "Commander Supremo Chrome Forces" had been quick to fan the flames. "I heard from Andrew Lauder that you've been playing *Alien Soundtracks* on your show. Well we just wanted to thank you for the support," he wrote to Peel, "I'll send you advance copies of our third album as soon as it's finished." *Half Machine Lip Moves* (1979) was even better that *Alien Soundtracks*, and received rabid reviews in the English music press.

Tuxedomoon, on the other hand, were frequent live performers on the San Francisco scene. Formed in 1977, conceptually they were close to The Residents in that they sought to combine art, music, theatre and film, and their music was moody, textural and explorative. There had been early line-up changes, but by 1979 the core was settled and the music - avant-rock blended with classical motifs on violin and clarinet, a steady bass pulse and electronics - began to find its way into mature expression.

Alongside these two excellent and distinctive groups, MX-80 Sound were something of an oddity, playing sub-metal rhythms that sounded as if their portion of *Subterranean Modern* was some kind of pressing error. It was neither innovative, experimental or in any way avant-garde.

As for The Residents, they contributed three excellent tracks specially recorded for the project, and the best reading of *I Left My Heart In San Francisco* (Chrome hissed out some white noise, Tuxedomoon contributed a telephone call for welfare whilst the melody was buzzed out on harmonica in the background, and MX-80 Sound gave it a heavy, turgid instrumental reading). Three quarters of *Subterranean Modern*, with its fantastic Gary Panter cover art (the first Ralph sleeve not done by Pornographics) was, as Andy Gill wrote in the *New Musical Express*, "Light-years ahead of any comparable compilation release this year."

Tuxedomoon and MX-80 Sound were signed to Ralph Records, but, whilst Chrome was offered a deal, Damon Edge haggled so much that Ralph eventually withdrew their offer. This did not bother Edge as, by then, *Half Machine Lip Moves* had received a five star rating in the English music press and he was able to negotiate terms with Beggars Banquet, who had scored a massive hit with Gary Numan's *Are Friends Electric* and were looking for bands with similar potential.

At the time it was felt that MX-80 Sound had commercial appeal. In 1977, when based in Bloomington, Indiana, they'd sent a demo tape to Island records in England at a time when record companies were signing anything hard and fast. The demo was released as *Hard Attack* and sold twenty five thousand copies on the back of rabid reviews – "The Bloomington sound the next big thing?" wrote Chas De Whalley in the *New Musical Express* in December 1977. Unable, though, to promote their LP with a tour – the band all had day jobs – the arrival of the real next big thing in the new wave left them high and dry. Island dropped them, the band relocated to San Francisco and eventually they fell into the arms of Ralph Records as one of The Cryptic Corporation was a big fan of the band, "MX-80 were a very popular band in San Francisco due to their new expression of metal guitar and poetry. We weren't shopping for Residents clones. MX-80 just weren't trendy enough for the black-clad new wave or punk safety-pin crowd. That made them just right for Ralph."

The Cryptic Corporation's reasoning behind expansion was sound. By building a label of like-minded artists they could widen the appeal of Ralph Records and expected that the interest generated by The Residents would rub off on their label-mates. By this time, The Residents had established a devoted and rabid fan-base who would simply buy anything that Ralph Records released, and the plan was to turn it into a large, flourishing and successful independent record label.

As Jay Clem explained at that time, Ralph Records already had everything they needed. "For one thing, we have a lot of facilities right here in the building. We have a complete graphics facility for doing our own album covers. We have our own recording studio. When you have your own studio, you don't have to go out and pay $50,000 or something to rent one. Another thing is we don't spend a lot of frill money the way other record companies do. We can't. We just don't have it. The people who work here work, in large part, as a labour of love. Nobody is paid a fair market value for their services."

He continued, "We also do our own distribution. We do use other distributors as well, but we are the distributor to the distributors, as opposed to selling the master to someone in a licensing deal. Doing that we would cut our profits down to half, if not a third or a fourth. We service some stores directly, and we have our own mail-order operation, so we also get some of the retailer profits. Even though the volumes are all very low, it adds up enough that we are allowed to continue. We have found that, in spite of what everybody in the world will tell you, you can make an album for a decent amount of money."

With expansion, The Cryptic Corporation found themselves taking on additional staff. Close friend Helen Hall was brought in and later served as Art Director due to the increased output of the label, but the first person to be employed from outside of the magic circle was Tom Timony, who got to hear of the job through Jay Clem's girlfriend. As he was interviewed by Clem at 444 Grove Street, "Everybody else, sort of peered down – there was this balcony – looking at me. I guess they gave the nod of approval and I was hired." At first, working at Ralph was strange as everybody else had long established relationships, "...for years they were an in house co-op. There was never any outside world connection. I was someone they let in."

Timony was around twenty six years old, and his original role was as a general assistant. "I initially helped Jay Clem as we had two buildings, 444 Grove and 460 Grove, and I worked in 460 Grove when I first started, in an office next to Jay. I would go over to 444 Grove Street to help with mail order and I would also help purchase stuff. Just doing everything, from scrubbing toilets to getting shit sent in on the truck." (not, I hasten to add dear reader, to put down the toilet bowl in order that Timony could clean it again)

At Grove Street Timony also had to suffer the various musical tastes of his lords and masters that were played on the in house stereo system. African tribal percussion, Indonesian Gamelan, film scores and Ennio Morricone he could take. However, "One of The Residents loved Led Zeppelin. They used to drive me *crazy* playing Led Zeppelin albums." This was, presumably, the person who loved MX-80 Sound.

As an outsider, Timony can provide us with some perspective, "When I came in it was a free for all. Lots of money being spent, lots of product being made, just way out of proportion. There was a big independent scene... The Residents were in the right place at the right time to be caught up in that. It was like a playland – "We'll write all these cheques". They were riding on a lot of the money The Residents were making, people put money into the company. I came into the company as a non-business person and thought, "What the Hell are these people doing?""

The Cryptic Corporation did not just sign bands, they also gave them advances in the region of $10,000 - $20,000. Jay Clem, who handled this aspect, was concerned about being scrupulously fair. So much so that the contracts he drew up *allegedly* ran up to fifty pages and covered such esoteric areas as the division of royalties from sales made on American army bases. The thought of Marines having the opportunity to buy *Meet The Residents* at the PX really boggles the mind! When Tuxedomoon could not afford to pay a lawyer to read through the contract, Clem arranged for Ralph Records to lend the band the money to hire one. This lawyer then proceeded to advise his clients to seek more favourable terms from Ralph, who were meeting his fees!

There was also a heavy investment in promotion. One innovative idea was the series of *Buy Or Die* 7" EPs. These were, in effect, miniature *Subterranean Moderns,* featuring four tracks taken from the latest Ralph releases. In effect, an aural edition of the earlier mail order *Buy Or Die* catalogues, with inner sleeves that promoted Ralph artists. The EPs were offered in a large-scale advertising campaign restricted to the United States and Canada - *Billboard, Rolling Stone* and so on - for the token price of $1.00, which included postage and packaging. Even though Ralph would lose money on each of the records sold, it was hoped that in the long term they would recoup on their investment through subsequent purchases of singles and albums by their artists.

The first *Buy Or Die* featured excerpts from the then current LP releases by Snakefinger, MX-80 Sound, Tuxedomoon and The Residents. Tom Timony recalls that they certainly added to the frantic workload, "Helen (Hall) and I worked really hard to push The Residents. We would work night and day, doing so much mail order. Like the *Buy Or Dies*, there were literally thousands of them to mail out." There were three *Buy Or Die* EPs pressed between 1980 and 1981, each corresponding to the relevant mail order catalogue, and around twelve to fifteen thousand copies of each were pressed. Sometimes hundreds would be mailed out in a single day. Artwork for all three was done by Gary Panter, who also ended up releasing a single on his own label with some musical contributions from The Residents.

In the long run, the *Buy Or Die* EPs did work as a marketing tool, and the cost of producing them was recouped by mail order and direct sales. Indeed, a number of *Buy Or Die* EPs were pressed in later years to promote Ralph and New Ralph artists. A lot of established Residents fans bought releases by these new Ralph acts on faith, their reasoning being simple and sound - if it was on The Residents' label then they must like it, so it must be good. In many respects they were, and even the MX-80 Sound LP *Out Of The Tunnel* had its merits. Most of the early Ralph releases were excellent, from the aural soundscapes of the now seminal *Half Mute* by Tuxedemoon to the eclectic guitar work of Fred Frith, who had been signed via Chris Cutler and the Henry Cow connection (the two also recorded together as the Art Bears with Dagmar Krause). Later on there was also the electronic wizardry of Yello.

But the most significant Ralph release by another artist around this time was Snakefinger's debut album, *Chewing Hides The Sound*. Residents fans snapped it up as the album was essentially a collaboration between Snakefinger and the band, who had co-written, performed and produced it. The record began with the first ever cover version of Kraftwerk's *The Model*, and also included a cover of Ennio Morricone's *Magic and Ecstasy*, but the rest of the album was made up of co-written songs like *Picnic In The Jungle* and *Kill The Great Raven*, which showcased Snakefinger's distinctive vocals and guitar style.

Chewing Hides The Sound was licensed to Virgin records in the UK, with whom The Cryptic Corporation had built up a relationship which resulted in the 1979 Virgin release of a Residents sampler LP called *Nibbles*, accompanied by some press release nonsense - "The Residents, those lovable eccentrics from San Francisco, have almost consented to the release of an album through Virgin Records. With characteristic disregard for protocol, Virgin have chosen to interpret silence as agreement and release *Nibbles* on 13th July". This LP was, in fact, the same as a Residents radio sampler titled *Please Do Not Steal It*, which had been compiled and sent out to American radio stations with a press release penned by Cryptic engineer Hardy Fox:

"Due to the distinctive qualities of this music, not all stations are prepared to deal with this inventiveness."

According to Bill Reinhardt, The Residents' decision to target radio stations with these samplers was partially due to him, "I did many specials on the band, and when they did the radio sampler they did that with me in mind to air it first."

Although Tuxedomoon and MX-80 Sound came from the flourishing San Francisco scene, and Fred Frith and Art Bears through their connection with Chris Cutler, other Ralph acts were signed in the traditional sense. The Residents had always received tapes, either demos or fans attempting to cover their material, and as early as February 1978, in their third mail order catalogue, were asking these tapes to be restricted to "your most interesting selections" and advising that "editing is no sin". But it was through this medium that The Cryptic Corporation signed two experimental groups from Europe, Renaldo and The Loaf and Yello.

Renaldo And the Loaf were based in Portsmouth, England. Like The Residents, Brian "Renaldo" Poole and Dave "The Loaf" Janssen were less of a band than two people interested in making tapes in the evenings and at the weekends, and eventually, in 1979, these self-produced noises made it onto their own privately released tape, *Renaldo And The Loaf Play Struve And Sneff*. Amongst other things, Poole and Janssen were such rabid Residents fans that they even wrote a song in response to the formation of The Residents' fan club, seeking the meanings of "W.E.I.R.D" – Walk Energetically In Rubber Dungarees, Watch Escapism It's Rather Daft, Waste Eleven Iron Rubber Dummies and so on. Their first appearance on vinyl was on *South Specific,* a sampler LP of local Portsmouth talent released in August 1980, but this was only the beginning. When Brain Poole went on a fly-drive holiday to America with some friends, "We stopped off in San Francisco for a couple of days and, being into The Residents, I was naturally curious to see where 444 Grove Street was and what it looked like. Found it. Just rang the doorbell and went in. Apparently – I was told retrospectively – I was lucky, very lucky. It was only because I'd come all the way from England that I was allowed in. I dropped a copy of my tape in."

What happened next was the dream of all artists dropping demos into a record company, "The person I'd actually handed the tape to at Grove Street happened to be a Resident who was at Ralph HQ on that day." He told Poole that he would play it there and then, and Brian had the uncomfortable experience of listening to his songs with one of his unseen idols lending an ear. "This is excellent," was the reaction, and, as well at letting out a huge sigh of relief, Poole states that subsequently, "it was The Residents' own request that we were brought onto Ralph. They liked what they heard." Later, Jay Clem came to England to sign the band, who, prodded by The Residents themselves and inspired to be on the same label as their heroes, produced the additional material that became their debut LP, *Songs For Swinging Larvae.* After signing to Ralph, Poole returned to San Francisco with his musical partner and got an insight into the hive of activity around the label, "When Dave and I were there, Tuxedomoon were shooting a video. I also remember that a black cat lived there and he wore a bow tie. It is now part of the mythology of Ralph Records, but the cat did have a bow tie on that day."

It was a similar story with Swiss electronic duo Yello. TV repairman Boris Blank and musical associate Carlos Peron dropped in a demo tape of songs at Grove Street and the people they happened to meet were The Residents. "We told them we had come from Switzerland," Boris Blank told Matt Johnson of The The in 2014 (who had *also* sent Ralph demo tapes) "and they said, "Oh, *Sweden*, right?"" The famous Geographical inexactitude of Americans aside, The Residents liked the music "even though the tape hiss was louder than the music itself" and later sent Yello a contract to record an LP, which would become *Solid Pleasure*, a totally original rhythmic electronic soundscape featuring the distinctive vocals of globe trotting artist Dieter Meier. So began the musical career of one of Switzerland's biggest exports since banking, tax evasion and watches.

Tuxedomoon and Yello both met with critical acclaim and, even Renaldo and the Loaf's debut LP made money for the parent company. Whether the left-field cartwheels of Chris Cutler's Art Bears or Fred Frith showed a profit is unknown, but they were challenging and important records in their own right, and part of the European improvisation scene that Ralph brought to a wider audience in America.

Ralph Records were, however, conscious of the fact that they were operating, especially in America, outside of the normal industry parameters and with music that was in no way suited to the commercial mainstream. In the early 1980s, an era of Blondie, Queen, Michael Jackson, Diana Ross and Kenny Rogers, independent music had to work hard for sales. True, Ralph was building a solid relationship with the College radio station network across America (*Please Do Not Steal It* had been mailed to eight hundred and fifty stations) as well as a number of record shops, but they wanted to explore as many avenues of promotion as possible. Therefore, as well as the *Buy Or Die* EPs, they also began to produce short promotional films.

Given The Residents' early experiments in this medium, it was an obvious avenue to explore. *Vileness Fats*, for all of its troubles, had taught them a lot about lighting and film techniques, and in 1977 this had led to a fantastic promotional film for *Third Reich And Roll*, produced for an early, innovative video programme in Australia called *Flashez*. This short promo was described by Michael Shore in *The Rolling Stone Book Of Rock Video* as "The most utterly, exuberantly original and bizarre performance video ever." Even today, I cannot better his description of "four maniacs in neo-Ku Klux Klan hoods and robes made out of newspapers, banging on trash cans and oil drums in a futuristic-tribal trash compactor mutilation of the Sixties rock classic *Land of A Thousand Dances*."

The Residents already owned lights and a 16mm camera, and Grove Street had ample warehouse space to use for indoor location shooting. They even had a close friend and collaborator in Graeme Whifler, who already had an office in Grove Street and was given a remit to produce and direct these promotional films for Ralph's new artists, as well as The Residents themselves. Whifler set about his task with relish, "I was a one man band, conceptualising, casting, constructing the sets and lighting, shooting and editing the films," as he told me. "Producing and directing the short films for artists like Tuxedomoon and Renaldo And The Loaf was simply sublime, like being a kid in the ultimate playpen with unlimited toys and daydreams. I'd listen to a song over and over 'til it oozed out of my pores, then cook up a concept, usually anchored in psychological trauma. Then I'd start the slow process of set construction, prop building, wardrobe wrangling and, of course, casting. After weeks, I'd be ready to shoot, which would usually take one bone crushingly long day with a full crew. On set I was both director and director of photography, so it was beyond physically demanding, but I got the framing I wanted and we could move fast. After that it was weeks in a primitive 16mm editing room, getting the picture lock, then sending the negative out to be conformed. For the film to tape transfer I'd go to Los Angeles because the colorists there were the world's best. And then, after they were done, it was the darndest thing - people really liked them. They were fun, grueling and scary to do because I never knew whether they'd turn out good or I'd crash and burn."

But filming was not without its problems. In one instance, a $6000 dollar Renaldo and The Loaf film had to be reshot after it was discovered that the footage was out of focus! "There was a lens seating problem with the first day's shoot that was discovered when the film came back from the lab," Whifler recalls, "The equipment rental house gave us another free day rental and we reshot. However, a few takes were so good from the first day that I used them, even with a tiny focus flaw that is visible for just a few frames." This and other production expenses eventually saw the cost reach $21,000, and the band don't even appear in the video, which is somewhat surreal given that a singing, life-sized cat does. A Cryptic officer later shared with me that, "Spending $21,000 on a film for Renaldo And The Loaf that would never be shown in any promotional aspect was absurd. The film cost more to make than the album did and caused Ralph to go into the red on the project." Whifler also made promotional films for Snakefinger's *Man In The Dark Sedan* (taken from his second LP), Tuxedomoon's *Jinx* and MX-80 Sound's *Why Are We Here?*

Whifler's technique was inspired by TV rather than cinema, as he told *Record* magazine in 1985, "Even though we were working in film, I was well aware of the dynamic of the tube (TV), which could withstand wide angles, and I was, in several cases, intending to parody commercials while promoting the music... I never went for a lot of post-production, low budgets notwithstanding. If it's not on the film it's not there. You should do it all with the camera."

Whifler's first piece for The Residents was *Hello Skinny*, produced in 1980 and intended to be the first in a series of short promotional films based around *Duck Stab/Buster And Glen.* The star of the film was Bridget Terris. As Homer Flynn told an audience at *The Museum Of Modern Art* in 1992, "Graeme brought in this guy around about the time the film was happening and he was dressed in, like, black gay leather drag. He'd just been released from a mental institution. He had been put inside because he thought he was Bridget Bardot. Everybody called him Bridget..."

Bridget was perfect for the part. As the lyrics to the song stated, he was "incredibly thin" although Whifler recalls today that he was also incredibly lucky to be in a position to finish the film at all. "Making Hello Skinny was like playing with razors. Bridget, who played Skinny, was a guy I found in my old Bernal Heights neighborhood in San Francisco - basically, most of my casting was done from regulars at the local dyke bar that was my second home. Bridget was living in a group home for mostly older men with mental disabilities, and the owner was an evil transvestite who stole all the old men's money and kept them living in filth. I'd seen her parade her 'boys' down Cortland, the local drag, got my first glimpse of Bridget and was just overwhelmed by his star potential. I sought him out and convinced him that becoming a film star would be a wonderful thing. He auditioned and I gave him the part."

But after only a few scenes were shot, Bridget decided to leave San Francisco and go back to live with his mother out East. "I begged him for a few hours before his Greyhound bus was set to leave, and brought him into the studio for a session of head shots. I shot several rolls of 35mm black and white stills before he insisted on leaving for the bus. So, camera in hand, I followed him down to the bus station and kept shooting 'til his bus finally left and he was gone forever." Thus Whifler crafted the film out of a series of black and white photographs of Bridget, Resident eyeball montages and the brief snippets of colour footage shot before Bridget decamped. The finished film, with its dark compelling visuals, was a perfect counterpart to the eerie throbbing music of the song.

Produced a year before the innovative but conservative, AOR-minded MTV hit the airwaves, *Hello Skinny*, like many promotional films, mainly received exposure in art houses, University campuses and film festivals in America, as well as limited exposure on more broadminded European TV. However, there was critical acclaim heaped upon Whifler's work, with one commentator stating that, "There's a very distinctive personality, a point of view to Whifler's mastery of camerawork, colour schemes and lighting."

At the end of the day, however, it was all about selling records, and poor sales for some of the new artists on Ralph, and the high cost of producing these short films, slowly saw their production come to a halt. In an attempt to retain his brilliant visual sense, The Residents later offered Whifler $1,500 a month (the same amount they were paying themselves at the time) to direct the Mole Show project. As he'd never directed a live show, Whifler was uncomfortable with the idea, especially as The Residents already had a good idea of what they wanted. There was an amicable parting and Whifler moved to Los Angeles, where he worked on a number of video promos and TV programmes, including *Ripley's Believe It Or Not*. He also wrote and directed the 2005 film *Neighborhood Watch*.

Whether Whifler's films actually encouraged sales is a moot point. They're certainly not centered upon artists performing their songs, and the video as promo was in its infancy. However, the films were innovative, visually compelling and, as Homer Flynn pertly stated in 1992, "Everything to do with advancing a fledgling art form. The Ralph videos were definitely in line with our aesthetic."

The Commercial Album

"The Residents' Commercial Album consists of forty tracks – each exactly sixty seconds long – that sound less like songs than hit and run advertisements for the alien musical expansion of this San Francisco-based group's early records." - Rolling Stone LP review.

"I once had dinner some twenty years ago with a feller who claimed to be the manager of The Residents. I can't for the hell of me remember why he came to Swindon, but all he did all night long was boast about how big his penis was. Very disturbing when you're tucking into a vegetarian spring roll." - Andy Partridge (XTC), February 2015

Whilst all of this expansion was taking place, The Residents had not been idle. Indeed, they were attempting to sell themselves to the mainstream, albeit on their own terms. The way they chose to do this was by recording *The Commercial Album,* an LP of forty one-minute songs.

There was a lot of available material to work with. As Hardy Fox told *Keyboard* magazine in 1982, "*Eskimo* had been a very dominating project for a long time, and it didn't allow an outlet for a lot of things that were being written. There were piles of things, so *The Commercial Album* was an efficient way of getting rid of them."

The LP was possibly inspired by avant-garde composer John Cage's late Fifties composition lecture series *Indeterminacy*, where a series of thirty stories and anecdotes were read out, each lasting one-minute. It was also intended to make, as Jay Clem said, "a direct comment on the superficiality of pop music by incorporating more substance in one minute than most pop songs do in three or four." Or, as another Cryptic source later stated, "*The Commercial Album* was not an attempt to be commercial. It was just a run-screaming-from-the-likes-of-*Eskimo* project. Mainstream? Even The Residents aren't that out of touch with reality."

Unlike the long drawn out slog of *Eskimo*, *The Commercial Album* was put together in an intensive ten-month period between September

1979 and July 1980. As for how songs were kept down to exactly a minute in this pre-digital age, Hardy Fox was very clear, "Basically, each song was worked on without regard to its length. Then it was a matter of starting to edit it using a stopwatch. Sections would be knocked out, or bars, or individual beats, until finally a basic cue track was written that was as close to one minute long as possible. From there, further operations were done with tape recorder speed and things like that to make the exact length."

As usual there were a number of collaborators on the project. Parts laid down by Chris Cutler and Fred Frith were heavily used, and Lene Lovich recorded the vocals for *Picnic Boy* under the subterfuge of the assumed name Sandy Sandwich. Another guest was Andy Partridge, lead singer and guitarist with XTC, who can vividly recall how he came to contribute to the LP.

"It was the whirl of touring" he laughs down the phone, "We were playing San Francisco, and it was two gigs at the one venue (The Old Waldorf). When you're on tour it all becomes one long gig. I can't remember how they approached me, but it may have been backstage after the gig. I think Brian Eno and David Byrne turned up, and I have a funny feeling that Todd Rundgren turned up as well."

Whatever was said by The Residents made a positive impression on Partridge, who already owned a copy of *Duck Stab/Buster And Glen,* "I found myself jumping in a taxi the next morning and heading over to this rather nondescript building that, I'm guessing, was some kind of small manufacturing works. Some small place that used to make stuff, with offices attached. Well, inside was this... well, to say "funky" would be putting it politely. It looked like a little demo studio, with scraps of carpet on the floor and posters pinned up on the walls, odd looking instruments and funny looking objects d'art stood around. I had no idea what they wanted me to sing, and there was no kind of run through or anything. It was "You go in there and put the headphones on and we will send you the track". There was no "This is the melody" or "This is how it goes" or anything like that. It was just, "Right GO!" They pointed at me and I just kind of started. It was all *very* thrilling and great fun. I just grabbed a melody or a voice out of thin air."

Partridge greatly enjoyed the experience, especially as the band loaded him up with T-shirts and other goodies after the session – "I think I wore Residents T-shirts for the next ten years" – although today he finds the whole experience somewhat surreal. "It was a dream-like experience. My head was in the touring thing where you just spend all of your time being permanently tired and half-asleep, so if someone had told me that I hadn't done it and just dreamed it, well it would not have surprised me. *But I did do it.*"

The Commercial Album became the first Residents record to be licensed overseas (the *Nibbles* compilation aside). Prior to this, Ralph had exported finished albums to various distributors in America, the UK and Europe, but *The Commercial Album* was licensed to labels in England, France, Germany, Australia and New Zealand. Despite being courted by Virgin and Radar, in the UK The Cryptic Corporation signed with PRE, which was a subsidiary of the large, established Charisma label. As well as putting out the LP, PRE also released an eight track *Commercial Single* that included two tracks, *Shut Up Shut Up* and *And I Was Alone*, which were unreleased recordings from *The Commercial Album* sessions.

The Commercial Album was heavily promoted in each country by the respective licensees and sold well. After all, it was an extremely melodic album featuring tracks like *Moisture* (uplifted by a tremendous short Snakefinger guitar solo) and *The Act Of Being Polite*. In their native San Francisco, Jay Clem used the novel marketing device of booking forty one-minute slots of advertising space on local radio station KFRC-AM, therefore cunningly playing the entire LP in a day. When it came to talking about the strategy to *Billboard* magazine, Clem was on fire, "The conception, execution and marketing of the LP was intended to be more commercial than anything we've done so far. When it came time to make the choice of a station for the world premiere, we really had only one choice since KFRC is the top rated forty station in the market and is a consistent national award winner. Because the album has forty cuts we wanted to premiere on a Top forty station, and we have also pressed forty thousand copies."

There were also promotional films financed by Phonogram and Celluloid Records in Europe, whose generous budgets allowed a great deal of work to go into them. *Moisture* and *The Simple Song* were directed by Graeme Whifler, and *The Act Of Being Polite* and *Perfect Love* by The Residents themselves. Again, *The Rolling Stone Book Of Video* perfectly sums up the beauty of the films, "Petite pinnacles of haunting, dreamlike symbolism, each clip evoking serious otherworldly ritual... all four videos are stunning, because of The Residents' incredible imagery and Whifler's equally awesome use of camera angles and movement, cutting and colour. Rock video doesn't come much better than this. Once seen, the *One Minute Movies* cannot be forgotten."

The pick of the bunch is *The Act Of Being Polite*, particularly the arresting image of the blonde-haired girl dressed all in red with a huge eyeball for a head. *Simple Song* features The Residents strolling dance, in full tuxedo and eyeball regalia, around a pig roasting in the yard at the back of their Grove Street building. "The pig was on a gimbal," recalls Graeme Whifler, "and to get it to move we had the very young daughter of the hippie pig wrangler crouching at the base of the pig, dressed in a protective fire suit, spinning the pig. Surrounded by a sea of flaming red flares, somehow during the shot she was getting burned by dripping sulphur. So the music played, the camera rolled, the dancers danced and the pig spun, and we could all hear the muffled crying of the little girl inside her fire suit. She was a trooper." Readers will be delighted to discover that the little girl was unharmed by her ordeal, and the pig was taken away and eaten by the wrangler. On the subject of animals, Whifler recalls that he "had some props made using animal intestines, and they were okay for the first few days, but by the time we got around to shooting the odor of death was like a mist hanging on everything."

The film for *Moisture* is full of death symbolism and features a hilarious attempt by a Resident to energetically mime Snakefinger's guitar solo. "We dressed him up all funny," recalls Whifler, "handed him an instrument, and he came out and exploded with a spot on performance." *Perfect Love* - the weakest, to my mind, of all four – suggests, in a David Lynch manner, what *can* happen if you watch too much TV.

Today, Whifler is proud that, not only the *One Minute Movies* but all of the films he made with The Residents, have stood the test of time, "In all modesty, I can humbly say that Renaldo And The Loaf's *Songs For Swinging Larvae* is, if not the best, then one of the very best rock videos ever made. That was all a long time ago. What's the most fun and gratifying for me is when people tell me that their childhoods were seriously scarred by watching my videos, that the nightmares I gifted them with lasted."

Rock 'N' Mole

"Mark Of The Mole may well be the '2001' of avant-garde rock. Only difference being that this odyssey takes us underground, not to outer space, which may say something profound about the nineteen eighties. I will leave that question open. Let the mythologists among you decide." - Tom Padilla, Phoenix Magazine, 1981

"The Mole Show... is probably the worst business decision The Residents ever made, or at least the worst one we at The Cryptic Corporation allowed them to make." - Homer Flynn, some time later

As far back as 1973, The Residents had often played 'live' in the studio, and the fact that they'd only played three live dates in the ten years of their existence was less due to reticence than the fact that, as they progressed, it was virtually impossible to recreate their multi-textual music in live performance. Their music was created in the studio for the sole purpose of being released on record, and it was never intended for live performance. However, with the advent of their popularity, The Residents began to contemplate touring, not only to promote themselves, but also to find out what it would be like to play live for an extended period. It was something they hadn't done, and they were curious about sailing out into these uncharted waters.

There had been tentative plans to take *Eskimo* onto the road in spectacular operatic style, and at one point The Residents had designed a mock-up of how the set might look, but the project never got off the ground. But there was something in the air by 1981, when they began taking the possibility of going on the road seriously. Brian Poole, who was in San Francisco at this time with David Janssen, saw an unusual sight, "I have recollections of rehearsals going on for translating their music for potential live performance... rehearsing the songs we all know and love, to see how four people could perform them on stage. Whether the music, which, in itself, was created solely in a studio context, could be translated live. Various versions of things like *Birthday Boy* and *Hello Skinny*."

Nothing came of these rehearsals, although some years later these *Assorted Secrets* were released and gave fans a fascinating insight in how The Residents had boiled down songs like *God Song*, *The Letter*, *Birthday Boy*, *Bach Is Dead* and, amazingly, *Ship's A'Going Down* into music that could be performed on bass, synthesizer, guitar, percussion and vocals by a live band. The Residents sounded like a garage band - in other words, *great.*

Eventually, technology came to the rescue when, in 1981, a small company called EM-U Systems of California began marketing the Emulator onto an unsuspecting market. What EM-U had developed was the first major music technological advance since the introduction of the synthesiser some fifteen years previously. The Emulator was one of the first samplers - consisting of a small computer connected to a piano keyboard, it didn't generate any sound itself, but allowed a user to record two seconds of sound through a microphone input and then replay this 'sample' across each of the twelve tones and across four octaves. The sound source could be *anything*. A dog barking, a handclap, two steel pipes banged together, a cough, a car exhaust, a regular instrument or even music from a record. All of these samples could be stored on small floppy discs and replayed perfectly via the keyboard. A further nuance was that each sample could be sped up or slowed down.

The groundbreaking versatility of this instrument was first demonstrated to a wide audience in the film *Blade Runner*, for which the composer Vangelis used, among other things, an Emulator to create parts of the soundtrack. The Residents were aware of this, and one of them even went to see the film specifically to tape the music in order to study the various unusual sounds produced on the Emulator. It's worth noting that Vangelis refused to sanction the official release of the original score from *Blade Runner* until 1994.

The Emulator cost $10,000 in 1981, and after reading the promotional literature The Residents put in an order. They duly received one of the first machines off the production line - serial number 005 - and locked themselves in the studio for six days, only venturing out to grab anything in Grove Street that they could sample.

At first they saw this new studio toy as simply another compositional tool. Indeed, they used it extensively on their next recording project, which was part two of the Mole Trilogy. Although the first album, 1981's *The Mark Of The Mole*, had been recorded using traditional instruments, by the time it came to the second part, *The Tunes Of Two Cities* (1982), The Residents owned and used an Emulator. As Joshua Raoul Brody states, the new tool allowed the band to "make really remarkable music that sounded like nothing else, because they were drawing from a palette that was not available to anybody else." The Emulator proved perfect for *The Tunes Of Two Cities* as each side of the LP reflected the music of two warring cultures, which the Emulator allowed to be realised. In a bizarre musical twist, The Chubs were partial to Stan Kenton, whose track *Eager Beaver* was twisted into *Mousetrap*, whilst *Happy Home* tips the eyeball to Kenton's *Machito*. *Serenade For Missy* was, however, a Residential original and a lost beauty. The Moles were a little more primitive in their tastes, and tracks like *The Secret Seed* and *Smokebeams* sounded like traditional Residents tracks.

Eventually, though, The Residents realised that, by judicious use of a couple of Emulators, they could not only play live but, rather than produce a poor imitation of their recorded selves, they could take the authentic sound of The Residents out onto the road with them, stored on computer discs.

The next step was to plan what kind of show they were going to put on. They had no interest in offering up some kind of rock 'n' roll performance or playing songs like *Constantinople*, *Numb Erone* or *Blue Rosebuds*, which fans would consider to be The Residents' Greatest Hits. Instead, they envisaged something operatic and spectacular, and the *Mark Of The Mole* material was ideal for theatrical production. That LP, released after *The Commercial Album* in 1981, had been an ambitious, serious-mined concept album inspired by the Great Depression of the 1930s and dealt with the friction between two cultures after natural disaster had forced one - The Moles - to migrate to the land of the other - The Chubs. It was a fantastic LP and featured some of the most powerful music The Residents had yet recorded, and although it had been played on normal instruments these sounds were ripe to be sampled and augmented in a live setting. Better still, in dealing with the problems of assimilation, exploitation and conflict, *Mark Of The Mole* was ripe to be acted out on stage using a variety of props and backdrops, set to a musical accompaniment.

In a pre-tour interview with *Keyboard* magazine, Hardy Fox set the scene, "It's more of a theatrical presentation. A group of dancers will be acting out the story... and The Residents will be in a sort of booth at the back playing the music. Except for the overture, intermission music and the finale, which will be taped, all the music will be done live, and it will be overwhelmingly keyboards, although there will probably be a couple of guitars as well."

The Residents set to work planning and constructing the show. They set themselves no financial constraints - they didn't need to. By September 1980, Ralph Records had raked in, before expenses, over $500,000. On the face of it this looks like a lot of money – half a million bucks! – but it should be borne in mind that this was based on sales alone, and did not take into consideration any expenses such as the manufacturing costs of records, the printing of sleeves, purchase of musical equipment, living expenses, salaries, servicing the Grove Street mortgage or paying any taxes due. It should also be noted that this figure covered all sales from 1972 onwards - this was not simply one year's income. Still, it was a nice tidy sum and most of it had been generated between 1978 and 1980.

As artists, The Residents thought more about what they were going to put into the show than what they were going to get out of it. The Cryptic Corporation went along with everything, expecting that, as the level of interest in The Residents was so high, the show would comfortably pay for itself. Grove Street became a workshop where twenty one huge, eighteen foot high backdrops were designed by The Residents and painted by themselves and a number of enthusiastic friends. Costumes were also made, and full size Moles and Chubs were designed and manufactured. As for the musical aspect, The Residents rehearsed for the shows with two Emulators and full technical back-up from E-MU systems, who were gratified to have their technology showcased by a band who were already using their products to their full potential and were equally keen to see how their equipment would fare on the road. Indeed, E-MU even named their Research and Development room after The Residents and, later on, Cryptic engineer Hardy Fox would actually demonstrate the versatility of the Emulator at musical trade shows.

As this was a theatrical performance, dancers would be required, so an advert was placed in a local dance studio. One of the people who read this note was Carol LeMaitre. "The audition notice was pretty bizarre," she told me, "Avant-garde band needs dancers. Possible European tour."

Sarah McLennan, who was to become one of LeMaitre's dancing partners on the tour, also told me that, "Dancers are notoriously unfamiliar with music, especially modern music, and I don't think any of them recognised who The Residents were, apart from me and a couple of other people." They both went down to Grove Street for the audition, and, as the understated LeMaitre told me, "It was obviously not a dance studio. These guys were standing around." The audition, run by Kathleen French, who was choreographing the show on behalf of The Residents, was a typical dance audition in that she demonstrated the movements and the dancers who had showed up followed. At the end of the audition four were hired to dance on the tour.

Next, to make things clear for anybody attending the show who might be unfamiliar with the obscure concept of the Moles and the Chubs and their conflict - even Rick Wakeman hadn't gone *this* far out

- The Residents decided to employ a narrator, who, at suitable junctures in the performance, would explain to the audience what was happening on stage. Although famous now, at that time Penn Jillette was a struggling artist who came to the attention of The Residents, with his partner Teller, during the long running, madcap *Asparagus Valley* revue in San Francisco. Jillette was not only hired as the narrator for the Mole Show but, to get up to speed with their output, was tasked with recording the hilarious *Ralph Records 10th Anniversary Radio Special*, wherein he was locked in a motel room for six days and forced to listen to every Residents and Ralph Records release. As for his role in the Mole Show, he told the English music press in 1983, before the Hammersmith Odeon date, "I was handed a script from a word processor that had all the lyrics to all the songs, what the songs were about, an abstract description of the dances... and then the spaces for what I was supposed to do."

Putting aside the fact that The Residents seem to have owned a word processor as early as 1983, Jillette also stated that his primary function was, "...just coming out and essentially talking in those sections - which had times on them incidentally - a minute, two minutes. Do a minute and a half here, get irritated here, go crazy and so on and you'll be tied up here..."

Jillette was a one-man Greek chorus, and, as a comedian, would also be expected to inject some humour into a performance that Hardy Fox said in a pre-tour interview would be "reasonably intense. They don't want the audience to sit back and have a good time. The Residents will not be disappointed if some people have to get up and leave because they can't take it. Those who stay will have to go through some unpleasant things because that's reality. The Residents feel a responsibility to be entertaining too. It will be more than just simple entertainment." The dancers and Jillette would enable the performance to project some personality as The Residents intended to remain behind a netted screen at the back of the stage, in keeping with their reticent reputation.

Even the lighting would be different from the norm. This side of the show was entrusted to Phil Perkins, a cinematographer who had helped light *Hello Skinny* and the *One Minute Movies*. As he told me in 1992, "I thought from the beginning that I did not want it to look like a current rock concert. At that time, people lit rock concerts with hundreds of parcams and it just seemed to me like the shotgun approach. That's not lighting, that's illumination. Just turn the switches on and kaboom! You flash the blue ones, then you flash the red ones and turn on the smoke machine and that's considered lighting. Well, that's ridiculous." As, "it was supposed to be a dark, powerful, operatic type of show," Perkins lit it accordingly. "Rock shows tend to be lit like old fashioned television, the lighting is frontal and high. We lit our show back and low." There was one spotlight though – to illuminate Jillette for his walk-on parts.

The cost of the Mole Show was colossal, and no expense was spared. Including The Residents themselves there would be some thirteen people on stage – four dancers (slimmed to three in Europe), Jillette and four backdrop movers. There were also lighting and sound people, as well as a road crew, so by the time the Mole Show toured Europe it was around twenty people strong. But The Residents did not care - to them, this was not merely a series of live performances but an artistic showcase of everything they stood for. Music, art and theatre rolled into one. As Hardy Fox told the *Los Angeles Herald Examiner* in 1982, "They wanted to do something big – something that hadn't been done before. They wanted to do something real scary. Doing a live show seemed to be the scary thing to do."

The first performance of the Mole Show was a low-key warm-up gig at The House in Santa Monica, southern California, on the 10th April 1982. None of the dancers or props was used, the show was merely intended to run some of the music through its paces and see if the Emulators were equal to the task of live performance as The Residents performed behind a white sheet in a totally darkened room to an audience of sixty or so people, The show went well, with no real problems, and six months of intense preparation later – on 26th October – the Mole Show officially went overground with two sold out shows in the Kabuki Theatre in San Francisco, followed by four shows in Los Angeles and one Halloween show at Perkins Palace, Pasadena.

The show received very positive press reviews, with *The San Francisco Chronicle* commenting that, "The art-school crowd assembled on Tuesday at the Kabuki sat in rapt attention while dancers frolicked on a stage flanked by giant cartoon-like paintings, sporting various weird props, as the band worked its way through an obscure allegory about moles and their culture." The fact that The Residents had finally played live was a story in itself, and many reviews not only took the trouble to explain the concept being presented but also to comment on how Jillette's role helped translate the performance. "He would eventually go on to play a more active role in the proceedings," stated the *Los Angeles Times*, "and his glib delivery and gradual disintegration helped keep The Mole Show from going over the brink of esoteric."

At the Pasadena show, The Residents had their first brush with rock 'n' roll petulance. They were on a double bill with Wall Of Voodoo, a synth-rock band who, at that time, were on the brink of MTV-fuelled one-hit-wonderdom with the track *Mexican Radio*. It had been agreed in advance that The Residents would headline the show and perform last, it being Halloween, but, as show time approached, Wall

Of Voodoo decided they didn't want to play second fiddle to a bunch of wackos droning on about Moles and dug in their heels, insisting that they headline. When presented with this problem, The Residents were blasé. "This band with guitars and drums want to go on after The Mole Show?" said one Resident. "Sure, we'll go first." When this was related to Wall Of Voodoo, however, they changed their minds. Either they feared, in rock parlance, being blown off the stage, or they felt a sudden compassion for their loyal fans. Either way, The Residents closed the show.

These first Mole Show concerts were negotiated without any major problems, apart from the Emulator disc drives having a tendency to overheat as there were some eighty-five disc changes throughout the show. Also, as San Francisco, Los Angeles and Pasadena were all reasonably close together on the West Coast, transporting the props and backdrops didn't present a major logistical problem. So, the following May The Residents took the Mole Show to Europe for thirty dates, and into the teeth of a disaster.

The European tour was a double-sided coin. The performances went well, and, even if The Residents and their party were indoctrinated into the tough touring rituals of long drives, boredom and food poisoning, the shows were enthusiastically received by sell-out audiences everywhere and reviews were very favorable. However, the tour lost a bundle of money. How could this have happened?

There had been some financial worries at Grove Street before the troupe flew to Europe. There were a staggering amount of props and backdrops to transport, and the travel cases were so large that they could only fit into the hold of a 747 Jumbo Jet, meaning it cost a tremendous amount of money to fly them across the Atlantic Ocean and transport them from venue to venue. Then there was the number of people involved – twenty people had to be fed, watered, put up in hotels and have their salaries paid. The Cryptic Corporation tried to cover a lack of experience by signing business manager Bill Gerber, who, at that time, also looked after Devo, Tom Petty and The Cars. He told The Residents not to worry, they would recoup all of their expenses and outlay when selling out in Europe. Of course, this was not the case, and even though the European tour was a solid sold-out success The Residents still lost money. Why?

Firstly there was no large record company behind The Residents to pick up the tab for such an extravagant show. At this time, major labels like CBS, Island, EMI and even Motown would sign bands to a deal including 'tour support', which would help pay for hotels and other expenses as they toured in an effort to break their early releases into the charts. But The Cryptic Corporation, Ralph Records and, ultimately, The Residents, had to find the money themselves. As they realised that the numbers might not stack up in their favour until after the tour, and in order to generate some much needed cash flow before the tour got under way, The Cryptic Corporation sold the merchandising rights for the entire European trip for $10,000, including the Pore Know Graphics team's original designs for T-shirts and other promotional material. At every concert this merchandise sold like hot cakes, but The Residents, as per their contract, only received the agreed sum of $10,000.

Although at that time the sale of promotional items at concerts was not the big business it is today, it was still a very important source of revenue. Ironically, up until that point The Residents had maintained a strong hands-on policy towards merchandising, and their own T-shirts, from the first *Meet The Residents* design through to *Eskimo*, had sold strongly through their own well-established and well oiled mail order operation. They even had Tom Timony on tour with them, and had The Residents manufactured and put T-shirts onto a 747 along with the backdrops the tour would not have ended as a financial Waterloo. Of course, hindsight is a wonderful thing, and at the time an advance of $10,000 for merchanding seemed too juicy a carrot to refuse. But it was a mistake. "Licensing for our product was sold too cheap," Tom Timony states today, "and The Residents, T-shirt wise, just *killed* at every show in Europe. They sold tons and tons of those things."

Once they got to Europe, The Residents got their first taste of the hard-drinking English road crew that their tour organiser had employed. Used to dealing with rock bands who enjoyed drink, drugs and blowjobs, the crew found the low-key approach of The Residents' touring party somewhat taxing. It should be borne in mind that the (eldest) Residents were in their late thirties at this time, and that their days of sex and drugs and rock and roll, whilst not over, were certainly not in the forefront of their minds or libidos. The roadies also didn't enjoy having to wear boiler suits and Groucho Marx spectacle and moustache combinations like the rest of the touring party to protect the identities of the band backstage. They developed a problem with Penn Jillette too, who was no fan of smoking and drinking. Consequently the two European tour mini-buses became a tale of two cities themselves, with the party bus led by the road crew and the library bus, where alcohol, cigarettes and other smoldering substances were banned, led by Jillette. Those who didn't belong to either faction floated amongst the two as the mood took them.

Although I don't know all of the details, another cause of the financial pit that The Residents fell into during the European tour was the apparent abuse of the touring kitty. Although it cannot be verified, it appears this occurred to such an extent that one member of the road crew flew in his girlfriend from Europe and put her up at a hotel - all at The Residents' expense! As for Resident/Roadie relations, they hit their nadir when the road crew pulled out all of the instrument patches at the end of the prestigious Hammersmith Odeon concert in London, so that when The Residents attempted an encore there was no power, and consequently no sound. It took over five minutes to prise the roadies from their beer cans to grudgingly restore power so the band could play *Smack Your Lips*.

Of course, it wasn't all doom and gloom, even if there were road accidents, equipment theft and Penn Jillettte nearly dying of a gastric complaint in a Spanish hospital. For some, the tour was a great experience and allowed sightseeing in all manner of wonderful European towns and cities, from Utrecht to Paris. As Carol LeMatrie told me, "We were not so much aware of the financial problems, so we were having a good time and the pressure was less on us, as opposed to The Cryptic Corporation who were watching their children's life savings going down the drain. They weren't having so much fun."

This was true, and, looking back from the vantage point of today, Homer Flynn recalls, "It was pretty horrible really. Ultimately it was a bad decision based on even worse advice. Everybody was completely inexperienced at that point and relying upon advice from other people, and a lot of that was not really good. But, as they say, the things that don't kill you make you stronger..."

As with the American dates, the tour received a rapturous reception from fans, and very positive reviews, but after the last date, at Leicester Polytechnic in England on July 1st 1983, The Residents flew back to America vowing never to tour again. As Phil Perkins told me, they had been "raped by promoters and killed on merchandise." All The Residents had to show from staging and presenting one of the most ambitious pieces of performance art ever staged in European rock venues were huge debts that threatened to capsize the entire Ralph Records operation. Things were so bad that The Residents even had to ask their families for money to help meet financial obligations. "We came out from the Mole Show," recalls Tom Timony, "with sold out shows that basically put us $30,000 in debt, versus coming back with a pile of money."

Of course, when it rains it pours, and at this time Jay Clem and John Kennedy prepared to leave The Cryptic Corporation. From the outset, Clem had been the mouthpiece of the organisation, and his departure in July 1982 was a big blow. Why did he leave? Were there personality clashes, or did he simply, as Tom Timony told me, "Get frustrated with the biz. I think he wanted to be a big businessman. A powerbroker." As the overall boss of Ralph Records, perhaps he was tired of the day to day running of the business, the hassles with distributors and having to continually chase up late payments and monies owed, as well as having to sort out payments for the label's running expenses. The fact that he planned to manage Yello suggested, however, a bright future in the music business, although it must be stated that he found it very hard to leave, as he wrote at the time.

"Things have been really insane for some time now. It's been really hard to function in the environment that developed around me... I'm leaving Ralph/Cryptic... It was very difficult and painful, and I think, the best for all concerned. I still love my partners and The Residents, et al"

Bearing in mind that Clem had moved to the San Francisco area along with his friends in the late '60s, it must have been very hard to leave not only the partnership but also deep-rooted personal relationships behind. He was around long enough to help publicise the early dates of the Mole Tour, and was speaking to journalists as late as October 1982 as loose ends were tied up. However, shortly after The Residents' 10th Anniversary package was produced – custom made golf balls, pizza pan holders, *Santa Dog* sponge forehead thermometers and false locks of Residents hair – he bowed out to establish his own management company and look after Yello, shattering the myth that he was a Resident once and for all.

Clem's departure left a hole. Of all of the Cryptic officials he was the one most in touch with the music business, and had supervised the expansion of the label, as well as negotiating most of the licensing agreements with European and Far Eastern record labels. He'd also conducted a good share of interviews with journalists to promote The Residents' brand, and if Clem had remained with The Cryptic Corporation during the European Mole tour he may have been able to deploy his skills and accountancy know-how to minimise the financial problems. Who knows?

John Kennedy also left The Cryptic Corporation shortly after the performances at the Kabuki Theatre, leaving Homer Flynn, the graphic designer, and Hardy Fox, the engineer, to deal with The Residents' business affairs. His timing could not have been worse, although he was keen to stress to me in 1992 that he had "pumped a lot of money into the record company and the record company soaked up the money." When it was discovered that the proposed Mole tour of Europe promised to consume even more money, he decided that enough was enough. In his eyes, his involvement in the project had run its course. "We were making some money," he told me, "I would not say we were profitable, certainly it was not paying back the purchase of the property... Once it (Ralph) had been set up it was managing to maintain a cash flow. It even required refinancing. We would borrow money to permit certain projects... We had done a decade of it and produced many recordings and a film had been attempted. That had been enough."

Kennedy's departure was complicated. Unlike Clem, who, in leaving the Corporation took an agreed sum of money and the American rights to Yello and their first two LPs, Kennedy had invested a lot of money in Ralph and so wanted more. At one point he asked for the rights to all of The Residents' recordings made up until that date, but, after protracted negotiations with the remaining Cryptic officers, acquired something more valuable - 444 Grove Street. The building was owned by The Cryptic Corporation and was sold to Kennedy in return for his stock in the organisation. What price he paid is not known, but one imagines that it was a nominal sum for legal purposes. Part of the agreement was that The Residents had to leave. "I did not kick them out in any way," he told me, "but we had to establish a fair market value – rent agreement – which was above Ralph Records' ability to pay."

There was a reasonable notice period for The Residents to find suitable alternative premises, but it was a traumatic time for Flynn and Fox, who thought they would be in Grove Street forever. They later moved The Cryptic Corporation into a building next to the freeway in Clementina Street, but, due to its smaller size, had to jettison a huge amount of material, including all of the costumes and sets from *Vileness Fats* and other memorabilia, in a huge garage sale. Worse still, the studio in which every Residents recording from parts of *Fingerprince* to *The Tunes Of Two Cities* had been made needed to be dismantled and reconfigured in new surroundings.

Eventually, some succor, at least from financial pressures, came from an unexpected source - an offer to stage the Mole Show one last time at the opening night of the New Music America Festival in Washington DC. The Residents at first refused, but when the financial carrot got bigger they were not in a position to turn it down. It would help to clear some of their debts.

However, the European tour still hung around their necks like the Ancient Mariner's albatross, and all of their instruments had been confiscated by a shipping company in England for non-payment. Their tour manager had been supposed to pay the bill, but, like the entire tour, he'd run out of money. The dispute dragged on until the shipping company refused to send the equipment back unless The Residents sent them the $16,000 owed. It may have been at this point that The Residents had to approach their families and ask to borrow money. They finally paid $10,000 and agreed to pay the balance after they played the Washington show, but the agent accepted the first payment and then refused to send the instruments until he received the final $6000 owed. Meanwhile, show-time was approaching.

To make matters worse, The Residents were supposed to be the curtain-raising act of the two-week festival, which was staged in a different city each year. The promoters had taken an "aesthetic gamble" by booking the band, as their music was unlike anything else on the bill. The Residents did not tell the promoters about their problems, naively clinging to the belief that the shipping agent would release the instruments and everything would be fine. As Phil Perkins recalls, the band arrived in Washington "with no instruments, no props, no sets and no costumes and had to break that to them." He told The Residents that the show would probably have to be cancelled and was told by a Resident that "We were going to do a show even if it meant standing out there in our underwear with a slide projector."

So everything was built from scratch. Backdrops were made, and those that couldn't be fabricated were represented by slides that could be projected onto the stage. Moles and Chubs were constructed, and a local ballet school was contacted and their young dancers commissioned to give the show colour. Attempts were made to get Penn Jillette to the show, but airline schedules confounded him, and in the end The Residents' manager played the protagonist. Perkins recalls the mad rush to pull a show together, "The band, trying to rehearse the whole deal, rehearsed the chorography in a couple of rooms in the local YMCA, and in the vacant lot next door there was an army of people from California spray paining things and trying to build all the props on the street in time for the opening."

Joshua Raoul Brody was one of the spray paint army, "In DC I got involved in some of the last-minute scrambling to create replacements for the props that got stuck in Europe. I was aware that there was grousing about the inconvenience, but I didn't know anything about the depth or breath of the financial issues. I recall drawing a couple of top hatted eyeballs on fibre-board and attaching them to sticks, and since that's all I remember doing my guess is someone from PornoGraphix took one look at my efforts and figured I'd be better suited to making a coffee run!"

There was also the issue of instruments, and, as Perkins states, there began a "Statewide search for what, at the time, was very rare equipment - two Emulators, programmable synths..." The Emulators were only obtained after Hardy Fox rang EM-U systems and got a local dealer to lend out their demo model. Ironically, the equipment from England arrived hours before showtime (their manager, Bill Gerber, in England for a wedding, had taken a detour to go and threaten the shipping agent). 'We literally hopped into a station wagon and went down to Baltimore airport, and I pulled out what we really needed," recalls Tom Timony, "Which was the Resitar - a guitar whose strings were all tuned to E, which was really indispensable - the synthesisers and a few other things." The rest of the gear was left there, to be flown back to San Francisco at a later date.

The show would go on, although, as Perkins recalls, "The dress rehearsal was just awful. Not only was it awful sounding, it broke down a couple of times. We couldn't even keep the show going. It had to stop." However, on the night things were different, "The Residents came out and they killed. Of all the Mole performances I was involved in, it was the most passionate, the most colourful, the most varied. Precise enough, but with something very dangerous and angry going on, which was what the Mole show was all about." Joshua Raoul Brody also recalls that it went well, especially for him, "Nessie Lessons (Helen Hall) came down with laryngitis, so I ended up stepping in for her on *Happy Home* (dressed up like Uncle Sam), in addition to schlepping set pieces as I had done in California."

With the show over, The Residents flew back to California to lick their wounds. As for The Cryptic Corporation, they had more pressing problems - keeping Ralph Records solvent.

And If I Recover
Will You Be My Comfort?

"Initially, it all worked out on paper that it was feasible, but in the end they came back $30,000 short. It really boiled down to the fact that basically people in England fucked us over." - Tom Timony

"One thing that has always stuck in my mind was an evening when we went to a Resident's house for dinner. You have to remember this is 1981. The Resident asked whether we'd like to see his hot tub. I had no idea what a hot tub was and was thinking, "Why does he want to show us his washing machine?" So the evening ended with Brian, myself and two Residents sitting naked in a hot tub. One Resident dryly remarked, "Now, you'll be able to say that you recognise The Residents by their penises."" - Dave Janssen

In order for Ralph Records and The Cryptic Corporation to survive, it was imperative for all concerned to make money. The Uncle Sam Mole Show, for all of its trials and tribulations, had, at least, brought in some much needed cash, and around this time more money was raised by Tom Timony - now running the record label - selling a large amount of surplus stock to a cut-price dealer. These records were sold for a fraction of their value, but the money received helped with cash flow at a critical time. Whilst Ralph might have hoped to sell the records through distributors or by mail order, this would have taken some time, and, by 1983, the bottom was beginning to fall out of the American independent scene. Also, there was less space at the new premises for storing records, so getting rid of inventory seemed to be good business sense. Like many small labels, Ralph was now struggling to survive - things were so bad Timony recalls that, "People pressing the records and stuff wanted cash up front. It got to the point where we had to establish credit with people and things like that. It was a very difficult time."

After Kennedy and Clem left the organisation it was also decided to make a clean start and rename Ralph Records, which became New

Ralph and even sported a new logo. There may have been legal reasons for this rebranding after the Flynn/Fox/Clem/Kennedy partnership was dissolved, or perhaps Fox and Flynn just wanted the label to have a new start. Also, for the first time there was a compromise in the quality of packaging. "Instead of doing everything in four colour separation with gatefold and picture sleeves we toned it down to either one or two colours, and that saved a lot of money in the initial cost," recalls Timony, "We were just trying financially to keep it together. We were also owed a lot of money and got stiffed there by a lot of people."

There were also more creative ways to raise money. The *Buy Or Die* catalogue of April 1983 auctioned off items like one of the original asbestos suits used it early promotional pictures (minimum bid $150), a guitar "broken by a Resident on stage in Dusseldorf" (minimum bid $300), "Resident signed" brown vinyl copies of Mark Of The Mole ($30 each), test pressings, posters and some archive copies of vinyl rarities like *Santa Dog, Babyfingers* and the first pressing of *Meet The Residents*. This policy of auctioning off rare items to maintain cashflow would continue with subsequent mail order catalogues and, along with garage sales, really helped to generate revenue. Timony also had a brainwave that generated another flow of dollars, "I said, "We have $36,000 of film sitting on the shelves in the studio,"" he recalls, "So we put out a video called *Ralph Records Volume 1* with Tuxedomoon, Renaldo And The Loaf, The One-Minute Movies and other things like that. We transferred it to video and I found this guy in San Francisco who fronted us product. We would do fifty at a time and started with Beta, then went onto VHS." At that time videos were a luxury, selling for $45, so Timony sold *Ralph Records Volume 1* for $50, with initial copies coming in hand-made Xeroxed paper covers to save money. "That helped create cashflow because *everybody* who was a fan bought them." Later on, these videos were housed in more expensive colour covers.

Fortunately, to generate an even thicker blood flow of dollars, New Ralph was able to rush release another very unusual Residents LP, a collaboration with label-mates Renaldo And The Loaf named *Title In Limbo*. The original sessions for this album had taken place as far back as March 1981, when Brian Poole and Dave Janssen visited Ralph Records shortly after being signed to the label. Today Janssen recalls the experience, "We got to talk about how The Residents achieved some of the sounds and effects they used on their recordings, listen to rarities and of course, do some recording." Brian Poole takes up the story, "We were just hanging out in San Francisco for most of that time. The Residents were always in and out of Ralph headquarters and at one point said, "Let's see what happens if we went into the studio together.""

That was right at the tail end of our stay, and we just piled into this small studio and did stuff. There was a notional discussion of doing an album in four days. Obviously it didn't happen."

As Poole and Janssen were experienced studio explorers, there was no trepidation or angst about the recording. "I don't have any memory of being nervous," Poole recalls, "We were sitting in the same space as people whose records we really dug, but we'd also got to know them as people, and as people they were not scary, so we weren't scared in a musical sense. We were always made to feel very at ease, and it was really like a bunch of mates sitting down and messing around." Janssen confirms the informal nature of what took place, "We all sat in the studio, I was playing a guitar and mostly concentrating on that. I've no specific memories of what anybody else was doing. It was only afterwards that the idea was floated of trying to turn what we had into an album in the remaining four days we had in San Francisco".

The result was a forty five minute long tape upon which one of The Residents did a small amount of post-production before sending copies to Poole and Janssen for review. At that point the tape was put in The Residents' archive. However, two years later The Residents were in Hammersmith, "After the Mole Show in London we went backstage to say "Hello" and it was mentioned that perhaps we should finish that project off as it had potential," recalls Poole. "We know, in retrospect, that Ralph at that time was going through financial difficulty and it was a potential Residents release that might not take too long to do, but it was discussed at that point about doing it."

Janssen couldn't make the subsequent recording session as he had plans to go walking in Wales, but Poole flew out to San Francisco in September 1983 to work on the project. Upon arriving and recovering from jetlag, Poole saw that the new studio in The Residents' new building in Clementina Street was pretty basic, "The impression I was given was that it was not a proper studio and that it was a temporary situation. The recording area was separated from the office by only one partition, so it was all one space. Controlled studio conditions did not exist in Clementina."

Poole and The Residents quickly got down to business. "It was just a case of listening to (the original tapes) and using them as templates to build pieces on," recalls Poole, "In some instances the original stuff from the jam session comes through on the recordings, in others it has totally disappeared and been replaced by something else."

At this point the instruments that The Residents had used on the European tour – their Emulators and synthesisers – were still in transit back to San Francisco, so the amount on instrumentation was limited, but the chemistry between Poole and The Residents was evident and the sessions went very well. Looking back today, Homer Flynn recalls that, despite the financial pressures on The Cryptic Corporation, The Residents greatly enjoyed the collaboration, "It was a really positive experience for them and it was an unusual thing in that regard, but they had always felt a kind of kinship and connection with Renaldo and The Loaf that in some ways they never felt with anyone else. The Residents are not trained musicians, and in a lot of ways, rather than see themselves as musicians, they see themselves more like experimentalists or musical constructionists, and they felt that Renaldo And The Loaf came at music from the same point of view."

Like Chris Cutler, Poole recalled that this chemistry was linked to hard work with "a strict regime of working. Discipline. I just got weekends off." Thus everybody was expected to come in at nine, break for lunch and work until six in the evening. Even an attack of influenza did not prevent The Singing Resident, these days better known as Randy, from fulfilling his vocal chores. How sick he was can be heard on the track *Woman's Weapon*, during which he was "laying on the floor with the microphone next to him." Of course, when he was in finer fettle it was a different matter, and Poole has a vivid recollection that "The lyrics to the songs... were acted out at the same time... obviously not dancing around the studio, but in front of the mic a definite emotion and gestures of emotion... over and above what a singer would do to pump themselves up. Crouching down around the microphone and acting it out as if on stage."

As for how The Residents worked in the studio, Poole saw that they would built up things gradually, although chance was also an important element, "When they decided that a bit of Snakefinger would sound good here they simply rang him up and he came down to the studio."

Although Poole had met Snakefinger backstage in Hammersmith after the Mole Show, he still recalls a mixture of fear and trepidation about what happened the first time the guitarist came in to work on the Renaldo and The Residents material, "He was warming up and he said, "Do you want to jam?" I thought "Yes" but, because I was not the world's best instrumentalist, "What am I going to do?" But I had my bouzouki so we sat there and I played a drone for him to play over the top of. I didn't play the blues or anything like that, and he was obviously a wizard on the guitar - I was just playing and watching him. It only lasted a few minutes, but he did not make me feel like it was beneath him and that I was sitting down with this great guitarist. He was the perfect gentleman."

The Residents too were perfect gentlemen, especially when Poole was having trouble with a bouzouki part and they left him to wrestle on and went and had a coffee whilst he operated the tape machine and laid down the parts and the overdubs himself.

The finished LP, *Title in Limbo*, was released in November 1983, and, as well as generating cash, was an important addition to The Residents' discography. Indeed, it nestles in the top ten of many fans' favourite Residents albums. It's easy to see why - the organic nature of songs like *Crashing*, *Horizontal Logic* and *Sitting On The Sand* show the strength of the connection between the two bands. The Residents were certainly pleased with it, and even played the track *Monkey and Bunny* on their 13th Anniversary Tour. Also, Poole and Janssen were treated very fairly financially - although they didn't see the artwork until the record was released, they shared fifty per cent of the profits, and Poole recalls, "With our half we were able to buy an eight track Tascam, a sixteen channel mixer and a couple of bits of early digital outboard equipment. It was the biggest earner we ever had. For our album on Ralph we barely got a few hundred quid, but for this LP it must have been around £800, which back then was quite a lot of money."

As for the next Residents project, after the financial disaster of the European leg of the Mole tour they felt little desire to complete part three of the trilogy, and chose instead to put that behind them and move on to something else. Therefore work commenced on another ambitious project that had been on the back boiler of their collective imagination for some time. This was to be their *American Composers Series*.

The idea behind the series was simple - The Residents would offer up their own phonetic interpretations of the seminal music of various American composers. This would not be confined to classical music as, in their eyes, Captain Beefheart, Sun Ra, Smokey Robinson, Harry Nilsson and Bob Dylan were just as important as Charles Ives and Harry Partch. In total, The Residents intended to cover the works of no less than twenty composers over the next sixteen years, completing the entire project by 2001. Each LP would feature the music of two composers, one on each side. A list was drawn up and work commenced.

The first fruit of the project, released in March 1984, was *George And James*, wherein various keynote compositions of George Gershwin and James Brown were interpreted. At the time of release I recall being totally underwhelmed by the album, although as time has progressed it has become a more interesting and engaging listening experience. It was certainly bold of The Residents to attack Gershwin's *Rhapsody In Blue*, *I Got Rhythm* and *Summertime* with respect rather than the abrasive nature of their treatment of some cover versions in the past.

Also, rather than play it safe with James Brown, The Residents chose to cover the seminal *Live At The Apollo* album - one of *the* great early soul and funk recordings of all time. At least one of The Residents had a strong connection to the music of Brown, and Randy later recalled on stage that, in 1965, he'd actually met the great man briefly after a show in the South and helped guide his car back to the highway. As for The Residents' reflection of Brown's *Apollo*, the 'live' audience was taken from the Mole Show in Holland, and the vocals sound like they were slowed down to give them an echo of Brown's distinctive delivery. Some of the backing vocals were also delivered by Joshua Raoul Brody, "about three or four vocals, all sung by me in about two takes I think."

There was also a single released to promote the record, and *It's A Man's Man's Man's World* was a successful meeting between the Godfather of Soul and the Masters of the Underground. For this recording, the slowed and slurred vocals of the LP were abandoned in favour of the usual Residents delivery, and the music was fantastic. The first four thousand copies were pressed on white vinyl and featured a large iris in the centre, so that they resembled what was by now the trademark eyeball icon.

A video was made for the single, financed by Warner Brothers to promote the LP in Western Europe. The generous budget allowed The Residents to rent a studio for a day and shoot some live action footage with Phil Perkins, and they acquired a video computer called Mindset for $3700, upon which they constructed animated segments using *Lumina* a graphics package designed by Time Arts. "We saw Mindset at a computer graphics show in southern California," Hardy Fox told *PC World* in March 1985, "and decided that the machine was in a class by itself. For the money, it has great resolution and it's extremely fast." Homer Flynn was equally enthusiastic as it was certainly better than the early Commodore computer they'd originally used, "The important thing is that the Mindset has an output that supports a standard TV signal. Using a composite monitor we can run the output directly to video."

The animated footage was combined with live-action depicting a grey-faced Resident with flashing, medusa-like orange hair singing out of synch to the song, and the purely computer generated images shadowed the lyrics as cars dissolved into roads, trains, weights, electric lights and so on. The film showcased The Residents' tremendous visual flair at a time when there was a boom in the use of video to promote music - by 1984, it was de rigeur for singles to be accompanied by a promotional film. The Residents had anticipated this trend but were no longer in a position to exploit the medium - it was not a question of ideas but money, and the main outlet in America, and soon the world, was the now hugely successful MTV, which was mostly interested in showing videos of hit songs, or actually creating hit songs by strong rotation of videos. True, innovative videos could and did break hit singles and new acts, but they usually reflected a certain type of music and visual style and were made by large record companies with money to throw at video production in order to showcase the talent of bands they had made a big investment in. Thus, in 1984 the top MTV videos were for acts like Madonna, David Bowie, U2, Twisted Sister and new kids on the block Depeche Mode. There was very little scope for the promotion of music from outside of the mainstream, and experimental videos by cult artists like The Residents got very little public exposure.

The fact that they were on the outside looking in had never bothered The Residents, but there was now no escaping the fact that they were no longer in a strong enough financial position to finance their own promotional videos, or those of other Ralph acts. The European Mole Show disaster, the dissolution of The Cryptic Corporation and the decline of the independent music scene in England and America combined to flatten the idea of attempting to build Ralph into a flourishing company with a wide range of acts, and additional staff that had been recruited during Ralph's expansion, such as Helen Hall and Doug Krol, left the company as there simply was not the money to pay them. New Ralph did, however, maintain a small roster, experimenting with new releases by artists like Nash The Slash, Rhythm And Noise, Hajime Tachibana and Bill Spooner, and even licensing King Kurt's mini-LP *Road To Rack And Ruin.* However, these were usually one-off affairs, with minimal promotion outside of the *Buy Or Die* catalogues, and generally sold poorly, although the 1987 debut by Voice Farm did sell well. The fact that Yello were garnering international success away from Ralph must have also helped, but, whoever the label signed, The Residents were New Ralph's bread and butter.

The Residents themselves were still brimming with ideas, but hampered by limited resources. If they were going to continue to express visual ideas on film and video then they would have to find sponsorship from other sources and try to sell art to business. With this is mind, they floated a proposal to produce a series of Science Fiction's Greatest Hits, wherein original footage from 1950s science fiction movies would be coloured, edited and enhanced with modern computer graphics. The end product would be a series of short, two to four minute long features that could be shown on TV and MTV or released on videocassette. All of the accompanying music, of course, would be provided by The Residents.

With a view to soliciting funding for this project, they produced a demonstration tape, and the 1956 film *Earth Vs. The Flying Saucers* was treated accordingly. The results were, for the time, stunning and totally original, and The Cryptic Corporation entered into negotiations with interested parties in the film industry, but a deal could not be struck. There was an immediate problem with copyright - most of the rights to the films they wanted to use were owned by different studios and it would be too expensive to acquire them all. Eventually, the music for *Earth Vs. The Flying Saucers* was given away as a free one-sided single with the first edition of the 1986 *Cryptic Guide To The Residents*, an updated version of the 1981 fan club book.

The Residents had always been keen to work on film soundtracks, but most producers found their music too weird and therefore avoided using them. But this changed in 1985, when they were commissioned to score a low budget horror flick called *The Census Taker*. The Residents were not the first choice for this project. Indeed, by the time they got involved two soundtracks had already been commissioned and rejected, so they were recommended to the producers by their friend Penn Jillette.

The commission was hardly ideal. Time restraints allowed very little material to be freshly recorded, so the bulk of The Residents' contribution came from selective editing of existing material like *Margaret Freeman*, *The Simple Song* and *Easter Woman* from *The Commercial Album*, although some new material was included. In 2015, Charles Bobuck, aka Chuck, who composed most of The Residents' music, revealed that he wrote *Hellno* for his former wife Helen Hall, aka Nellie Lessons, who sang on it. The Residents liked their soundtrack, which was released on Episode Records, but not the film.

In the three years since the release of *The Tunes Of Two Cities* in 1982, there had been a rash of supplementary releases associated with the Mole series, all proclaiming that they were *not* the third and final installment of the Trilogy. These included *Intermission* (the intermission music played during the tour), a live LP, a low quality video recording and official and unofficial bootlegs of Mole show concerts, and even rehearsals.

There was also a series of comic books, produced by illustrator and fan Matt Howarth and based on the fictional mole characters. As Howarth told me, "I originally did the first issue of *The Comix Of Two Cities* as a tangent of silliness which I felt compelled to pursue upon hearing The Residents' *The Tunes Of Two Cities*. The first issue made its debut at a San Francisco concert in the early '80s and was swiftly followed by five more issues of the comic, co-published by Howski Studios and Ralph Records."

A limited edition was even produced in Germany, and the complete story ran to twelve issues, although issues seven to twelve were never published as standalones but were folded into a book with the first six. Howarth is an artist with a unique and individual graphic style and a fertile imagination, and in order to "bridge the comic book field with the field of alternative music" he also later featured musicians in the adventures of his greatest creation, Savage Henry. As he related to me, "Each guest in the Savage Henry comic book happened for different reasons, but obviously such guest appearances were incited by my personal interest in the bands' music. The decision to invite them to appear as guest stars was a welcome escalation of my desire to blend comics and music, mixing reality with fiction. Since Savage Henry is a guitarist whose inter-dimensional travels can take him anywhere, each guest's story could be designed to tailor-fit band eccentricities or musical style. The Residents got to be sonic wizards with a thousand different faces."

Eventually, in October 1985, The Residents did finally release the next installment of the Mole trilogy. But this was not, as expected, part three but part four! The Residents had perversely decided, rather than finishing the project, to extend it to six parts, with part one, three and five being political and parts two, four and six being social. The newly issued fourth part was entitled *The Big Bubble*, and upon release the cover art caused a great stir as it featured four men in white tuxedos with their faces exposed, leading many to think that The Residents had finally tired of their anonymity and revealed themselves. But this was another Residential hoax - the four people on the front cover were not The Residents but actors hired to portray a mythical band called The Big Bubble, who had grown out of a union of the Moles and the Chubs.

As for the music, it was intended to be a series of short Mole/Chub garage songs, but, in fact, it sounded as if The Residents were painfully exorcising the demons of the entire European Mole Show debacle. Songs like *Gotta Gotta Get* and *Go Where Ya Wanna Go* are disturbing cries of naked emotional pain, a sense that was enhanced by the way that the album was recorded. As Hardy Fox related to *Sonics* magazine in November 1986, "The vocalist would sing the song first without instruments or rhythm, and the arrangement would be worked out on that improvised structure. The timing of the singing is very erratic, so it required laying a grid behind the vocal to find the points where things would fall."

Today, Homer Flynn recalls, "That was really an experiment in recording all those vocals, a lot of which were done very loosely and improvised, and then building tracks around that. It was a very interesting experiment." The entire LP is dominated by cries, shrieks, groans and a host of vocal effects. Some of it works, whilst a large part borders on self-indulgence, with much repetition of nonsensical babbling and vocal histrionics. Some fans loved, it but many remained less than keen.

With *The Big Bubble*, for the first time in their career The Residents sounded as if they were treading water. Perhaps it was their increasing dependence upon the Emulator, sampling and synthesiser technology, which seemed to bland out the rough edges that had always personalised their music. But what do I know?

"I believe it is where The Residents finally grew up and stopped making that juvenile hippy punk grungier stuff. It is compositionally more mature and sophisticated. You should live with that album a bit more. It will creep into your brain!!"

Who said that? Someone from *inside* the bubble?

Enter The Professor...

"They did a tour in 1983, a European tour that went berserk financially and lost a lot of money, and they said they would never tour again..." - Hein "The Professor" Fokker

After the European tour debacle, The Residents had agreed never to go out on the road again. But, a couple of years down the line they needed to promote their work in order to sell units. As they were anonymous and not a mainstream act they were at the mercy of reviewers, and, although Homer Flynn and Hardy Fox gave interviews as members of The Cryptic Corporation, they always spoke about The Residents in the third person, which was unlikely to generate compelling copy that got underneath the skin of The Residents' working practices, or their private lives. They did, for example, open up to *Computer Comments* magazine in 1984, but only to wax lyrical about how their computer system allowed them to manage their mail order business. "Our audience is a special interest group," stated Hardy Fox, "The problem is trying to reach them, because they are scattered all over the world. We try to keep in touch with every fan, no matter where they are, so they can buy our products and keep the business running. That's the reason computers have become so handy." Computers aside, touring was, for most bands, not only the best way to make money but also to keep in touch with fans, help with self-promotion, shift units and win new followers to add to the computer database.

In early 1985, The Residents were approached by Wave records, their Japanese label, with an offer to tour the country. At first, The Residents were not interested, citing the financial and emotional cost of the European leg of the Mole tour as the principal reason. But Wave remained persistent and offered to bear all financial responsibilities, including airfare, accommodation and the shipping of all instruments and props. It was a very juicy carrot and slowly The Residents began to sniff at it.

Finally, they agreed - with everything taken care of financially, as well as their being paid to perform, they could hardly refuse – and set about creating an economical performance they would be comfortable with. There was no talk of backdrops, narration, props and playing heavy conceptual music. Rather they decided that these four dates in Kyoto and Tokyo would be a musical celebration of thirteen years of activity, featuring material from their vast back catalogue of music recorded in the studio but never played live. They also decided to take Snakefinger with them to really make the dates special.

Of course, there had to be *some* kind of floorshow, so, as well as having the traditional focal point of a lead singer – which they had not had during the Mole show - there would also be two dancers, who, like the singer, would go through a variety of costume changes. There would also be various hand-held props and inflatable animals, which would be cheap and easy to transport and set up on stage, and lighting would be minimal and revolve around the creative use of car and loft inspection lamps. The Residents set about programming their synthesisers, rehearsing and getting ready to put on a show.

At this point, Rich Shupe appeared on the scene. Shupe was a long-time fan and had heavily featured the music of his heroes on his weekly College radio programme. Like many hardcore fans, he'd persistently pestered Ralph Records for information on The Residents and forthcoming releases, and over a period of time had established an ongoing mail and telephone relationship with John Kennedy. In April 1982, when Snakefinger's third LP, *Manual Of Errors*, came out, Shupe rang Ralph with a view to doing a radio special on the guitarist and other new releases on the label. He was informed that Snakefinger was going to tour to promote the record, and in his enthusiasm Shupe found himself offering to actually promote a Snakefinger concert in his native Baltimore. When the date of the gig came, he even went as far as putting Snakefinger and his band up.

As Shupe recalls, "The whole band came to my house and we had, like, a barbeque and everything. Snakefinger did some laundry and lost one of his socks in the dryer. He's at the gig getting ready and he says, "I seem to have lost one of my favourite socks, can you check and see if it's at home?" So, I mailed it back to Ralph and they thought that was the funniest thing in the world, that Snakefinger's sock arrived in the mail from this fan. So I called the next week and said, "Is John Kennedy there?" and Hardy (Fox), who rarely answered the phone, said, "I know you, you're the one that mailed Snakefinger's sock!""

That was the friendly nudge which saw Shupe accepted by The Cryptic Corporation, and their relationship was cemented when he helped paint backdrops and assisted with security for the Uncle Sam Mole Show in Washington.

When Shupe rang Fox and was told about the dates in Japan, a thought struck him, which he verbalised - "If you've got something you can put on an airplane and take to Japan why can't you put it on a bus and take it to America?" He boldly offered to attempt to try and put something together in the two and a half weeks that The Residents were away in Japan, and The Residents agreed to review the situation when they returned.

The short Japanese tour was a huge success - The Residents were royally treated by Wave, who spared no expense and even constructed a huge sculpture of the band in their record store to honour the visit. They even set up a few live TV appearances, and in one of these The Residents performed an interpretation of *Jailhouse Rock*. The four performances – one in Kyoto and three in Tokyo – were exceptionally well received, and, more importantly, The Residents and Snakefinger greatly enjoyed performing them.

Shupe had been busy, and upon their return "there were far more shows than they ever wanted to do available to them." The Residents set about pruning down the list and establishing a proper itinerary for a club tour, which they also wanted Shupe to manage. This presented him with a dilemma - not only had he never managed a tour before, but he was also an undergraduate at College, and managing a three-month tour between December 1985 and February 1986 would mean missing two College terms. It was a hard choice, but there was only one possible outcome - The Residents were his favourite band, and at nineteen he became their tour manager. The next three months would be, for him, a "non-stop thrill."

Unlike the Mole Show, everything about the 13th Anniversary tour was based on strict economics. Everything – musicians, dancers, tour manager, equipment and props – was crammed into one large touring recreational vehicle. "It was not luxurious by any means," recalls Shupe, "It was more like a big family thing. The bathroom was full of equipment!" The only slight problem was Snakefinger's enjoyment of smoldering substances, which saw him frequently disappear to the back of the bus so as not to annoy the majority, who were non-smokers. Snakefinger greatly enjoyed the experience, and was much loved by the other performers. He was, "Just a really fabulous person," recalls dancer Carol LeMaitre, "Just his dignity on the road. That was his life and that was his home - travelling."

The 13th Anniversary Tour was also much looser than the Mole trip, with emphasis upon playing music and having fun rather than trying to project some musical concept piece. "The studio that had been their freedom had become their jail," Hardy Fox related to *Now Magazine* in 1986, when promoting the tour, "All the freedom and ease of work, with time to try this and that and experiment, got so it wasn't satisfying because it wasn't scary enough. They felt they should be on stage in a situation where there was real time and see what they could do and what would come out of it. Even after the Mole Show, they felt they were still too far removed, because that show was a theatrical piece. They thought they would try the club scene to see what that would be like, and they're not trying to make any statements of any type."

On stage, two dancers wore a variety of costumes, including full white tuxedoes and eyeball regalia, although actually dancing in the eyeballs was somewhat cumbersome. There was, as Sarah McLennan told me, a "Very small line of vision, no vision down, you can't see your feet or four feet in front of your feet." There was also, "No oxygen in those eyeballs... very heavy and no way to breathe." They found that they could perform in the eyeballs for a maximum of twenty minutes, but, unlike the Mole Show, the dancers had much more input into this tour's choreography. The Residents gave them only very vague dynamic direction rather than specifics, and let them work things out for themselves. Sarah McLennan reveals that there was, "a trust in the performers, and also an interest in what chance will give you... Let's take these people, put them together, give this limited direction and see what we come up with and call it a piece."

The lead singer, somewhat stifled behind a screen and having to play instruments on the Mole tour, revelled in being the focal point of the show. As well as radiating charisma like a nuclear reactor, he took great pleasure in wearing a range of teasing disguises that almost revealed his identity to the audience - wigs, false ears and a variety of tantalising masks.

The American tour was a great success - The Residents played in New York for the first time, and their two shows at the Ritzy were sellouts. Indeed, in 1985 The Residents played the third biggest grossing show at the venue after Jerry Garcia and Eric Clapton, and *The Concert Pulse* of February 1986 saw The Residents crash into the chart with an average gross of $13,212 per show. Top of the pile was ZZ Top, with an average gross of $259,946, but it's amusing to see that The Residents were listed above Bonnie Raitt ($12, 819), Husker Du ($6,634) and the Red Hot Chilli Peppers, who were only grossing an average of $4,252 per show at that time. Crucially, The Residents made sure they were in control of the merchandise, and at the three sold-out San Francisco shows Tom Timony hawked from a stock of a hundred and six different items and nearly sold out of everything, much to the surprise of the venue owner.

Of course, as the tour progressed there were one or two venues that presented a challenge, like a pool hall in Lawrence, Kansas near the local University. "You got twelve people clustered at the front while people were playing pool and ordering drinks at the back," recalls Sarah McLennan. At another venue in the Midwest, The Residents played what was to be the venue's last concert before the promoter transformed it into a Gentleman's Sports bar offering female topless basketball. As Don King was fond of saying, Only In America!

There were also dates in Australia and New Zealand, but, although Shupe did a great job, returning to Europe gave The Residents cause for concern. They required a battle-hardened professional to manage their affairs. Enter The Professor.

The Residents had sent a fax to their record company in Holland telling them that were contemplating a tour of Europe, but after their experience of English tour managers and English road crews they wanted someone that they could trust and who spoke the language. This fax ended up on the desk of Hein Fokker, who had actually seen the Mole show when a friend dragged him to a date in Holland against his will and had enjoyed it so much that he'd bought four T-shirts. "I planned to go to America three weeks later," Fokker told me about receiving the fax, "to visit the world championship bike racing in Colorado Springs, so I made a detour over to San Francisco and they played a show for me in their rehearsing room. At the end of the show they asked me, "Well?" I said, "What well?" Well, ever since, I have been working with them."

Fokker agreed to sort out the European tour but, importantly, was very clear as to how things were going to be, "I told them, "Well, if do this job I make the decisions on all kinds of things, of course in co-operation with you guys but on the road and with the production *I am the guy*. There are no BUTS and no IFS – of course there is proper discussion and agreement and stuff, but no hassle. *I will take the decisions.*" They said, "Fine, that is exactly what we need!" I said, "You guys focus on what you have to do, your hour and a half show every day, and as for the rest let me do the hassle." Well, they loved that! Ever since, it has been a complete situation of trust."

Audience reaction in Europe – as it had been in America - was hugely enthusiastic. In many respects, this was the show that fans had wanted to see all along - The Residents playing some of their most-loved recordings live, a solid-gold collection of classics. *Lizard Lady*, *Semolina*, *Hello Skinny* and *Constantinople* were all radically restructured for performance and mostly played from behind a bank of Emulator technology by one Resident, resplendent in a skull mask (Mr Skull's eyeball was stolen after a Los Angeles show on December 26th 1985 and, although it was returned, it had been damaged and was retired from touring). *Smelly Tongues*, *Ship's A'Goin Down* and *Water Westinghouse*, from the *Babyfingers* EP, also got airings, and there was even some material from the recently released *The Big Bubble.*

Snakefinger also made a significant contribution to the show on guitar, and, as most of the music was synthesised, sampled and structured, his searing guitar parts and subtle accompaniment gave the show tremendous excitement and strength. The Residents obviously enjoyed playing with him on a protracted basis, and the feeling was warmly reciprocated. Indeed, he and Hardy Fox also gave a number of interviews as the tour progressed, and, during one of these, Snakefinger related how the band kept him on his toes:

"The Residents... don't believe in timing. I'm a career musician, basically. Everything I play in any band has very obvious timing and you know where you are. So, it's a little tricky with The Residents at first... you have to have a certain amount of telepathy going on. There is no logical timing. No four counts."

Hein Fokker proved the perfect tour manager, and even when the backline and costumes did not arrive in Norway did not miss a beat. "They all looked at me and said, "What now?" I said, "We all go into town and we start shopping." We went to all kinds of crazy shops with costumes, bought all kinds of things and started working in the hotel to make new costumes and masks and those kind of things, and it turned out to be fantastic. They were hilarious shows in Norway, and when we arrived back in Oslo the backline had arrived so we could continue. That was the first mark I made." Fokker also made his mark at the front of house. "Hein is my best friend," Maarten Postma recently told me, "we have now been friends for forty years this year. Anyway, he was touring with The Residents on their 13th Anniversary Show and the merchandising guy ran out on him. Something like that, and so they needed someone to sell the merchandise. So I got a phonecall in Holland. "Maarten, can you come out tomorrow?" That was somewhere in Germany. I said, "Of course." That is what I did, and I *never left*!"

Once the European dates were completed, The Residents returned to San Francisco. "The whole thing made a pretty good sum of profit," states Shupe, "it was a financial success, the exact opposite experience of the Mole Show."

As with the Mole Show, a live LP of the tour (recorded in Japan) was released, with a fantastic cover by Japanese artist Tiger Tateishi. This did not, however, feature all of the songs played on the tour, so Ralph later released a limited edition double cassette and CD of the entire Minneapolis show, as well as one featuring music from the Amsterdam show. As the digital age progressed, The Residents have also made available downloads of shows from New York and Cleveland, and there have long been several bootlegs in circulation between fans.

Stars & Hank

"I have one approach to playing the guitar... and that's to be that familiar with it and that good that I can play anything and not be bound within any tight time structure. I'm working towards that. And... trying to keep the random thing happening so I'm not so familiar that I know what I'm going to do all the time." - Snakefinger

EDWIN POUNCEY: Have they ever met Sun Ra?
HARDY FOX: Yeah... but I don't know if meeting would be the right word. Sun Ra was making a film in San Francisco and The Residents hired themselves out as busboys in order to work on the set, because they were really curious about being around Sun Ra and what he was like when he wasn't performing. So they did meet him, but in the guise of busboys. They talked to him as they were cleaning his dishes and stuff. They found out that he wasn't just a performer... he was like that all the time!"

With their second tour complete, The Residents went back into the studio to work upon the second part of their *American Composers Series*, this time based around the music of the legendary country musician Hank Williams and the composer John Philip Sousa.

Entitled *Stars & Hank Forever*, the LP was something of a schizophrenic affair. The Hank side was absolutely fantastic, and gave wonderful renditions of some of Williams' most famed songs, each an absolute gem. *Hey Good Lookin'*, *Six More Miles To The Graveyard*, *Ramblin' Man* and *Jambalaya* are all excellent, and the strength of the project was demonstrated by the fact that there were three songs recorded but not used until later issued on the fan club CD *Daydream B-Liver* (UWEB 005). The outstanding track on the LP, though, was the disco version of *Kaw-Liga*, which was also released as a single.

Kaw-Liga begins with a typical touch of Residential humour, a plundered sample of the opening bars of Michael Jackson's Billie Jean – a sly reference to the fact that Williams' second wife shared the same name – before a drum machine takes over the beat and a powerful electric guitar joins in with vocals straight from the swamps of the Deep South. The song sold so well in Europe that a house mix 12" was released, although Hardy Fox was initially perplexed about an emerging dance style, "I don't think they've ever heard of Acid House. I just heard about Acid House myself in Holland for the first time. I don't know what it means!"

Pleasingly, the entire *Hank* side was some of the most accessible and commercial music The Residents had ever recorded. It also marked a move towards using more traditionally sampled instruments rather than self-created sounds. In fact, The Residents had simply tired of sampling and deploying unusual sounds for the sake of it, as Hardy Fox related to *Sonics* magazine in 1986, "They sampled everything when they first got it (the Emulator). But once samplers became common and the exotic charm of having one was gone, they moved away from it. They've started going for traditional instrumental sounds, very high quality digital sounds. They get professionals to record the sounds they want."

The only problem with *Stars & Hank Forever* was the other side of the LP! It was quite a jolt to flip the disc over and have to sit through twenty-three minutes of American marching music. It was not as if the Sousa side was poorly realised – it was extremely well done – but that it presented such a stark contrast. Of course, it could have been The Residents' intention to offer two extremes of music to the listener to challenge their preconceptions, and when it came to interviews The Cryptic Corporation were more than prepared to fight Sousa's corner. "He's one of the most solid, totally American composers there is," Hardy Fox told *Spin* magazine in April 1986, "He was a true original. He virtually invented American patriotic music and during his lifetime he was The Beatles, he was the most popular musician of his time." Homer Flynn then jumped into the fray, "At that time marching bands were where it was at, and he had the hottest one. But the music, if you listen to it, is very intricate, very baroque."

Most reviewers in the rock press had no time for classical music and treated the LP as if it was two separate releases, responding warmly to Williams but remaining lukewarm towards Sousa. "Get it for the sake of Hank..." wrote a reviewer in the *Melody Maker* in the UK, "Just for God's sake don't turn it over."

Stars & Hank sold strongly on the strength of the *Hank* side, and the *Kaw-Liga* single also sold well, although there was no money to film a promotional video to try and push it into the heartland of the mainstream. A shame, because if anything was going ferry The Residents across the waters into that uncharted territory it would have been *Kaw-Liga*. Then again, they had no interest in being anything but themselves.

Sadly, *Stars & Hank* was to be the last release in the *American Composer Series*. The Residents did not over promise and under deliver but were – ironically – ambushed by technology when, by 1987, the CD revolution began to wipe out vinyl as the main format on which music was bought in America. This meant that the idea of covering two artists on each side of an LP was negated - it simply couldn't be done on a CD as one would have to follow another. Secondly, and more significantly, the advent of the CD led to a rush of reissues and, therefore, revised royalty payments for previously released material. If The Residents were to continue with the project they would have to pay high royalties to the composers of the original songs. As sales of the albums were relatively low (from *George and James* onwards they sold in the region of twenty to fifty thousand units) the idea became financially unfeasible.

The next proposed album in the *American Composers Series* was *The Trouble With Harrys* – retoolings of the music of Harry Partch and Harry Nilsson, a wonderful meeting of unlikely artists. Also, as Homer Flynn recalls, "They definitely wanted to do Sun Ra, and they did some experiments on that, and at one point they even proposed doing an album of Bob Dylan stuff, and even had a connection to one of Dylan's sons. The whole point was to try and get Bob Dylan in the studio and have him create samples – guitar notes, piano notes and voice, whatever – and then they would create an album of Bob Dylan songs based on samples that Bob himself had created. Crazy ideas they would throw out there that are great ideas, but it is not always possible to work out how to make these things happen."

In general, however, the abandonment of the series was no great loss. True, it would have been interesting to see what The Residents would have done to the music of Stevie Wonder, Barry White, Scott Joplin or Captain Beefheart, but it would have been time consuming and would have prevented them from recording new material. In any event, they continued recording selected cover versions in the future, and even dropped anchor in the unlikely port of Prince's *1999*.

Stars & Hank not only marked the end of the *American Composer Series* but also, with the 13th Anniversary Show LP release, the end of The Cryptic Corporation's control of New Ralph. They no longer wanted to run a record company and mail order business, and so handed it over lock, stock and barrel to Tom Timony and his wife Sheenah (who were running it anyway) for nothing. As well as receiving all of the liabilities, Timony's newly formed TEC Tones was allowed to use the New Ralph name for five years. "I wanted to add different things to the label, and it did not feel that it was Ralph anymore... and at that point we went into TEC Tones, which had a different sound," recalls Timony. "They knew things were changing in the indie world. We had no problems; the object was for all to stay solvent. They found new deals on CDs with Ryko and overseas and I experimented with new acts. I did continue to press Residents vinyl and pay royalties." TEC Tones operated as a separate entity in the same building as The Cryptic Corporation, and to say that Timony ran with the project would be an understatement - he added new bands to the roster as well as establishing a number of fan clubs, like The Residents' UWEB and another for Sonic Youth.

Snakefinger's contribution to the Hank Williams project had been some typically inventive guitar licks on *Hey, Good Lookin'*, but, regretfully, this was the last time he would work with The Residents. Whilst touring Europe to promote his fifth solo LP, *Night Of Desirable Objects*, he had a fatal heart attack in Linz and passed away in his sleep on the night of 1st July 1987. He was 38 years old.

Lithman had always had a heart problem - a heart attack in Australia in 1980 had put him in hospital for six months – but his condition did not stop him from pursuing the life he wished to lead. Everybody I have ever spoken to about him told me he was a very easy going, friendly person. Quietly spoken and courteous. "A true guy," says Edwin Pouncey, who knew him well, "Really sincere." He was a musician to his fingertips, who could not imagine any life other than the one he led - his heart condition only made him perform it with even more gusto. He'd taken up residence in San Francisco and loved the city. Whenever he came over to England he would meet up with Pouncey and tell him, "How great it was to live in San Francisco as he would never have to suffer another bloody London winter." His home in San Francisco was at The Residents' old Sycamore Street address, and his living space was, aptly, their original studio.

Despite his solo career, Snakefinger had always existed in The Residents' shadow. This was no fault of theirs, it was simply that his unique guitar sound – slide or strapped on - was so deeply associated with some of their most seminal recordings. His first two solo LPs were also recorded in conjunction with The Residents, who played, produced and assisted with composition on the excellent *Chewing Hides The Sound* and *Greener Postures*. He then went on to record with his own band, and with subsequent tours and releases established his own musical personality. His most ambitious project was *Snakefinger's History Of The Blues*, and Joshua Raoul Brody, who played piano on that tour and the resulting live LP, issued in 1984, summed that project up very well.

"He was going through a phase where he was tired of being pigeon-holed as an avant-garde musician and really wanted to do something a lot more earthy and emotional than the music he was notorious for. So he put together this ten-piece blues band – no synthesisers, no electronics, no fancy stuff – all traditional blues... and demonstrated what a fantastic guitarist he was. He really copped the style of each of the blues artists he was covering."

Philip 'Snakefinger' Lithman was buried in London. Edwin Pouncey attended the funeral and recalls it being a "Foul, horrible, shitty day," and had a strong feeling that he "...wasn't glad to be back, really." The Residents did not attend the funeral, but paid their own tribute by holding a musical wake to their dearly beloved lost friend. In black, they played a heart-felt rendition of Hank Williams' *Six More Miles To The Graveyard* and a series of renditions of old English laments. Several large balloons were filled with helium, wrapped in black netting and attached to a number of tiny mementos brought forward by Snakefinger's friends. These were then released into the heavens. Hardy Fox, "It was necessary to put an ending to a friend who died. When the balloons were released and disappeared it was like letting go of a period of grieving. It was time to go on with life and prepare to meet your own death at some point."

Snakefinger was dearly missed by The Residents. He was a close personal friend first and a collaborator second, and left a six-string hole that was not filled musically until Nolan Cook appeared on the scene nearly two decades later.

"When Snakefinger died it was a real kind of blow to The Residents," states Edwin Pouncey, "because they had lost one of the star attractions of the show... he just let rip with that guitar. It was extraordinary. He was not playing normal, boring rock guitar, he was playing something else. Very, very experimental."

Since his death, through reissues of his music, both solo and with The Residents, Snakefinger lives on.

God In Three Persons

"Now there was this thing about them that caused me at times to doubt them, or created conflict in my mind. Usually there was a he one, and there also was a she one, but somehow they came out differently. And one of them, when she was she, would smile and burn a hole in me; a hole that was too hard for me to hide." - lyrics from 'God In Three Persons'

Snakefinger had been penciled in to contribute some guitar parts to The Residents' next project, which was being completed at the time of his death. This was to be an ambitious, spoken-word opera called *God In Three Persons*, and when it was released in 1988 the guitar parts were played instead by Richard Mariott from the Clubfoot Orchestra – on trombone.

God In Three Persons saw The Residents return to the conceptual arena, and if *Hank* was a return to musical form then this was The Residents moving to the next level, breaking the glass ceiling and challenging their fans to take the journey with them. This time, the music was subservient to the story, which concerned Mr. X, a kind of Colonel Parker-type faith healing hustler, and his relationship with two young conjoined twins who he exploits and serves. It's a poignant story of lust, sexual confusion, devotion and darkness, and, significantly, was the first time the poetic lyricism and storytelling of The Residents had been showcased in an extended form. The words are clear, rhythmic and easily understood, and there was even an accompanying booklet of the narration as a reference for the listener.

Some parts of *God In Three Persons* are extremely disturbing to listen to, whilst others are extremely sensual. Overall, it's is an amazing and mature piece of work, and the huge emotional investment by the Resident who wrote the narration comes across in the delivery and recording. It was also the first time that, Laurie Amat, a singer gifted with extreme vocal qualities, worked with The Residents on an extended piece for the first time. "I met them in 1986," she recalls today, "When I did my first work for *Hit The Road Jack*. Joshua Raoul Brody, who I had been working with on theatre pieces, called me and said, "Do you want to come in and do a session?" I said, "Sure." He said it was for The Residents. I said "OK." I did not know who they were – I'd seen an article in a newspaper once about a band in eyeballs but that was it. I went home and said to my roommate that I was doing a session for a band called The Residents. My roommate went crazy. "You're going to work with The Residents. Don't you know who they are?" They pulled out all of these albums - two of them were the composers series - and said, "You need to listen to this!" So I lay down on the couch, put the headphones on and put the music on and totally fell asleep." It was so relaxing to me. My friend said, "I can't believe you fell asleep to The Residents!""

When it came to the session, Amat was there to do backing vocals with some other singers, "They (one of The Residents) said there is a little solo so I would like each of you to sing it. I said, "What do you want?" They said, "Whatever you want. As crazy as you want to get." That was a kind of clarion call to me. So I did my solo and that's what ended up on *Hit The Road Jack*. As I walked out the door I said, "If you ever need a voice, call me."

A year or so later, The Residents called Amat about working on *God In Three Persons*, where her role was to sing the opening credits and act as a kind of Greek chorus, commenting upon the action. Even today she can recall the power of the music, "That whole album, for me, was a very sensual and sexual album. You could feel it throughout the music, and the story itself had that desire going under the whole thing, so I got to sing that desire and it worked out really well." In fact, it worked out a little too well for Amat.

"They'd given me a cassette of the roughs and I was listening to it on my Walkman in Tower Records. I was listening to the end piece where Mr. X tries to separate the twins, this big bloody sexual epiphany, and I was in the store – and you can say this, I don't mind – I was so turned on I had to leave the store! And I was sat outside going, "Oh my God! Oh my God! Oh my God! This is fantastic!" I was kind of on fire. That end part, I was like... Wow! *That worked*."

On release, *God In Three Persons* split hardcore Residents fans down the middle. Some loved it, whilst others were far from musically aroused and felt annoyed that the constant narration detracted from the beautiful – just listen to those trombones! – sonic tapestry beneath. And it's true, the supporting music is exceptionally strong, especially as old analogue synthesisers had been dragged out and dusted down. The composing Resident also made cunning use of the Swinging Medallions' hit *Doubleshot* – first covered on *Third Reich And Roll* – and the old hymn *Holy Holy Holy* as recurring thematic motifs. Detractors of the overpowering narration were missing the point that the powerful music was intended to compliment the narrative like a movie soundtrack, but, of course, The Residents also later released an LP of the soundtrack music on its own, so fans could have it both ways and The Residents could open up a secondary revenue stream from the material.

Reviews were – as you might expect – mixed, although *Rolling Stone* described it as "No less than a Residential *Tommy*." *Reflex* Magazine actually put The Residents on the cover and ran a six page feature on the album which read as if Lester Bangs and H.P. Lovecraft were conjoined twins, although when writer Sam Ryder - who was very close to the band - toned down the purple prose he was quite astute, "It's cool the way the story just sort of floats in the music, which wraps around and reinforces it in a real soundtrack kind of way. The more you hear, the more you start to see it like a movie in your head, especially when you listen to it with the headphones on."

Of course, what any reviewer thought was superfluous - *God In Three Persons* was the best album The Residents had produced for some time, and perfect for the new CD format. Homer Flynn and Hardy Fox worked hard to promote the LP with a number of interviews, and Flynn summed things up succinctly when speaking to *Music And Sound Output*, "It's probably the most sophisticated thing they've done. In terms of impact, this is easily the strongest thing since *Eskimo* and *The Commercial Album*, and maybe The Residents' most powerful work of all."

Ironically, despite their love of technology, The Residents were initially reticent about getting involved with the advances offered by digital recording and computer generated music. One reason was expense, but they were also comfortable with their existing sixteen-track Tascam machine, so *God In Three Persons* was recorded on tape - "It's actually played!! Amazing!! No wonder it was so hard to make" – and laborious multi-tracking and tape splicing was an important part of the working processes, "There's virtually no tape that goes through the studio that doesn't get razor-bladed at some point," Hardy Fox explained at the time, and that probably accounted for his permanent stubble.

The Residents were worried that by embracing direct digital recording they would lose the hands-on ingredient that made their music so unique, but circumstances forced them to update their facilities in 1987, when they were commissioned to score some episodes of *Pee Wee Herman's Playhouse*. Hardy Fox recalled, "The first show had eighty one cues and there was only a week to do them! You can't do that amount of work and expect to synch a video without a computer..." Of course, once they dipped their toes into the waters and found them warm they immersed themselves in this new recording technology, and soon went totally MIDI. Their original Macintosh Plus was upgraded to a Mac II, and they then acquired a Southworth Jambox 4 synchroniser cum MIDI processer and some sequencer software.

This technology, and the demands of writing for a TV show, gave The Residents an entirely new skill set. As Hardy Fox related to *Music & Sound Output Magazine*, 'The Residents had to doctor things that had been written for a given episode to create music for other episodes. You can write one thing, then flop it around, change instruments, slow it down, and it becomes another cue. By the time they finished their third show – pulling their hair out because it really is work – they were developing pieces that became themes and little jingles for things in the show. They were developing a language for visual expression. It was fascinating."

Pee Wee Herman's Playhouse was a red-hot show, and, like a lot of children TV, was surreal enough to appeal to adults. That Gary Panter designed the sets shows how visually edgy it was, and The Residents, as musical contributors, were in good company with Mark Mothersbaugh from Devo, Todd Rundgren and even Dweezil Zappa. Even though they only scored four shows (Mothersbaugh did thirty seven of the forty five) children were exposed to The Residents' music during segments like the *Puppet Dance*, and the commission certainly pushed their music into the mainstream by the subversive route of TV.

Their love of technology also saw The Residents embrace the Compact Disc, and *God In Three Persons* was envisioned as a CD only release (although it later made it onto a 2-LP set). Despite the fact that the emergence of CD had helped to kill off the *American Composers Series*, the medium was one The Residents were eager to explore, due to its longer playing time and the possibilities for thematic development. As Hardy Fox gushed in 1988, "With vinyl you think in terms of a strong start and a strong ending for each side. The CD presents an entirely different structure. You don't have to worry about whether you have too many long songs on one side, or too may short ones on the other – especially since The Residents' songs vary between a few seconds and several minutes long."

The digital sound of the CD also gave a greater clarity and brought out certain harmonics, especially in the re-mastering of their back catalogue, which had not been evident on the initial vinyl release. Hardy Fox was delighted with the results when Residents albums began to be re-issued on CD, "It's great to hear the CDs sound so much like the master tapes. It's a real pleasure." As with the entire music business, The Residents found that they could sell their back catalogue to their fans again in a new format, with the addition of rare and bonus tracks of course. These CD releases were initially helmed by East Side Digital in America and Torso in Europe, but as time has passed there have been reissues by a number of other companies.

God In Three Persons was an excellent and challenging concept piece, but by this time The Residents' image was becoming counterproductive. Not only had the eyeball icon of the *Eskimo* period grown the wings of an albatross, but the self-generated mythology of The Residents had backfired in the sense that it had marginalised the music. Features or reviews concentrated upon the theme of obscurists in tuxedoes with eyeballs on their heads, whose identities were something that required the skills of Sherlock Holmes to unravel. The music they were making was an adjunct to the story, and was invariably described as 'weird' or 'wacky'. The Residents were becoming marginalised. Indeed, it was only touring that kept them in the public eye and won new converts outside of their large and devoted hardcore following.

For this segment of the market, a new fan club named UWEB (Uncle Willie's Eyeball Buddies) was established in 1988. Unlike W.E.I.R.D., it was set up and run with The Residents' approval, and because of this there was a regular flow of members only CD releases, ranging from rare recordings of live and studio work to a disc containing the *Snakey Wake* played for Phillip Lithman. UWEB also issued a quarterly newsletter, as well as updated recordings of *Santa Dog*. Tom Timony did most of the heavy lifting for this, although he made some mistakes, "35 Montana Street was my home. I would have guys banging on my door at 2am shouting "*Uncle Willie! Unclie Willie!*" I was not Uncle Willie, but getting my address printed on the newsletters was not the greatest idea!"

God In Three Persons spawned two singles, *Holy Kiss Of Flesh* (a remix of a track from the album) and *Double Shot*. There were also plans to tour the project in operatic form, and an overture was even written. Although abandoned, this is one project that The Residents would still like to see on the stage, as Homer Flynn recently told me, "In a lot of ways I think it was conceived as that. The Residents have always been trying to move into musical theatre, and in a lot of ways *God In Three Persons* was intended as a musical theatrical piece."

The next Residents project, however, would be a perfect piece of musical theatre that, like Jack, would hit the road.

Cube-E

"This show has more dancing, more costumes, more lighting effects, a bigger sound, computers and musicians and weird things." - UWEB newsletter.

"This show was probably one of The Residents' better business decisions, and the reason it was such a good business decision was because they put so much energy into merchandising... What happened with The Residents when they toured, they did about seventy five to eighty performances of the show and, a far as the actual tour went, they probably showed a profit of oh... maybe four or five thousand dollars. But the merchandising was gangbusters! Ultimately, what it amounts to is the show becomes a promotional device for a T-shirt selling business." - Homer Flynn.

Unlike the Mole Show and the 13th Anniversary Tour, the *Cube-E* project of 1988-90 was not conceived as one long performance piece, but came together slowly.

At some point, one of The Residents discovered an authentic book of cowboy poems and songs. Intrigued, he researched further and they slowly constructed a short suite of songs around the theme of the Old West in their newly installed MIDI studio. This became *Buckeroo Blues*, which was first heard by fan club members when released on a CD (UWEB 003) which also contained the overture for the abandoned *God In Three Persons* opera. The piece was then premiered at a party for Boudisque (Torso) Records, their European label, in Amsterdam on November 18th 1987, where The Residents performed, and was subsequently performed live on German TV for Tele 5 in April 1988. This half hour show was set up by The Residents' German distributor Guido Randzio, who told me, "That was an idea proposed to me by Christian Eckert of Tele 5, and we just made it happen." The performance was fleshed out with cover versions of Hank Williams' *Jambalaya* and Elvis' *Burning Love*. Filmed in front of a live audience and a static camera, The Residents also presented an early version of the choreography for the *Buckeroo Blues* segment of the *Cube-E* show, dressed in black cowboy suits.

With the vague idea of constructing a new touring performance around a thematic history of American music, a second piece slowly developed around the contribution of black music – primarily jazz and blues – which became *Black Barry*, and the two suites were performed live at New York's Lincoln Centre (Alice Tully Hall) on 21st July 1989.

It was decided that the third part of the show would be a medley of Elvis Presley songs. But the band had difficulty with the staging of this segment, and there was a difference of opinion as one member of the band thought they would not be able to pull it off in live performance. At this point they spent two nights in a motel room brainstorming over how to present this part of the show, and came up with the idea of a medley of Elvis songs performed by a grandfather Elvis imitator. With the presentation and staging resolved the band could proceed with staging the show.

It was now a question of designing costumes, working out choreography and building up the theatrics of the entire performance. Unlike their previous two tours, *Cube-E* was not a concept or a concert performance but a theatrical piece with musical accompaniment. The lead singer would not simply sing the songs but, in conjunction with two dancers, would act out each piece. Thus he would dance, perform and, like Elvis before him, mop his brow with silk scarves and throw them out into the audience. Movement was worked out by the lead singer in conjunction with the two dancers, Sarah McLennan and Carol LeMaitre, and, as McLennan recalls, it was a very interactive process, "Watching (him) move and then taking that and exaggerating it or suggesting new things or different things or choreography... it was a real exchange of ideas between all of us. Generally we were given an idea of what was going to happen and what the props and what the set were and we would fill in the blanks."

McLennan also recalls that the finished choreography was designed to be "very focused and slow moving at the beginning, pick up a little and then kind of blow out at the end, so that the audience could get an emotional release." McLennan and Lemaitre both danced on the tour, and found working with The Residents highly stimulating because of the creative freedom they encouraged, "A typical dancer will rehearse for six months and perform once or twice," McLennan recalls, "With this group you can rehearse for two weeks and perform a hundred times. It's a great opportunity to get to do the same show over and over and find more depth in it. And that, to me, is the most exciting thing about working with The Residents, in that things change and grow and evolve in performance, and they're very open to that. A show develops, as opposed to developing in rehearsal."

As with the Mole Show, The Residents did not want to have

typical rock lighting – instead it had to be theatrical and supportive to the performance, and they turned to stage lighting expert Chris McGregor. McGregor had seen the 13th Anniversary Show and had been appalled by the minimal lighting – he knew he could do better, and with The Residents' blessing he set out to prove it.

The nature of *Cube-E* meant that the three sections could be played and acted out against coloured backdrops, upon which different back projections could be made to visually compliment and enhance the performance. In order to emphasise the actions of the performers, a decision was made to use ultra-violet black light, created by placing filters over fluorescent tubes to filter out colour, so that the only light emitted is ultra-violet black light. Any material responsive to this type of light glows as if light is coming from within it, whilst non-responsive material remains barely visible, creating what McGregor describes as a "Very powerful, intense effect." To achieve this stunning visual effect for *Cube-E*, a dozen powerful sodium vapour and mercury lighting units were laid out in front of the stage like footlights and covered with very intense filters. This meant that the performers could go anywhere and the light sensitive materials on their specially designed costumes would pick up the ultra-violet light.

The costumes for all three parts of the performance were designed and manufactured to enhance this effect. For example, in the *Buckeroo Blues* sequence the singer and the two dancers wore totally black costumes with huge black ten-gallon hats, whilst red light sensitive material was stitched onto their chests. The singer also sported huge white lips on his mask, and two penlights, supported by glasses, served as white, glowing eyes.

McGregor worked closely with The Residents to maximise the dynamics offered by this creative use of lighting and tweaked the show during performances to accommodate local conditions, as well as adding new effects to enhance the performance. For example, when a cinema screen proved unresponsive to black light it was discovered that the Elvis portion of the show worked much better with total darkness behind the performers rather than back projections, and a black curtain was incorporated into the show to obtain that effect. "It was like creating a piece of art and then watching it metamorphosise over the two and a half year period we toured," McGregor recalls.

The first fully integrated three part performance of *Cube E* took place in San Francisco, at the Cowell Theatre on September 21st 1989, and received a standing ovation. In total, The Residents played six sell-out shows in four days at the four hundred seat theatre before heading off on a European tour, where they received equally enthusiastic responses from sell-out crowds. "It was a big production," recalls Hein Fokker, "We had two trucks, two drivers, big merchandise and some extra people for the stage. We went on the road with around twelve people, but all had been calculated before. The great thing about The Residents is that you can always have a calculation that takes into account that the merchandising is very good. That helps to make it cohesive financially. That worked out great."

One of the strongest features of *Cube-E* was that it did not require any pre-knowledge of The Residents, their music or their past. Even the eyeball was abandoned in favour of newly designed cubist eyeballs (Cube-Es) that only made a brief appearance. Apparently, The Residents were so fed up with the tuxedo and eyeball association that they specified in the contract for each performance that they would not wear them. *Cube-E* was a fully integrated theatrical performance piece that anybody could come see, understand and enjoy, and the music was not grating, unusual or weird but melodic and very easy on the ear. It was, in essence, a soundtrack to support a cinematic performance. "That's right, The Residents music is now accessible," wrote one reviewer.

And what a performance! After the 20th Century Fox fanfare, played from a ghetto blaster, the curtain parted to reveal three cowboys in huge ten gallon hats, sat around a glowing red campfire against a blue backdrop studded with white stars. As the music commenced, one cowboy stood and bow-leggedly sung *From The Plains Of Mexico* to his two companions and the audience. More songs, like *The Stampede*, *Bury Me Not* and *Saddle Sores*, followed, as well as cowboy dancing, a knife fight and the death and burial of Old Red.

Next, *Black Barry* saw the three main protagonists dressed in reflective white shirts and black body stockings, whilst the musical theme suggested that black America sold its music to win acceptance. This section culminated with the dramatic appearance of the huge, box-headed Black Barry figure, suggesting the rising up of black Americans from slavery.

The climax of *Cube-E* was, of course, Elvis. Once the audience had returned from the interval – "where merchandise *killed*" – they would hear *Thus Spake Zarathustra*, the trademark music Elvis used before taking the stage for his Las Vegas shows. The curtain would then part to reveal an old Elvis imitator asleep in a chair with his two puppet grandchildren, Shorty and Shirley, sitting on his lap. Waking up, he would relate the story of *The Baby King* – Elvis – to them. "I used to pretend that I was kind of part of it," he told them, "I'll show you guys a bit if you like... let's see if I can remember how it goes..." He would then stand up and, garbed in a fantastic light reflective costume and striking black and white face make-up, launch into *Don't Be Cruel*, *Devil In Disguise*, *Burning Love*, *Teddy Bear* and other seminal Elvis songs, delivered in typical Residential vocal style.

This part of *Cube-E* was stunning, especially when the two dancers portrayed Las Vegas showgirls (with red light reflective 'tits 'n' ass'), before forming their bodies into a heart of roses as Elvis donned a huge stomach and belt to signify his decline. The climax of the entire performance came when he was symbolically killed by blasts of music from The Beatles and The Rolling Stones – The English invasion. This was a typical Residential touch, and the perfect way to bring the performance to a close. There were no encores.

Taken as a whole, the performance was breathtaking and marked a high watermark in The Residents' career. *Cube-E* combined elements of music, theatre and performance into a compelling audio and visual spectacle, and audience reaction, especially in Europe, was fantastic. As Chris McGregor told me, "You pull into Athens and it's like you're with The Beatles. All of a sudden there's a riot on the street in front of the venue because they couldn't sell enough tickets and they're rocking police cars around. The band had to be covered up and run the gauntlet to the backstage entrance."

Even the performers were bowled over, as one eye on the wall stated, "In Berlin we got a standing ovation that lasted longer than the show. We were already completely broken down... we were wandering around in the crowd drinking beer and they were still applauding." Ah, Germany!

In Bologna the Italian promoter was unclear about the concept, and announced that there would be two intervals rather than one. At the end of the show The Residents left the stage and prepared for the curtain call, but when they took to the stage the lights were up and the auditorium virtually empty. "Everybody was out in the lobby smoking cigarettes and drinking cappuccino going, "How are they going to top that?"" laughs one of the performers today.

Despite the grand nature of the show, unlike the Mole experience there were no problems in Europe, and Hein Fokker exercised tight control over every aspect of the tour, from flight transfers to hotels, "There were more Dutch people on that tour than Americans, and they loved that because they were trustworthy people and there were no hidden agendas or forgotten financial obligations and that kind of thing. It went perfectly. They came over and rehearsed for a week with the PA companies that I booked and stayed in the special housing that I arranged, it was like a family gathering. That is the way it became and they loved that." Fokker also had to deal with ensuring that the band and their identities were protected, which, for one of The Residents, was a real concern. "In the early days it was always a huge hassle," states Fokker, "He would maintain the secrecy and hocus pocus backstage - he was really fucked up if someone came backstage, even if it was a technician. To be honest, whenever somebody comes (backstage) nobody would know who they are as they could be crew, they could be anyone. How many times have people come backstage and told me that I am one of The Residents!? I did not deny that of course..."

As for merchandise, there were all manner of goodies to be bought on every leg of the tour – T-shirts, posters, badges, aprons and cassette tapes to name a few – all of which could be taken home in specially branded *Cube-E* plastic bags. Sales, as you might imagine, were strong. "I know that we went to a place in Oslo," recalls European distributor Guido Randzio, "and a guy came up to me afterwards and said. "You broke Motorhead's record." I said, "Not selling beer, right?" He said, "With the merchandise!" I kind of liked that."

There were, as always, some minor speed bumps. Hein Fokker recalls that that "The Lumi electric drum our drummer played, almost every day it broke and had to be opened up and repaired. It was crazy." At one gig in Paris it gave up the ghost during the third segment and the drummer had to improvise his parts by banging on the buttons.

"The result is quite hilarious," Uncle Willie later related to fans in his newsletter, "...at first, but suddenly the band is fuelled by a kind of frenzied playing I have not witnessed before on the tour. They just go crazy, rearranging songs into new abstract sound. By the end the group has suddenly solidified into a unit of power more akin to the drive of hard rock than the usual delicate handling." The computer containing the sequenced music also crashed in New York, although computer expert Rich Shupe was on hand to sort it out, and on another occasion, on a train between Italy and Germany, a thief got into one of The Residents' compartments and stole cash from his money belt. The Resident was un-phased, "It's only money. It could have been something important." When the production played Tel Aviv, they faxed ahead their lighting requirements, flew in, did the show and flew out five hours later, members of the Israeli army having prepared the theatre for performance.

Back in America, The Residents played another string of sold-out shows at the Cowell theatre in San Francisco, culminating in a New Year's Eve performance at which every member of the audience received a free CD, titled *For Elsie*, of The Residents interpreting Beethoven. This recording, which takes one melodic and memorable piece and gives it several different and excellent interpretations, was also released as a one-sided collector's LP on vinyl, and stands – to my mind – head and shoulders above The Residents' interpretations of the music of George Gershwin and John Philip Sousa.

On the stroke of midnight in San Francisco, The Residents played the first and last *Cube-E* encore - a version of *Auld Lang Syne* - and a live version of *Santa Dog*. In the new year they moved onto the Florence Gould Hall, New York, for several shows, and appeared on David Sanborn's prestigious *Night Music* on 14th January 1990. The Residents had agreed to showcase a couple of tracks from *Cube-E*, but when Chris McGregor went into the *Night Music* studio with a long list of their lighting requirements, a disagreement ensured. The producers wanted The Residents to simply play like any other band, without any theatrical presentation. The Residents were, however, not like any other band, as Chris McGregor told me, "The Who or Genesis, with all of their huge systems, their lights and their explosions… could go into a studio and still make beautiful music and still please everybody. In fact, people would be thrilled to see that happen. But with The Residents, the visual is so much of the show. You can't take that away from them. It's not all about music, we're dealing with artists who have a whole vision of how the show is presented."

The producers and Sanborn relented after seeing one of the New York performances of *Cube-E*, but when it came to arranging the lighting of the two numbers to be performed there was still "much butting of heads" with the Union stagehands. Only when the lighting director Phil Hyams – an "old New York cigar smoking, raspy character" – arrived did things change. He was very understanding and interested in The Residents' creative use of lighting. Hyams barked out orders and got the ball rolling, and the audience got to see a fantastic version of *From The Plains Of Mexico* and a cover version of *Teddy Bear* that was, Rich Shupe recalls, "So aggressive they got more viewer mail than any other act… either extremely appreciative or extremely unappreciative." The Residents also got to twist with the late Conway Twitty, which was somewhat surreal.

Sadly, these two numbers were the only part of *Cube-E* properly filmed, apart from the embryonic German TV footage. Although the show was performed around eighty times, not a single performance was commercially filmed. This was a great shame as *Cube-E* was a truly groundbreaking show, and, considering The Residents' fascination with archiving their long career, well worth preserving. There were, apparently, some interested parties, but no one came up with the right financial package to make it happen. The Residents toyed with financing it themselves, but finally abandoned the idea. According to Chris McGregor, they were of the opinion that, "if something was going to be filmed it would not be *Cube-E*, because that, ultimately, had to be experienced live for it to carry across."

Cube-E was so successful that it ended up touring twice, and in 1990 more dates were played in Europe and America. This time, however, there was a mixed response. "In Europe there were big audiences, enthusiastic audiences. They were responsive and interested in this thing The Residents were doing," recalls McGregor, "The range of audiences was phenomenal - everything from expectant punks in black leather to old couples, to people wearing suits and hippies, a rich, broad range. Here (America) it was very much your College music audience. I think it might have been a little artsy for them. Some of them were very responsive, but most of them were into REM or the latest thing on the hit parade. It's scary to think somebody as avant-garde and revolutionary as The Residents are relegated to old fogey status by guys waiting for the next Peter Gabriel album."

Of course, by the second tour of Europe in 1990 the band were a little too familiar with the music, and maybe also tired of the intense schedule. This showed during a performance in Bologna when, according to an eye on the wall, they were, "Going through the motions. The singer was very disturbed by this, felt like he was carrying the whole show by himself, *and he let us know it*." Backstage, after the gig, he went eyeball-to-eyeball with the band, and when it came to the next show in Athens, "Inspired by the dressing-down we'd received in Bologna, we put our all into making up for it."

The final American dates were also dogged with misfortune. One Cleveland promoter declared himself bankrupt as The Residents stepped out onto the stage. As he was also promoting the next concert, they would in effect be playing for free as no one was there to pay them, so that performance was cancelled. The last performance of *Cube-E* took place in New York in November 1990, when a speaker cabinet fell from the stage and crashed into a fortunately unoccupied seat in the front row and a small fire broke out on stage. It was quickly extinguished, but The Residents, detecting that the *Mark Of The Mole* might be coming back to haunt them, flew back to San Francisco forthwith.

Bad Day At The Freak Show

AUDIENCE MEMBER: *"What's a CD-ROM?*
HOMER FLYNN: *"That's a good question and I'll get to that in a minute."*
(Museum Of Modern Art, New York, 1992)

"They populated their work with 'characters', closer by far to acting than to singing. These subjects 'spoke'. Musicians tend still to have an urge towards self-expression. The Residents were more interested in the invocation of characters." - Chris Cutler, File Under Popular, 1991

Instead of the typical 'Interface', in 'Gingerbread Man' you navigate through it's 'EnterEye.' The Residents have refused to authorise any instructions or specifications for using the EnterEye, accept (sic) to say that, "Given its name, when you see it, you should know what to do." – 'Gingerbread Man' booklet.

To coincide with the *Cube-E* tour, The Residents released *The King And Eye*, an LP of cover versions of Elvis Presley songs. In previous editions of this book I stated that it was a fairly uninspired affair, and, having recently endured it again, I see no reason to revise my opinion - some of the tracks are, in my view, *awful*, possibly due to the fact that *The King And Eye* was recorded in a commercial studio rather than their own - Different Fur Studios in San Francisco, The Residents wanted to see what it was like to actually work against the clock with a finite amount of expensive studio time, and they found out. Songs like *Blue Suede Shoes*, *All Shook Up*, *Devil In Disguise*, *Burning Love* and *Teddy Bear* are bland, flat and totally free of sparkle. One of the few notable things about the record is the use of a refrain from *Vileness Fats* on *Devil In Disguise*, and even Laurie Amat's vocal contributions and some guitar from Bruce Anderson of MX-80 Sound fail to help the musical soufflé rise. The cover art – depicting a crucified skeletal Elvis - is perhaps the most interesting thing about the LP.

The King And Eye saw an evolution in the art department. Pore

Know Graphics would still devise the cover art and images, but packaging was handed over to graphic designer Rex Ray. Ray was not the first (or last) to assist The Residents with their packaging - for five years in the early 1980s Helen Hall was the art director at Ralph Records, and also went under the name Nessie Lessons on some Residents recordings, including *The Tunes Of Two Cities* and *Title In Limbo*. As an aside, Chuck recently opened up to reveal that he and Hall were actually married before he met his current husband, Roman, which suggests that the private lives of The Residents contained ingredients usually reserved for soap opera. Anyway, Rex Ray also began to handle all of the UWEB fan club CD art, adding his personalised and distinctive style. As he did not have to worry about a "direct sales impact," he could do as he pleased.

Like Tom Timony before him, Ray started off in the Ralph mail order department, working part-time whilst studying Video and Conceptual Performance Arts at the San Francisco Art Institute. Ray also got the unique pleasure of impersonating a Resident in full eyeball regalia on an MTV promotional boat trip when one of the band was so sick that he couldn't attend. Ray was greatly enjoying the experience until Jefferson Starship, who were also on the boat, tried to drag him onto a small stage for an improvised jam. As Ray played no instrument he was afraid that if he accepted the guitar that was being thrust into his hands and attempted to play he would be revealed as an imposter. He graciously refused, although he later told me that he had been, "*Sorely* tempted."

Riding on the back of *Cube-E*, *The King And Eye* sold tremendously well. *Don't Be Cruel* was released as a single, and The Residents created a computer-generated video featuring a lot of disfigured Elvises and garishly coloured dollar bills to promote it. The song was so bland it was even shown on MTV.

These Elvis covers sounded much better in live performance, as demonstrated on the CD release of the *Cube-E* show *Live In Holland* and a later 2CD and DVD box set. Raw, rougher and obviously live, perhaps they revealed that *The King And Eye* was merely the studio-created template for the live show. To be brutal, the short voice-over that the singing Resident (playing Michael Jackson) and Laurie Amat (playing a pink rabbit) performed as Dangerous Puppets for MTV's *Liquid TV* was much more fun than *The King And Eye*.

Around this time, The Residents were receiving heavy rotation on MTV, although it wasn't one of their videos being shown. *Slow Bob In The Lower Dimensions* was a short, five-minute pilot for a new show by San Francisco based director Henry Sellick, who was responsible for animating a large number of the famous MTV logo identification pieces. The Residents scored the film, which led to them also scoring the five episodes of *The Adventures Of Thomas And Nordo* aired on MTV in 1992.

They also continued to produce music and, in 1991, released *Freak Show*. As the title suggests, this was a concept album based on the freak shows that had once toured America. The Residents no doubt drew inspiration from the considerable amount of literature available on the subject, especially *Freak Show* by Robert Boydan, *Freaks* by Daniel P. Mannix and *Human Oddities* by Martin Monestier. They were also inspired by the extraordinary 1932 movie *Freaks*, which controversially documented a group of disfigured and malformed performers, presenting them as real people with intellect and feelings rather than as sideshow attractions.

Considered by many as musical freaks themselves (and let's be honest, they played up to it on occasion) this was a logical area for Residential musical exploration. They did the concept justice with songs about a troupe of Resident-created freaks such as Benny The Bouncing Bump and Harry The Head. The record again featured the vocal talents of Laurie Amat, whose peculiar vocal qualities were perfect for the project. "We did not run my voice through any effects," she told me, "because I tried to do it all naturally." *Freak Show* was recorded in The Residents' own studio on a computer based MIDI system with the assistance of Tony Janssen, who had been responsible for the excellent sound on the *Cube-E* tour and CD release and whose sonic ideas strongly influenced the sound of the finished music.

Freak Show was to spin off so many tentacles that it is easy to overlook the fact that it is a fantastic Residents LP. In addition to Amat, Diana Alden and Tony Janssen also lent their voices to tracks like *Wanda The Worm Woman* ("Watch me! Watch me! *Watch me!*") and *Herman The Human Mole*, and the rich diversity of the vocals matched the broad sonic palette of the compelling music. Homer Flynn states that the sharing of vocal chores was part of a conscious process on the part of The Residents which led to the addition of Diane Alden to the mix.

"*Freak Show* was one of the first in a series of albums where there were a lot of different characters," he recalled, "And so rather than having one singer – Randy, The Residents' singer – they wanted a lot of different voices, so a lot of different people were recruited and she came along and she was great, she was really good. She was a friend of a friend. There was a guy called Mark Salvatore who performed on *Cube-E* and she was a good friend of his."

The concept of *Freak Show* was not confined to the music alone, and over the next few years the project spawned a whole host of other products in different media. Firstly there was the remarkable promotional video for the single *Harry The Head*, created by illustrator and computer graphics genius Jim Ludtke on an Apple Macintosh computer. The clip was so stunning that it was soon being used by Apple to demonstrate the graphic versatility of their computers. Lest we forget, at that moment in time their main market was in the graphic design field rather than in the burgeoning home PC market. iPhones, iPods and total market dominance were nearly two decades away.

There was also a *Freak Show* comic, published by Dark Horse in 1992 and a bold and imaginative creation. As Homer Flynn stated at that time, "The structure of the album is that each song is about a different freak, and so each of those has been rendered by a different artist." The artists featured were Brian Bolland, John Bolton, Matt Howarth, Dave McKean, Richard Sala, Savage Pencil, Les Dorscheid and Pore Know Graphics himself, and each artist contributed his own distinctive style to portray a unique vision of one of the freaks in the show.

"The band asked me to contribute," recalls Matt Howarth, "and assigned me Jello Jack. I listened to the song and worked from the overall mood of the music." As for Dave McKean, famed for his work with Neil Gaiman on the *Sandman* series of comics, "It may have been through Brian Bolland," he told me when I asked him how he got involved in the project, "who is a long time fan of The Residents. Or it may have been through the publisher Dark Horse directly. I vaguely remember meeting the band at a film studio. Could that be right? It's all a blur. I wasn't familiar with the music or the anonymity of the band, though I was aware of the eyeball/dinner-jacketed image, probably through shopping at Rough Trade. I wasn't sure how to approach them, it was such a hermetic world of references, characters and pose. I was an outsider."

But when he came to develop his strip he found that the subject matter lent itself to inspiration, "It was great, there were characters, and a loose narrative, so it was easy to expand into visuals. They didn't give me anything specific to follow, I was free to explore. I wanted it to feel like the music and have a hallucinatory, disturbing atmosphere. I wanted it to look hand-made, and full of the marks, scratches and fingerprints that sit on the surface of the images, but underneath the paint there's a blurry, indistinct feeling of the real world held in distorted and collaged photographs. This was one of the first pieces of work I did in this style, and I've returned to it many times since. It feels like we're balancing between two realms. The music has a superficial simplicity, but there is also a strange consistency to it. It all has its own internal logic. Once you get used to walking around in their world, the music couldn't be anything else really."

The lavishly produced comic was a wonderful promotional tool, not only for the *Freak Show* LP but also for a different market unfamiliar with The Residents' music. Two pages were devoted exclusively to the sale of Residents merchandise, including watches and a limited edition silkscreen portfolio of *Freak Show* comic art. Only KISS marketed this hard in their own comic books!

Also, on 15th November 1991, The Residents were hired for a twenty minute performance by computer giant NEC. The show took place in the Fairmont Hotel, San Jose in front of an invited audience of computer software experts, and The Residents were assisted on stage by Laurie Amat – "I loved wearing that white tutu". Featuring material from *Freak Show* (although the singing Resident was dressed in the Elvis costume from *Cube-E*), the concert was filmed and edited live by Todd Rundgren to demonstrate the effectiveness of new video editing equipment. This was the first time that Amat had performed live with The Residents and it was certainly memorable. "I remember wondering how I was going to sing higher and bigger over and over to the end!" she told me, "Yikes! And some guy kept trying to take flash pictures of me, so I kept moving my umbrella into his face. But it was incredible." A six-minute mix of this show was subsequently used for CD-ROM demonstration purposes by Apple, and given limited distribution on VHS video.

1992 marked twenty years of Residents activity since the release of the *Santa Dog* single in 1972, and to celebrate this anniversary there were – for The Residents - a series of low-key events. Homer Flynn gave a talk at the New York Museum of Modern Art entitled *Hissing And Kissing In The Wind*, which examined two decades of creativity and included a showing of original 16mm films of *Land Of 1000 Dances*, *Hello Skinny* and the *One Minute Movies*. Flynn also gave a sneak preview of work in progress for a Residents laser disc and the forthcoming *Freak Show* CD-ROM, which was a new media strand that The Residents were devoting time to with Jim Ludtke. "As you can see, he is an incredible 3-D modeler," stated Flynn, showing some of the graphics, "and all of this stuff is done on a Macintosh computer, which is hard to believe. The stuff that we are about to see he was working on as late as last week so you are looking at fresh, hot stuff..."

There was also a concurrent exhibition of Residents performance artifacts at The Kitchen, accompanied by music specially composed by the band, and the year was supposed to end in spectacular style with a fan convention and a Residents performance on the 26th December 1992 at the Cowell Theatre, San Francisco. This was, however, sadly cancelled due to the amount of time The Residents were spending working on the *Freak Show* CD-ROM project.

There was, of course, a special 20th Anniversary release. Resisting the temptation to release a repackaged collection of what fans would see as greatest hits, they chose to mix them all up in the computer, splice tracks together, re-record some parts and create something new out of old material. Working again with Tony Janssen, *Our Finest Flowers* took a year to come together before its release at the end of 1992. "Yes, these are new songs," stated the liner notes, "Just like all good pop music, there is something familiar about them..." Apparently, The Residents privately referred to this as the *Frankenstein Album*.

Significantly, this collection was issued on Ralph Records, which The Residents recovered from Tom Timony in 1991 after their five-year agreement with him had expired. Timony, who had already established his own TEC Tones label, was pleased to announce in his Spring 1993 catalogue not only that, "As most of you already know, that ol' Ralphie boy has re-emerged, preaching the joys of eyeball mania," but that TEC Tones and its offshoots would sail on and "Are being run by the same group of folks who have been serving you for all these many years." They also re-located to New York.

As for *Their Finest Flowers*, it's an interesting release. Those unfamiliar with The Residents' back catalogue won't recognise the complex, interwoven strands and motifs, whilst those who knew the catalogue inside out certainly will. It's much better than 1982's *Ten Years In Twenty Minutes*, wherein snatches of every single Residents song were stuck together to form one long, continuous suite of music. As time progressed the studio Resident grew rather fond of mash-ups of their own material, as numerous releases and downloads reveal. Personally, I like my rib eye Residential steak in its original form rather than reconstituted, except for *The King And Eye RMX*, which actually improved on the original.

In 1993 The Residents also decided to close down UWEB, due in large part to the creation of Ralph America, a mail order operation created to market their back catalogue, merchandise and new releases. This venture was established by Sarah McLennan, and later run by Dren McDonald, who had put together the *Eyesore: A Stab At The Residents* covers LP in 1996, and his wife Lorrieann (Lorrie) Murray, who he actually met when she was in one of the bands who contributed a cover version to the album. "You could definitely say The Residents brought us together!" states Murray today. "He first asked if the band I was in (Idiot Flesh) wanted to do a cover for *Eyesore*, and then when he found out I was a graphic designer he asked if I wanted to work on the packaging and do some illustrations for the 7". He's really easy to work with, and I don't say this just because we've been together twenty years. We got along really well running Ralph together, and not all couples can say that." Lorrie, who would become known as Mama

Ralph to many American Residents fans, "started off by redesigning the Ralph America catalogs, and then did the re-packaging for *Title In Limbo* and the *10th Anniversary Radio Special*." Her duties became wide ranging, and on the *Wormwood* tour she not only sold merchandise but also acted as stage manager and costume dresser for the lead singer on both the US and European jaunts.

A similar operation – Euro Ralph- was established in Hamburg, Germany and run by Guido Randzio, a long-time Residents fan who told me that he "First heard The Residents around 1978 when John Peel played their music on a show that was aired on BCBS in Germany. I was immediately fascinated." Randzio had been in a number of post-punk bands himself, and even recorded and released material as part of one called Vanity Fair. "At that time," he told me, "it became evident that I would prefer to sit on the other side of the table, and I started to work for a distribution company here in Germany called EFA, which was one of the top underground distribution companies in Europe. Pretty soon I was responsible for labels like Blast First. I worked very closely with a guy from Amsterdam at Boudisque, who also had Torso records. After a short while I began to work on The Residents, who I had for a long time been a fan of for the music and the concept. The Dutch guys were happy that there was someone to look after the group in Germany and Residents sales doubled and tripled. This was around 1986 to 1988, and the next time The Cryptic Corporation came to Amsterdam they wanted to know who this guy was in Germany selling all of their records!"

This led to Randzio meeting Homer Flynn and Hardy Fox, and over time they not only established a strong personal relationship but Randzio saw potential for even more growth. "Germany was an important market for The Residents," he says, "And when the *Cube-E* project became solid I undertook two or three voyages to San Francisco to prepare whatever needed to be prepared for the territories that I was responsible for. I had good contact with The Cryptic Corporation and could see that it was not working in their favour with Torso anymore – in my opinion – as they (Torso) were bringing stuff out just as regular product. I could foresee that packaging and putting special effort into the detail of the product would become more and more important. Therefore I proposed that we should set up a European branch of Cryptic/Ralph America in order to have control of how the products would look and sound." This led to the establishment of Euro Ralph, which Randzio ran, along with two other businesses in Hamburg, Bitzcore and Hit Thing, in conjunction with Jurgen Goldschmitt and Toby Dammit.

One of the first Residents albums that Randzio took his approach to was *Third Reich And Roll*, which had not been available in Germany for over ten years, "Because to show a Swastika in Germany was illegal, so we needed a Swastika free version." This not only led to a new sleeve design but also saw the German police take an active interest in Randzio as the LP still showed Hitler on the cover – "(They wondered) whether I was a Nazi, the Enoch Powell of the German underground" – although he was nothing of the sort! "That went down very well, and it helped fund other projects like the first Residents DVD. It has always been a hobby of mine to look at the new generation of consumer electronics and see what you can do with it." Ralph America and Euro Ralph issued and reissued a whole host of Residents material, including CDs, vinyl, T-shirts, a beer stein and other merchandise.

In 1991 The Cryptic Corporation had signed a deal with the Voyager Company. Voyager had been set up as early as 1984, and by 1991 was active in what was then termed "Electronic Interactive Publishing". The ability to place graphics and music on laserdisc and CD-ROM was seen as the next event horizon of the approaching digital age, and the driving force behind this union was Michael Nash, who had written extensively on art and video. As a curator at the Long Beach Museum of Art, he'd also been responsible for packaging a number of touring exhibitions of music video, and, as they'd been so innovative in this field, The Residents had featured extensively in these shows. Bob Stein at Voyager had seen one of Nash's exhibitions and liked his sensibility so much that he set up a meeting and convinced him that his future lay at Voyager in electronic publishing. "I brought a lot of my curatorial ideas and agenda to Voyager," Nash told me, "I had a list of people I thought it was absolutely essential to bring with me, and at top of that list was The Residents."

Nash arranged for Bob Stein to meet with The Cryptic Corporation in Santa Monica, where Voyager were based, and everybody agreed that The Residents and Voyager would be a perfect fit. The first fruit of this partnership was the release in 1992 of a Residents laserdisc entitled *Twenty Twisted Questions.* A laserdisc was effectively a 12" record that contained images and music, rather than just music, inside its grooves, and *Twenty Twisted Questions* contained most of The Residents' old promotional films as well as an exhaustive discography that allowed the viewer to look at sleeve art and hear a thirty second sample of the music from that particular release. But despite a lot of media attention, the laserdisc market never got off the ground as the equipment to play the discs on was very expensive, and within a year CD-ROM technology had advanced to consign it to the tech graveyard to keep BETAMAX company.

The second project with Voyager was much more ambitious in scale - The Residents aimed to transform *Freak Show* into an interactive

CD-ROM, in collaboration with Jim Ludtke, who had produced the stunning *Harry The Head* promotional video. Ludtke had tremendous computer modeling skills which would be able to bring the characters from the album alive, and Voyager was the ideal company to get behind The Residents and take this idea forward. As Nash told me, "They had an interactive design presentation they did for the whole company, and it was absolutely clear at that point that it was going to be an extraordinary project."

Although the budget was minimal - $40,000 – The Residents, who wrote the script and the music, and Ludtke, who created the visuals, were an ideal team. It was a very collaborative process and The Residents not only spoke to Ludtke (who was actually scheduled to appear with Flynn at the *Hissing And Kissing In The Wind* talk at MOMA until laid low by a shoulder injury) several times a day but, as he was based in the Bay area, would also meet with him once or twice a week. The finished project took three years to complete, but it became apparent to everybody that something special was being created: a breakthrough in interactive media.

"At that time in the CD-ROM area, people were primarily just reprocessing existing content and providing an interactive framework to have a richer experience," Michael Nash told me, "but The Residents had a vision of this world... a kind of character by character world with places that were inviting exploration, a mental landscape for the embodiment of the worlds of different characters. This was absolutely the foundation of all the significant work that has been done with interactive fiction in interactive media, and that idea had to be completely nailed down before anything could follow. *Freak Show* was really the project that demonstrated how it could be done."

The *Freak Show* CD-ROM was released in January 1994, and not only received rave reviews in specialist magazines – "The most arresting and innovative interactive CD-ROM... a multimedia masterpiece" (*CD Review*) - but also received coverage from journals as diverse as *Time* and *The Washington Post*, and would go on to win several prestigious industry awards. The success was in large part due to its groundbreaking approach - it was not a computer game but an interactive experience which was able to emotionally engage the participant. Freaks like Wanda the Worm Woman and Benny The Bump not only performed for you on stage but, once the show was over, had private lives, secrets and pasts which you could explore by slipping backstage and rummaging around inside their trailers. There was also an area where you could explore the past of The Residents themselves. For 1994, the graphics were superb and gave realism to the entire experience. *Freak Show* was literally a moving graphic novel. "The first time I tried it, it was amazing," recalls

Laurie Amat, although, "I confess that I was also going in to find the sound of myself." Having bought and explored *Freak Show* upon release, I can confirm that it was an exciting and immersive experience, and a stunning visual representation of The Residents' artistic sensibility.

Freak Show sold over 60,000 copies worldwide on both Mac and PC platforms, which was good business. The faith that Nash had put into the creative core of The Residents and Jim Ludtke was fully justified in financial as well as artistic terms, and the three years of development had been a solid investment for all parties. Significantly, *Freak Show* brought The Residents to the attention of a new generation who were growing up with computer games and interactive media. Those who explored The Residents' trailer and enjoyed their performance and clips could become hooked on this strange band and go out and further explore their music and mythology.

The success of *Freak Show* also opened doors in the developing Silicon Valley for The Residents. They were no longer perceived as a band who operated on the fringe of music but were now on the cutting edge of an interactive media that finally allowed them to combine their ideas of music and graphic content without artistic compromise. As Homer Flynn told Silicon Valley Radio in 1996, "They evolved these contacts, both creatively and technically, in the computer industry in the Bay Area, so that ultimately, by the time CD-ROM was really here, they were sort of in the right place at the right time career-wise for the first time. But you know, it was never really part of any plan, it's just kind of the way life evolves in its mysterious ways." Thus The Residents could finally reveal those "waking dreams" that Jon Savage had alluded to in an album review back in 1978. Everything pointed to the future and The Residents were eager to make another CD-ROM as soon as possible.

They were given the opportunity by Michael Nash, who left Voyager to set up a company called Inscape with powerful financial backing from Warner Brothers and Home Box Office (HBO). Nash believed that *Freak Show* was the model of the kind of product that could be creative, innovative and commercial. He wanted The Residents to produce a sequel and offered total artistic freedom over the new project, as well as a budget of $400,000. Jim Ludtke would again contribute his unique skills as lead illustrator and animator, and Iain Lamb would do the programming. Unlike *Freak Show*, *Bad Day On The Midway* was, "conceived from the get-go as a CD-ROM," as Homer Flynn told *Billboard* in July 1994. "The Residents felt like the *Freak Show* CD-ROM was the fullest realisation of that particular idea, so when it came time to start the next project, that seemed like the natural place to start – where the earlier project had evolved to."

Michael Nash also took time to bang the drum in the same article, "*Midway* is another part of this Disneyland of the Damned that exists in The Residents' imagination as their own little stop off the information highway. The *Midway* is populated by about a dozen characters, and the user plays the *Midway* as one of those characters and experiences things differently based on the character they have assumed."

Bad Day On The Midway would take up a significant amount of The Residents' time over the following year, but they were not musically idle. Once the *Freak Show* CD-ROM had been completed they set about working on a music only project called *The Gingerbread Man*. However, when the tracks had been completed a Los Angeles company called Ion made an offer to add multimedia content to create an expanded album.

The expanded album concept would later become par for the course, acting as a halfway house between a normal audio CD and a CD-ROM and allowing musical tracks to be combined with visual multimedia. This was an ideal way for record companies to visually promote their artists, their promotional videos and their back catalogue. Whilst the budget for *The Gingerbread Man's* interactive content was small, with some input from Jim Ludtke The Residents visually fleshed out some of the characters that appeared in the songs. Their heads were actually sculpted by Leigh Barbier and then photographed and digitised into computer graphics and, when selected on the options screen, would come to life and reveal details about their lives. The user could cut and paste the heads, change the backdrops and make the characters reveal their experiences, thoughts and fears. The Ageing Musician, for example, had shot his dog....

The music itself was based around the *Gingerbread Man* nursery rhyme, which was a musical motif that linked all nine pieces, from the lament of the Dying Oilman to the rants of The Sold-Out Artist. Setting aside the multi-media content, the music was a triumph – strong, vibrant and with a real edge to it. One reason for this was that *Freak Show* had engaged so much of The Residents' time and energy that it was a relief for them to work on something fresh. There is a real enthusiasm in the playing and singing, and it's a fantastic album in its own right.

Again, The Residents used additional people to provide voices to represent the different characters, including Laurie Amat and Diana Alden, who had both appeared on *Freak Show*. Isabelle Barbier also appeared, as did Molly Harvey, who was to play a big part in future projects. One of the most interesting contributions, though, came from Todd Rundgren, best known for his lush production work, including Meat Loaf's *Bat Out Of Hell* and XTC's *Skylarking*, as well as being an established multi-instrumentalist and songwriter. The Residents had meet him back in 1991 during the demonstration of real time editing video equipment and thought he would be an ideal choice to represent a character. Fortunately, they were able to re-establish contact through Ty Roberts, who was Rundgren's friend and also, conveniently, ran Ion, the company scheduled to release *The Gingerbread Man.* Rundgren visited The Residents' studio one evening and got to deliver the immortal line "God Damn MTV!". According to Homer Flynn, "I think they (The Residents) were very impressed with basically how talented he was in that he basically came in and he got what they wanted and gave them what they wanted. The Ageing Musician that he did I thought was great, he did an amazing interpretation of that."

Although *Freak Show* had been a CD, a comic book, a CD-ROM and all manner of official Residents merchandise, there was one format that had not, as yet been explored - live performance. The Residents had discussed taking *Freak Show* onto the road, and had even performed a few numbers at trade shows, but with *Bad Day on The Midway* requiring a lot of time and creative energy there was no time in their schedule to plan, rehearse and tour it. But it did end up on stage as a theatrical piece, and Laurie Amat, whose parents were of Czechoslovakian origin, was instrumental in the project. As she told me, "I introduced them to Už Jsme Doma when we brought the first group of artists to San Francisco after the wall came down (in 1989)." Už Jsme Doma started life playing secret concerts in the Communist state, and had built an underground following that went overground when there was a peaceful transition to democracy in 1990. Amat continues, "We did an exchange festival, and Už Jsme Doma said, "We want to meet The Residents, introduce us to The Residents." So I introduced them and they became firm friends, their theatrical technique and sensibilities meshed together very very well."

Back in Czechoslovakia, plans were being made to revitalise the Archa Theatre in Prague by collaborating with artists with an international reputation, and Amat, who had been back to the Czech Republic, pushed for The Residents to get involved, "I kept saying to them "I really want you to come over, I really want you to do this piece in Prague. It would be beautiful, people love you there"". The idea intrigued The Residents, and after a visit to Prague they committed to the project. "I wrote the grant application, and it was brutal, but I got it," adds Amat about the funding from the Czech government, "It was the perfect place to put that show on because we had a gorgeous new theatre, the director was a Residents fan and they had hooked up with Už Jsme Doma, who were massive – the Resident were a big influence on them – so it was perfect. They had never played Prague – before that Prague was behind the Wall, so no-one was playing it."

It took two years for everything to come together, and firstly The Residents had to get their heads around how to transfer *Freak Show* into a live theatrical performance. In many respects this show was to be the most ambitious of all the projects spun off from the *Freak Show* album, and, significantly, The Residents would not be performing themselves. Instead, they would write the script, partially direct the performance and score the music, and were very excited about staging *Freak Show* with real actors, singers and musicians. They were also shocked when around sixty journalists turned up at the press conference in Prague announcing the performances. After all, they'd never had an official release in Czechoslovakia. Who said home taping was killing music?

Like all theatrical productions, there were many teething problems, and the most pressing from The Residents' perspective was timing - they were working on *Freak Show Live* and *Bad Day On The Midway* simultaneously. In fact, *Bad Day* was scheduled for release on Halloween, October 31st 1995, and the curtain would go up in Prague on the 1st November. As a result, The Residents had to miss the last six weeks of work on *Bad Day* and fly out to Prague to whip the show into shape. By that time *Bad Day* was being Beta tested, and they implicitly trusted producer Sharon Ludtke's decision-making and judgment. They would, however, miss the press calls for the release.

During these six weeks in Prague, The Residents took part in intense rehearsals as the mainly Czech actors learned their lines, movement and cues, and Laurie Amat worked with them to coach the two singers. "They were very enthusiastic," she recalls "and they were willing to do anything I asked them to do." Of course, there was one thing that they could not do, "I had to kind of let loose from them sounding like me as no-one can sing like me."

As The Residents did not read or write music, the original notation for the eight-piece band had to be written by a computer program at their studio in San Francisco. However, when the parts were handed to musical director Miroslav Wanek (leader of Už Jsme Doma) there were problems. The Residents took for granted the ability of the computer to allow them to manipulate sound as they saw fit, and so had created sounds beyond the range of the traditional instruments that would be played. In the end, Wanek had to rewrite the parts for each musician within the accepted guidelines of their instruments tonal range.

When The Residents and The Cryptic Corporation heard the music and saw the completed production performed for the first time, their reaction was mixed. Whilst Homer Flynn appreciated the endeavor, "My initial thoughts upon seeing *Freak Show* in Prague were that I completely understood the old cliché of producers and directors preferring to be in a bar across the street instead of being in the audience for the opening night performance. As the director all you can do is sit there cringing at every mistake or missed cue while feeling completely helpless to do anything about it."

Freak Show Live played a total of twenty-two performances during November, in a theatre which seated four hundred people, and each night was almost a total sell-out. The performance was split into two acts: the first was about forty minutes long and saw Tex The Barker, played by American actor Wayne Doba, introduce the various freaks, all of whom were played by actors, except for Harry The Head and Jello Jack, who were portrayed by props. Amat states that Doba's role was crucial to the show as, "You were taking an album and expanding it into a full evening show, so there had to be more drama. The ringmaster carried it because of his energy, and what he was doing really carried a lot of the sensibility of the CD-ROM." In the second act, the curtains parted to reveal four trailers on the stage, the walls of each made out of scrim, which allowed them to reveal the freaks inside. This part of the performance was designed to show the characters personal sides and, according to Homer Flynn, allowed the audience to see "how the people inside these freaks aren't that different from the rest of us." Puppets were used to tell Harry and Wanda's stories.

As the show was performed in English for a predominantly Czech speaking audience, there was a screen on one side of the stage showing Czech subtitles. Disconcerting for the actors to deliver their lines whilst the audience was looking in another direction to read what they were saying, perhaps, but the performances were very well received. As well as being vocal director, Laurie Amat also performed with the singers each night, and thoroughly enjoyed the experience, "I loved it. I never got tired of singing *Harry* every night, and I almost cried every time because I believed the story so much. When I go to perform things I just take them on. I guess my philosophy is that if I believe it there is a good chance that the audience will believe it."

Freak Show Live was filmed and shown on Czechoslovakian TV, and a documentary was made on the development of the show, whih can now be viewed in its entirety on YouTube.

Like *Freak Show* before it, *Bad Day On The Midway* received glowing reviews on release – "This game is the best example of interactive story-telling yet" – and was much more sophisticated due to budget, programming expertise and the experience gained by all parties when producing *Freak Show*. Set in a dark, decrepit carnival world, *Bad Day* was a murder mystery starring a young boy named Timmy, and what made the game particularly interesting was that you could slip into other characters and see things from their viewpoint and perspective. They each had their own agendas and secrets, and interaction with Dagmar, Otto, Ted and Dixie determined the future plot development of the game. A number of Midway attractions invited exploration, and also acted as springboards for graphic novels by illustrators like Richard Sala, Peter Kuper and Dave McKean.

"By then I'd met them again in San Francisco," recalls McKean, "And I think we were both intrigued by interactive media, and both trying to work out what it was and how best to use it. Again, they were very open, and allowed me to explore the story in my own way. There seems to be a strain of American surrealism that's about spoiled dreams, and the Freak Show as a phenomenon really seems to express this idea of simple circus family entertainment gone wrong. You can see this mix of nostalgia and unease in David Lynch's films, in Witkin's photos, and I think it's there in The Residents' music as well. I was very happy to explore this mood. The link between the butterfly and the human ears occurred to me as I made notes in my sketchbook. I tend to draw lots of ideas, anything that occurs to me, and then mulch them down and see what comes through as the strongest or most appropriate images."

Bad Day On The Midway eventually sold in the region of sixty thousand copies worldwide at an average price of $50, so generated a gross of around $3 million. Thus, as well as winning industry awards, it generated a profit on the original $400,000 investment. The Residents were keen to build on this success and began work on their next interactive CD-ROM, entitled *I Murdered Mommy* and based around the adventures of a thirteen year old boy. Thus they dedicated over a year to a project that was never to be completed, primarily due to the bursting of the dot com bubble burst and the advance of computer games rather than CD-ROMs as the next step forward in interactive home media, which led to the collapse of Inscape, who were funding, and intended to release, the project. Although they had been paid for their work, as *I Murdered Mommy* would never be released The Residents were left needing to find other ways to generate revenue.

This, of course, led to a decision to begin touring again.

Demons Dance Alone With Jesus

"If you decide to become Dixie… Wander the Midway and speak to as many characters as possible. Around 4 pm, you'll probably run into the IRS Man, who will inform you that he's giving you two hours to find all of the Midway's tax records for the past five years. Where did Ike (the midway owner now in a coma) hide them? This is one of the subplots. For more details of Dixie's dilemma, head to the room above the Three-Headed Abominable Snowman Skeleton exhibit." - thecomputershow.com suggested walkway cheat sheet

"I wish I'd picked an alias! If I could do it all over again, I sure would've picked another name. I mean, how boring?" - Molly Harvey

Molly Harvey first met Homer Flynn when she was working as a waitress in a cocktail bar… I mean a café/bakery called Elsie's, near The Cryptic Corporation offices, in 1993. She struck up a conversation when he opened his wallet and she saw something with an eyeball on it, which she commented on. "It's weird that I connected 'Residents' with his wallet," she told me, "(it was) a medical illustration-type eyeball, not a Rez eyeball. I wasn't a big (or even slight) fan… so it's odd that my mind went there at all."

Harvey not only served Flynn, but also Hardy Fox and Sarah McLennan, who was working for The Cryptic Corporation at that time. One day, "Homer of Cryptic came in and I was really wound up, I'd probably had seventeen espressos, and I had in these buck teeth that the owner of the restaurant had given us to wear – they were supposed to be bunny teeth for Easter. Anyways, I'm highly caffeinated and have these buck teeth in, and I guess I was feeling really silly, and I just said something offhand like, "Can't you give me a job? I can do voices!" He said, "Well… can you do an old lady voice?"" Harvey not only said "Yes" but also rang home, "I told my mom that on the phone and she said, "Molly… RUN!" I don't know if she thought it was some sort of sex cult initiation or what, but fortunately she was wrong."

Harvey went into into The Residents' studio to record an old female voice for a track on the *Gingerbread Man* album, and was able to do it, "In a take or two - that's what College will get you. You can learn how to audition. The person recording me liked that I worked fast and didn't hem and haw too much, and I guess my old lady voice was good enough because they used it."

Harvey also played Dixie, one of the characters in the *Bad Day On The Midway* CD-ROM, and it was not long before she was working for The Cryptic Corporation after an artistic difference at Elsie's. "One day the owner of the café and I had a fight, and I quit. Sarah happened to be coming up right then, and I said something like, "I hope to see you again. I just quit this job." She told me she could use some help at Ralph, and that led to six years working side by side with Sarah. I started out just packing boxes, mostly LPs in those days, making post office runs, and eventually helping with daily operations and writing the Ralph catalogue. Lots of talking with fans on the phone (this was 1994-1999) about music."

With regards to The Residents, Harvey was thrown into the deep end in 1997 when they roped her in for a one-off filmed performance in Koln, Germany, which went under the name *Disfigured Night*. "That was arranged through Ralph Europe," recalls Hein Fokker today, "Guido Randizo arranged the whole thing and it was sponsored by Marlboro or something like that. It was crazy interesting, it was nice. I love those things, the special occasions and one-offs." In fact, The Residents' performance was part of the Popkomm festival/music fair, one of the biggest in the world at that time, and, according to Randzio, who then worked for a distribution company called EFA in Germany, "Each year they wanted something special and they had sponsors, and at that time (it was) Phillip Morris/Marlboro. So with our connection with VH1, who did the TV production part, we could set up something special." Thus The Residents were asked to appear, although as the main sponsors were a tobacco firm, according to Randizo they, "were not too pleased that there would be a group with a skull in the Marlboro context. But it was art and they had to swallow it. They did not like it but they did it."

As for how she moved from mail order to frontline action, Harvey told me that, "I can't remember the transition to doing the show in Germany as in the moment I went "Holy shit!" because it was a pretty mellow process of one thing leading to another. (Before that) we did a private thing at Adobe's headquarters in the eyeballs... no one gave a shit we were there, except one weird lady holding a little dog. But that was actually my first performance experience with The Residents."

Although Harvey did not sing during the *Disfigured Night* performance, she was told there'd be more dates at the Fillmore, back in San Francisco, to celebrate The Residents' 25th Anniversary, "And that I was going to sing. I'll never forget that." The first part took material from *The Gingerbread Man*, the second from *Freak Show* and the third a segment from *Disfigured Night* that included a rendition of *We Are The World*. From this point onwards, Harvey, who had studied theatre at University, became part of The Residents' studio and live set up.

The first project to fully integrate Harvey into The Residents' DNA was *Wormwood*. This was the latest in The Residents' brave and ambitious concept pieces, in which they decided to reinterpret tales from the Bible that "no-one remembers." This bold undertaking was intended not to dismiss or deride religion, but to give a deeper understanding to elements of one of the greatest storybooks of all time. Crucially, Homer Flynn states that 'The Residents wanted to do a concept album that they could take out on tour. I think at that time the Conservative religious right in America was just rising to power, and I won't say that the album is a statement about that, but I think that kind of influenced their interest. They just thought it would be interesting to show the Bible in a different light, and that idea came about and they started researching it. Most of them had not thought about the Bible since they were teenagers going to churches back in the South, and as they began to research it they found it more and more fascinating. Most of it *(Wormwwood)* is the Old Testament, the really interesting part, and the more they researched it the more fascinated they got. It was almost like this bizarre window into an alien culture. Very quickly any stimulation they got from the religious right and making a statement against that quickly faded into the background, just because the Bible became so interesting in itself." The Residents gleefully wrote songs around tales with a cast of characters including Moses, John The Baptist, Cain and other lesser-known revelators like Sisera and Absalom.

Those unfamiliar with *Wormwood* might think that this was very unpromising ground in which to plant musical crops, but the resulting CD, issued in 1998, was a fantastic marriage of music, song and narrative, including tracks like *How To Get A Head* (sung by Harvey), *Spilling The Seed*, *Melancholy Clumps* and the very catchy *I Hate Heaven*. Of course, there were some tracks that did not make it onto the album as they were deemed somewhat sensitive. Most of these featured vocalist and master percussionist Toby Dammit.

"I was asked anonymously to come in for a recording session with a group who were looking for someone to perform "in persona" as Jesus Christ on a new musical soundtrack," Dammit related to me. "They (Cryptic Corporation) were specifically looking for someone who could sing falsetto with a young boy's southern accent, which I could."

Although these tracks were completed, when it came to the sequencing and mastering of the album, The Residents decided not to use some material, as Dammit told me, "Particularly my tracks as Jesus Christ, which apparently were just too controversial lyrically. The entire Jesus Christ character had to be removed from the project altogether... come to think of it, the Bible would be an interesting book without Jesus Christ as a main character." As for The Cryptic view on the matter, Homer Flynn states simply that, "The Jesus mythology has so overshadowed the older material in contemporary culture that they felt like they had to acknowledge Jesus in some way. But Jesus has been done to death, so to speak, so finding an interesting way of approaching that material wasn't easy. Ultimately, after trying and rejecting a few things, approaching Jesus through the perspective of Judas seemed like an intriguing way to deal with it."

Wormwood was crying out to become a touring piece, and The Residents got the nod from above – The Cryptic Corporation – to take it out onto the road. In fact, as The Residents had been left high and dry by the collapse in the interactive CD-ROM market, there was not only a conscious decision to begin touring again but to also to recruit additional musicians to form a core band to play the music and supplement the core Residential line-up. As Homer Flynn told me:

"The *Cube-E* tour had been very successful but very demanding, and I think that after that they were ready to take a break from touring at that point. And then the CD-ROM era came along and there was not enough time to be touring, working on CD-ROMs and recording music at the same time, so they were happy to let six or seven years go by, but at some point they did make a conscious decision to return to touring."

Classically trained Carla Fabrizio was not only a gifted player and arranger but had toured with a number of groups. "I was in my cubicle at a dotcom tech job and got a phone call from Hardy Fox," she related to me, "I'd met him before at gamelan concerts, and found out much later that our paths had crossed much earlier. In his usual charming voice he said, "This is Hardy Fox from The Cryptic Corporation... and I've been watching you for a long time."" At this point, Fox described the kind of project he would like her to work on, which involved "Orchestrating and arranging accompanying music by The Residents for a chamber orchestra in Europe, sending them charts, then going to rehearse and prepare them for The Residents' arrival and eventual performance. It was pretty much a perfect fit for me. This was unbelievable timing because I'd been struggling with the security vs. freedom thing of having good health insurance and steady income but feeling like I was losing my creativity."

Fabrizio was quick to say "Yes", but on her first day on the job, and having started work on the arrangements, she was told that the project was not likely to happen, "But they had something different in mind for me. The new project was the *Wormwood* album, and I was given the title 'Assistant to The Residents'. I chose much of the instrumentation, wrote charts and pretty much directed all the guest musicians. I don't think people realise that most of the sounds on that album are actually real people and instead assume its MIDI. We did some weird stuff with my voice and made it sound like instruments, and vice versa. It was a blast, and the only time I can think of where each day I couldn't wait to go to work."

This decision to draft in musicians to help record *Wormwood* led to the recruitment of another vital cog in the retooled Residential machine - Nolan Cook. "Well, I used to make these four-track cassettes at home of experimental material, apart from the stuff I was doing in bands, and I would dub them, hand-design the insert cards and just give them to friends for the fun of it," he told me. "A couple of folks at The Cryptic Corporation wound up getting their hands on one of those and liked what they heard enough to invite me over for a meeting, as they happened to be looking for a guitarist to hire for three nights at the Fillmore, for the Halloween 1998 performances of *Wormwood: Curious Stories from the Bible.* We wound up getting on swimmingly, and I'm still working with them today."

Crucially, the *Wormwood* project also saw the recruitment of a number of other musicians who would feature in other 'band' tours in subsequent years. "Most of those people have just come about fairly organically through relationships that already existed," states Homer Flynn on The Residents' recruitment process, "Eric (Drew) Feldman played with Snakefinger for years, so there was already a relationship with Eric, and when it became time to expand the group in order to perform *Demons Dance Alone*, well he was just a natural person to ask. For someone like Toby Dammit, he was a friend of Carla's, so when it came to do *Wormwood* and they wanted a drummer, I think he had been with Iggy Pop and had just left, so he was looking for a gig. Carla suggested him and that worked out."

According to Dammit, it was a stroke of good fortune that got him onto the *Wormwood* tour bus, "I was contracted by The Cryptic Corporation on numerous occasions for recording sessions, initially as a session vocalist, but when it was time to take those sessions to the stage they mentioned they would soon be searching for a drummer. Only then was it mentioned I could offer that service as well."

The first presentation of *Wormwood* was the Halloween shows in October 1998, which saw not only the debuts of Nolan Cook and Toby Dammit but also of Carla Fabrizio. "Being a super appreciator (of

The Residents) since my somophore year in high school, and after having gone to all of the Fillmore shows of the previous year, it was both a humbling and exciting experience," states Fabrizio, "and it was emotional on another level too as I felt I'd found a new family. It wasn't my idea to add the live gamelan to the show, but I was proud to be able to contribute by arranging those tunes for Sekar Jaya to perform in the second half. The audience was shocked when the curtain opened after the intermission to see all the gongs and gamelan instruments on the stage with twelve more Residents, all in costume. Those strange arrangements kept morphing over the years, which is of course one of the classic and cool Residential things."

Visually *Wormwood* did not have many backdrops or the theatricality of *Cube E*, but cleverly placed three members of the band – guitar, keyboards and Emulator – on the right of stage and the massive drums and percussion set up on the left. Whilst the players wore eyeballs, top hats and ecclesiastical robes, the main singer started as Mr. Skull before costume changes saw him taking on the role of other characters to prowl the central stage space, which he shared with Molly Harvey, who sang, danced and acted out tracks like *How To Get A Head* and *Tent Peg In The Temple.* The singer and Harvey would also bring a number of large heads mounted on poles onto the stage to denote the religious figures depicted in each particular song.

That The Residents performed *Wormwood* with a taut live band gave the music a powerful edge that the singer and audience could feed from, and although the songs had Biblical origins this did not detract from the fact that they concerned the staple toolbox of rock bands - envy, sex and death. "*Wormwood* did wear on me," recalls Molly Harvey, "The subject matter, women getting abused and fucked over, again and again, night after night, got emotionally draining. Those stories told over and over became like a mantra."

As for the musical set up, "It was right for that time," states Nolan Cook of the line-up, "and was very exciting. The 'band' era began with *Wormwood*, as did my involvement, and just like that we found ourselves in front of massive rock festival audiences all around Europe." As one of the arrangers of the music for the show, Fabrizio saw it blossom on the road, "The show had evolved since the Fillmore Shows, maybe even a little more serious or mature, not that that's either good or bad. I worked hard on *Nober*, and I was the last one to admit it wasn't working and resisted it being dropped from the show. The idea of a musical overture for a show as grand as *Wormwood* seemed essential, plus it was a perfect overture, but at the time I didn't realise that audiences didn't respond well to that kind of thing. Maybe it's my classical background. I'm still in denial about it, even though I heard a bootleg recording from Boston and it really wasn't very good."

"Every show has its great moments," recalls Hein Fokker, "but *Wormwood* is still my all time favourite. There was a lot going on on stage there, there were a lot of costumes, and at the end of the show when he becomes the big guy, I still get goose pimples thinking about that." This number was *Judas Saves*, sung by Mr. Skull in white robes. The song starts slowly, both musically and vocally, in near darkness, before picking up momentum, and ends with Mr. Skull standing on a dias bathed in light as smoke rises up around him, arms lifted to the heavens and screaming out the vocals as a sampled choir back him with hallelujahs. This really was old time religion Residents style, and Molly Harvey loved it. "Touring *Wormwood* is my all-time favourite performance experience," she says, "Carrying those heads out onto the stage every night, singing about the wrath of God and man. It was epic. My favourite memory was in Thessaloniki, Greece, performing outside by a train track, a storm brewing, wind whipping... and us with this audience. It was as full as life gets." But life got too full for Nolan Cook at a gig in Athens, where he was actually hit on the head by a rock thrown from the audience. One assumes the assailant was either insane or mistook The Residents for Kiss.

As for Carla Fabrizio, as a central cog she eased herself into the Residential touring machinery, "Touring in the US was a little tough because I hadn't learned about how everyone would be on the road. It wasn't at all like other bands I'd toured with, so I was unprepared. For the next tour, I adjusted my way of thinking and had a much better time. I think one of the challenges on the *Wormwood* European tour was the number of people travelling, and also problems with gear." A guitar was broken, a bass caused problems and needed hard to find specific parts for repairs. Fabrizio again, "And then there was that huge set of drums that took hours to set up and line check and almost as long to break down. And the dangerous sharp wires that kept the eyeballs round at the bottom kept coming unglued and required a lot of maintenance. A high point was at the Arezzo Wave Festival, in a packed football field, when the curtain opened and thousands of fans screamed, so happy to see The Residents. I remember that was a great show and the entire crew backstage applauded as they left the stage (which rarely happens)."

In fact, many audience members would have happily applauded the drum set up deployed by Mr. Dammit on stage, which sounded as extravagant as it looked. "It was a lot of fun to work with (twelve large drums onstage!)," he told me, "but very expensive to transport worldwide for a year, so that was the only time such an extravagance was permitted by The Cryptic Corporation after they tallied all the costs. No one was more fascinated by it than James Brown himself when he crashed a soundcheck and couldn't stop asking me questions about how I managed it all."

The album and merchandise for *Wormwood* sold tremendously well, mainly due to the fact that The Residents' marketing machine was well oiled in both America and Europe. "Merchandise is always very good for any tour," states Maarten Postma, "and the best-selling item is always the eyeball T-shirt. Always. It is an evergreen and never goes out of style. I always have beautiful stuff to sell as they always make beautiful things, but the eyeball always sells two, three or four times more than the actual tour T-shirts." Later on, these "beautiful things" would extend to include limited edition CDs that sometimes only had a run of only a hundred or three hundred copies. "This was something Dren came up with and The Residents really jumped on board," states Lorrie Murray, "The idea was to make something very special, but it wasn't always conducive to mass production. It was also a way to gauge interest in a release and build excitement for the live show."

As well as tour merchandise there was also a spike in what is now known as online sales. "There the World Wide Web came into our favour," recalls Guido Randzio, "We had started to do sales online very early, before 1993. I had been the co-owner of what you would have called back then a multi-media agency, and I had the services to hand to produce online sales at a relatively overseeable cost. We initially had a list of around two thousand people (in Europe) who would be interested, and after a while we would not have to print catalogues and mail them out anymore, so it was good. I think that the *Wormwood* project, the tour and the *Roadworms* LP was the peak."

In many respects there was a similar situation across the Atlantic with Ralph America, "The online mailing list was around three and a half thousand folks," states Lorrie Murray, although in her opinion it was not until the *Demons Dance Alone* album that electronic ordering in America outweighed the traditional mail order model as "it took a few years for some longtime customers to adapt to the new system. Some folks still liked to call in their order, either because they didn't have a computer or didn't trust that it went through, or just wanted to talk to someone about the band."

When it came to talking about the band, Lorrie was certainly a go-to person as she was not only involved in Ralph America with her husband Dren McDonald, but was also out there in the field, either selling merchandise on tour or in other backstage roles. "I enjoyed it immensely and still do," she says, "Especially on tour. I love talking to the fans and listening to their stories. It makes you appreciate the special situation you're in. I think some of them (most fans are men) especially like being able to have a conversation with a girl who knows a lot about The Residents. That probably doesn't happen very often! Having the ability to make the personal connection really humanised the online sales experience as well. They knew when they were ordering that it was me or Dren taking care of them."

The Roadworms LP was recorded on 7th July 1999 on the twenty-date European leg of the *Wormwood* tour. The Residents had been invited to perform in the SFB Sendesaal studio in Berlin, "But the theatre was also home to a German radio broadcasting station," recalls Homer Flynn, "so it was actually set up as a recording studio. They created this opportunity to go in on a day off and just run through their entire set and record it in a way that is not normally done. Normally you have to do all of this with an audience, you can't do things a second time and there are lots of compromises that have to be made live, whereas to be able to go into this situation in a place that is set up without an audience, but still have a lot of the momentum and the energy that a group gets when they are performing something every day... what was interesting about that was to take that energy into that situation and record it."

The Residents greatly enjoyed the experience as it captured how well the songs of *Wormwood* had developed during the American and European touring cycle. "It was very prestigious to record in the studio," recalls Guido Randizo, "and they got the performance and we got the recording, so it was good for everybody." Whilst The Residents were no strangers to releasing albums of live material, this was certainly a different type of recording and highlighted the chops of the very cohesive band that they'd assembled. Molly Harvey recalls that, for the tour and this session, "It was so thrilling to be playing with all these talented musicians. There was no room to fuck up, and although I felt competently trained in performance I was not confident at all as a singer. Looking back I still can't believe it." That said, she recalls that the *Roadworms* LP was great fun to record, "Touring *Wormwood* was a marathon, so we'd completed our course and had the chance to relax and let our hair down and belt out some tunes."

Molly Harvey found working with The Residents very stimulating on a creative level, and gained an insight into how hard work was equally important as expression, "Artistically, the environment around Cryptic was really important to my understanding of what a work ethic looks like. Coming to work every day, no matter how many projects you do or don't have right at this moment," she told me, "There were no days off because of lack of inspiration." Fortunately, at this time inspiration was not in short supply. To celebrate their 30th Anniversary, The Residents returned to the road in 2001 to serve up the *Icky Flix* tour to America and Europe. This was a no holds barred celebration, a theatrical experience that revisited tracks like *Buckaroo Blues, Constantinople, The Gingerbread Man and Just For You*. Once again, Harvey was on the road and a central pillar of the live performance, "I had no problem touring and thanked the baby Jesus and my lucky stars every day!"

The tour was in Hamburg on 11th September 2001, and the shocking use of airliners as weapons of Jihadist attack, the destruction of the twin towers in New York and loss of life hit The Residents, like it did most Americans, as a deep psychological shock. For many years America had encountered terrorists away from the homeland, but to be subject to attack on home soil un-tethered their fundamental feeling of national and personal security. The Residents and those on the tour were keen to speak to loved ones and get home.

There has been much talk about how the 9/11 attacks fed into into the *Demons Dance Alone* material, especially the section later entitled *Loss*. Musically, The Residents' reflection upon this seismic event was more to do with emotions and feelings than any attempt to distill the national anger and confusion that found its most extreme (and misguided) expression in George Bush's invasion of Iraq and investment in Afghanistan. This was confirmed when I spoke to Homer Flynn recently to discuss *Demons Dance Alone*, "An interesting kind of sidebar to that story is that the last major earthquake in San Francisco was in 1989 and The Residents were also on tour and in Hamburg when it happened. So this was two major disasters, I suppose, that happened back in the States with The Residents in Hamburg, which is a really odd coincidence. The whole 9/11 thing was so disturbing on so many levels to so many people - not just people in the United States but everywhere were shocked that this could actually happen - and I think for the group to be on tour and away from home when all of that happened was hard. The tour was probably not even half over – I don't remember exactly – but there was a lot of tour left and there was just a great sense of vulnerability that went through the whole group, being so far away and this crazy stuff happening at home. If you think about that album from the point of view of all the characters that are portrayed in it, it's all about vulnerability, all of these characters are in vulnerable moments in their lives and the idea of doing an album about vulnerability was the correct outcome of 9/11"

Demons Dance Alone is a tremendously important Residents record. It was the waypoint, the transition towards a new sensibility and richness of musical and lyrical expression. As I'm dealing with a band that wraps part of its working practices in secrecy, I can only speculate as to how the music for *Demons* was constructed and put together, but there is litttle doubting the central role that Chuck played, with his ability to compose, create and blend music together. But the

First time on the road with the Mole Show (Courtesy of The Cryptic Corporation)

The 13th Anniversary Tour sees the light (Courtesy of The Cryptic Corporation)

Lead singer during the 13th Anniversary Show (Courtesy of The Cryptic Corporation)

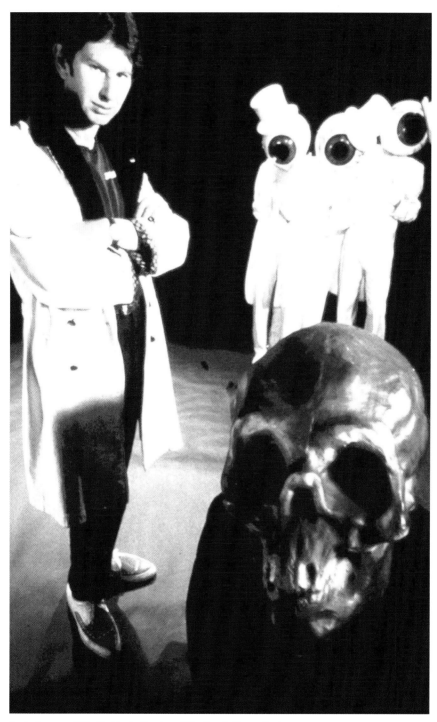

Snakefinger and The Residents (Courtesy of The Cryptic Corporation)

The Kitchen Exhibition New York (Courtesy of Ian Shirley)

Elvis rocks the house in *Cube-E* (Courtesy of The Cryptic Corporation)

The Residents museum (Courtesy of Andreas Mathews)

The Wormwood experience (Courtesy of The Cryptic Corporation)

Demons Dance Alone (Courtesy of The Cryptic Corporation)

Bob, Chuck and Randy! (Courtesy of The Cryptic Corporation)

Still going strong… (Courtesy of Dawid Laskowski)

addition of other familiar musicians like Carla Fabrizio, Nolan Cook, Toby Dammit and others added to the sonic palette that Chuck worked with, and therefore directly played a part in the compositional process. Toby Dammit was gracious enough to give an insight into how parts were used when he told me, "Often we would work on one thing and then the tracks would appear on completely different songs, having no relation to the initial structures... so song titles were nothing but a way of alphabetically filing the session results I suppose, until it was all reviewed later, then redesigned and renamed for purposes beyond my imagination. To my knowledge, Cryptic are continuing this activity even today." As for Carla Fabrizio, her contributions were sometimes infused with reverence, "Being a super Residents appreciator from a young age, I remember having to pinch myself when recording *Pestilence* and *Fire '99* on *Refused* and *Vileness Fats* for *Icky Flix*, where I got to sing those classic lyrics like "Bing bing, bing, bong bong bong" and "Kick a cat". It's because of that history that those moments were exceptional on a personal level."

As for Nolan Cook, he was the most important addition to The Residents' sound-box since Snakefinger. His first foray into the studio with the band was in 1999, adding a guitar part to the track *Matchmaker*, which was part of the *Knitting On The Roof* compilation, wherein different bands interpreted tracks from the musical *Fiddler On The Roof*. "That experience was a bit surreal," he recalls, "It was fun but I was not completely at ease sitting in that long-revered studio recording on a Residents track for the first time. I should add that it was just myself and one of the Cryptic producers that day - The Residents themselves were nowhere to be seen. I think I made two passes at it and we kept the second one."

From that tiny acorn a mighty oak grew, and on subsequent albums Cook's power, inventiveness and distinctive musical voice lifted the music to a higher level. As for his input, The Residents encouraged him. "Based on my own experience," he told me, "being part of the musical portion of their vast artistic terrain, be it onstage or in the studio, offers a rare and unique challenge. Early on, when I would ask about how I should approach a section of a tune, or even how to approach the task of being their guitarist, the answer would be, "That is for you to determine." They're less interested in providing guidelines to a collaborator than they are in allowing him or her to figure out how to balance their own artistic personality with that of the material at hand. As a guitarist it allowed me to apply all sorts of ideas that I never had this type of outlet for." In 2009, Cook went on to form his own band, Dimesland, along with his brother Drew. Their 2015 LP *Psychogenic Atrophy* received great reviews, and featured Carla Fabrizio. Sadly, Drew Cook died on in May 2015, after his other band, Wild Hunt, had released the LP *Before The Plane Of Angles* in 2012.

Again, Molly Harvey also played a central role on the *Demons Dance Alone* - I asked if she ever got to write any lyrics for any of the songs. "No, I definitely do not write any lyrics," she told me, "Those are handed down from the top." Well, the top, were certainly on fire on tracks like *Mickey Macaroni*, *Betty's Body* and *Caring*. The album also features one of the greatest Residents songs of all time - *Mr. Wonderful* – which not only showcases totally beguiling melody lines but also manages to convey experience, wistfulness, vulnerability, dignity, emotion and magic in its lyrics about a homeless man. It's a beautiful song, and one that the 9/11 shockwave generated. *The Car Thief* even sounds like something that might have been sung by Astrid Gilberto in the '60s, missing only Stan Getz's saxophone.

Demons Dance Alone was, in some respects, one of the most open of all Residents albums, and almost mainstream in its composition and directness. The songs are melodic and full of hooks. "I don't know if it was conceived as being accessible per se," ruminates Homer Flynn, "but I think there was a feeling that this sense of vulnerability was a universal feeling, and maybe they felt unconsciously that to convey that feeling it needed that accessibility, but I certainly don't remember that sort of dialogue going around."

As with *Disfigured Night* and *Wormwood*, the album's packaging was a joint effort between Lorrie Murray and Homer Flynn, and it looked so good as the result of good old fashioned friendly creative friction, "I really enjoyed collaborating with Homer," Murray recalls, "We have very different approaches to design and it certainly leads to lively debates, but I think we found a way to put both our personalities into those packages. I would say *Freak Show Deluxe* was the most fun of all. I think it took me eight hours just to find the typefaces I wanted."

Next, The Residents decided to tour the album, and between October 2002 and September 2003 embarked on three separate periods of touring, first in America and then twice in Europe. As Molly Harvey recalls, "*Demons* was a lot of fun to perform, but the lights in the eyes were fucking blinding!" The lighting set up was similar to that of *Cube-E*, with most of the illumination at the front of the stage directed at the performers. For the first time, The Residents decided to hire a male dancer, Paul Benney, who, in his red demon costume, interaction with Randy and Harvey and occasional, highly visual toots on a large trumpet, gave the show real panache and visual power. Considering how much he added to the shows, his recruitment was, according to Homer Flynn, pure chance, "It was such a serendipitous stroke of luck that he came along when he did. Paul was right on the cusp – he was in his mid to late 30s – of retiring as a dancer. He'd spent most of his career as a dancer with a female partner who had got married and had a child and quit dancing, and that kind of left him on his own."

Flynn continues, "The Residents were not so much looking for a dancer, they were looking for someone to hand-hold lights during the performance, and they thought that it would be good if that person was a dancer as that would be much more interesting to look at on stage. He brought so much to that performance, so much life, so much energy, so much creativity. I don't think they would ever have tried to cast the role for someone like that because they would not have thought they could ever find somebody who could do that. It was just a pure stroke of luck that that person happened to show up at that time, which added so much creative energy to the part. It was great."

"The guy who played the Demon was a very sweet guy," recalls Hein Fokker, "That was a great tour as well. That was the last tour with a lot of people on stage and a bigger production." Of course, the tours were there to make money, and like many other bands The Residents were subjected to grueling schedules. For example, the short European trip between 25th February 2003 and 15th March 2003 crammed in fifteen dates in nine different countries in eighteen days, and Molly Harvey's blog at this time was not only about the shows and audience reaction but early flights, lack of sleep, excellent to indifferent food and its gastric consequences, exhaustion, airing smelly costumes, elation and, one occasion, the band exceeding their collective baggage allowance so everyone had to carry costumes and props on their laps on the plane.

Despite bumping her head after being chased around the stage by the Demon in Holland, and the band hilariously being mistaken for a Swedish folk band at the airport by a promoter in Poland – "I just wish the miscommunication could've lasted long enough for us to get to the venue where the folk band was going to play" – Harvey enjoyed herself. The touring party was cohesive, with no grating egos. With regards The Residents on tour, Harvey told me that, "They are some of the most down to earth people you'd ever meet. I don't know that they'd be able to stay that way had they not been anonymous. They're very sane and they keep the insanity for the stage. There was nothing precious or pretentious."

She continues, "My background is theatre, and many stage actors are extremely superstitious, in that their warm-up exercises before a show are very important, and there's a lot of self-congratulatory stuff that goes on. With the Rez, we just did it. No group hugs, no warm ups (soundchecks would be the closest thing)... We'd eat a meal, maybe take a nap, and then hit the stage. We'd meet up afterwards on the bus, ask "How was that for you?" and go about our business. It created a bar for me in terms of professionalism, ego, all that." The other musicians concerned also enjoyed the experience. "*Demons Dance Alone* was an enjoyable experience onstage," recalls Toby Dammit, "yet embellished with deeper visibility concerns and acrobatics... None of us ever carried a camera, so we got along just fine."

Demons Dance Alone was a cohesive wrapper that was not only an album, a tour and, later, a DVD, but also a powerful demonstration that The Residents were still not only relevant but were creating fantastic music. That they were more than happy to repackage and re-release old material also kept their original albums in circulation. Of course, some of their mash-ups – *Their Finest Flowers* comes to mind - were not always well received by fans, but at other end of the scale their music was now being sampled by other musicians - The Residents' back catalogue was certainly fertile ground for those looking for inventive drums, percussion and music music to loop. This led to a strange situation when The Residents music appeared in TV adverts illegally in 2006.

"The story as I understand it," Homer Flynn told me," is that it (*Numb Erone* from *Meet The Residents*) appeared on two different commercials almost simultaneously, which is even stranger. One was Levi's and one was a T-Mobile commercial. It was a fan that originally heard it and informed us what was happening. Some DJ remix guy released it and that music was used in the ads. When he was approached about it his story was that he had just bought a collection of samples that he thought were cleared for royalties – they were royalty free samples and that was what he was using. We don't know if that is the truth or not, but that's what he put out."

What was also – legally - released in 2004 was a remix of *The King And Eye*. "That idea came from a guy in Germany," recalls Homer, "Called Guido Randzio, who used to run Euro Ralph and who was good friends with a guy who goes by the professional name of Paralyzer. Now Paralyzer was, and I am sure still is, a huge Elvis fan, so it was Guido and Paralyzer, their relationship, Guido's connection to The Residents and Paralyzer's connection to Elvis, that really created that."

According to Randzio, the project was also driven by the fact that the original magnetic master tapes of *The King And Eye* "were in a state and we needed to do something about it in order not to lose them. We used the services of my friend Arne (AKA Paralyzer), who transferred the tapes as he had a good studio (the famed Master And Servant) and was also a very successful pop and techno producer. We had been school buddies influenced by the first wave of post-punk, and The Residents were amongst those artists. He had a personal approach to the project and put a lot of energy into it. It appears that The Cryptic Corporation liked it enough that it became product."

What he created was the excellent *The King And Eye RMX* album, which might have baffled some Residents fans but delighted others. Personally, I think it is fantastic - he took one of the worst albums that The Residents had ever released and transformed it into a powerful and compelling collection of songs driven by a pounding techno beat! Viva Las Vegas! According to Randzio, there were plans to issue a whole host of RMX albums due to the necessity of transferring many of the original Residents master tapes that had begun to deteriorate with age and needed to be transferred. Although there was the *Warner Bros RMX* album, "We did not continue the series as we had planned to." Maybe part of the reason was that Randzio had health issues to attend to, which saw him - regretfully - take a back seat in the running of Euro Ralph.

Hein Fokker also took a back seat when the band was offered a series of five gigs in Australia in March 2005. "It was too good an offer to pass up," recalls Homer Flynn, "but the problem was that they didn't have a show, so they had to put something together in six weeks. Normally, when The Residents tour they spend a lot of time rehearsing and then they go out and will play twenty shows in four weeks or something like that, so they are performing a lot and it actually gets into a rhythm with the whole thing. With the Australian shows they never got to rehearse it much, never got to rehearse it on stage. By the time they got to Australia, took a few days to get over the jet lag and performed it again it had been a while since they had done it. They did a couple of shows and then had some days off before performing again, and then the shows were over. So they never got into a performance rhythm. There were technical problems on top of that, like microphones not working." To be fair, as the DVD release of what is known as *The Way We Were* shows, they were not bad shows visually and sonically, but as the Residents' performances were theatrical as well as musical they always required time, rehearsal and performance to bed themselves in.

Full Mute

"We lived together in San Mateo in a small apartment at first, he was bringing all his friends out there as when they first got out there they did not have apartments and stuff, so it was like an Irish flophouse, a bunch of people sleeping on blow up mattresses and things like that, you know?"

"No matter what they say in the beginning. No matter how much they love their husbands or their boyfriends or their wives or their kids or whatever; they eventually want more. More than I can give. More than they should have." – 'Tweedles' lyric

As an album, tour and live-in-the-studio recording of the live band, *Wormwood* had been a creative success and had shown that The Residents' creative teeth were still in full working order. It was, however, like many things Residents related, to lead indirectly to a new path and creative relationship for the band.

Robert Schilling was given a tape of *Wormwood* by a friend whilst studying at University in his native Romania, and after playing it his life changed. "To me it was like a blood infusion," he told me, "It was *that* serious." Schilling soon began playing the album non-stop, "When I started to listen to that LP it was like a scan of my brain. Everything was, to me, perfect and I understood every sound and every word as it was exactly what I wanted to hear. For three weeks I could not go to University. I just had to stay and listen to this album, probably thousands of times. I was obsessed."

It was not long before Schilling was sending money off to Ralph to order thirty or so Residents CDs, "And they all came three weeks later. It is one of my key memories, when I was happy opening them up." As you might imagine, Schilling began playing these albums non-stop as well, and became a dedicated Residents fan. When he later moved to England he decided that he wanted to work for Mute Records - the fact that there was no job for him was no deterrent, "I called them every two weeks asking for an interview, and it got to the stage when they said "Stop calling!"

I said "I just want to talk!"'" When Mute happened to need someone, Schilling was called in.

One of the people he was interviewed by was Daniel Miller, who had founded Mute to release his own 7", *T.V.O.D/Warm Leatherette*, back in 1978, around the same time he first heard The Residents. "I was in the Rough Trade shop in 1978 when I first heard their version of *Satisfaction*," he says, "I was extremely impressed by the sound, the concept, the humour and the Faustian echoes." As for Mute, that acorn not only grew to spread the music of Depeche Mode and Nick Cave throughout the world, but sub-divisions like The Grey Area also re-packaged the back catalogues of significant artists, such as Throbbing Gristle and Cabaret Voltaire. Miller casually asked Schilling who his favourite bands were. "Of course, I mentioned The Residents, Kraftwerk and things like that," Robert told me, "and Daniel was very excited by that. He said that he was also a big fan of The Residents and had all sorts of things by them as they were so important to the history of music, as well as electronic music."

Schilling was hired as Special Projects Manager, and played an important part in bringing The Residents to the Mute table. Although he is keen to stress that "My understanding is that before I came here there was interest floating around (in working with The Residents)" it was he who stormed the kingdom by reaching out to The Cryptic Corporation. As you might imagine, as Schilling had a severe dose of Resident-itis this was not your standard business call, "I spoke on the phone with the spokesman about the way I felt about The Residents. It was amazing that I was so crazy and passionate but not over the top."

One imagines that when Homer Flynn put the phone down the receiver was red-hot from Schilling's call from the heart. It did, however, open the door to the establishment of a deal. "At the time, as I understand it," Schilling recalls, "they were looking to co-operate with an indie label to help them with distribution... we did a worldwide deal for some of the albums. They were always very flexible with us and it was a very successful collaboration. For me personally there was an incredible connection and this incredible trust. This connection will stay with us forever, I hope."

Homer Flynn confirms that, for The Residents it was all about working with Schilling. "Almost entirely the reason why The Residents were working with Mute had to do with Robert Schilling, who was the product manager the entire time they were there. Robert felt that it was his calling in life to bring The Residents to the larger world if possible. He was extremely passionate about getting involved, supporting The Residents and getting the music out there, and so it really happened because of that relationship."

The Residents signed with Mute in a deal that also included the rights to reissue parts of the back catalogue. They were willing to sign a worldwide agreement due to the fact that Euro Ralph and Ralph America were being closed down and advancing download speeds were undermining the music industry. "The whole way to sell records changed," recalls Guido Randzio. "We had an operation here with a staff of ten to fifteen people, but as DSL sales went up you could see that our back catalogue sales would completely go down, even our Residents stuff where you had a solid base of people who would buy more or less everything. If the whole distribution structure crashed you could not put advances into product anymore. You run into problems, and if you have personal health problems like I did it is too much. I just had to make a decision to live as opposed to producing records." By signing to Mute, The Residents not only secured a financial advance but, in dealing with only one label for distribution, allowed their creative energies to be focused on their music and visual ideas. As for Daniel Miller, he was "Honoured and privileged that they chose Mute to be their partners."

The first fruit of this partnership was the *Animal Lover* album, released in 2005. The gestation of this album was very lengthy, mainly due to the fact that after *Wormwood* The Residents invested time and energy into a project that was later abandoned. "At one point there was a lot of discussion about doing an album about the American Civil War," recalls Flynn, "so there was a certain amount of development that went into that. It became a project that never really gained enough momentum to be realised, and ultimately that energy switched to *Animal Lover*." A number of backing tracks were recorded for the Civil War project, and were later made available for download in 2015. As for *Animal Lover*, a lot of studio time and creative energy went into the project, but the *Icky Flix* DVD, CD and tour, and then The Residents' reaction to the 9/11 attacks leading directly to *Demons Dance Alone*, placed these recordings on the back burner. At one point this material could have ended up as a lost project like *I Murdered Mommy* or the American Civil War recordings, but when the digital folder was re-opened it was seen that there was considerable merit in the tracks, which were eventually finished, sequenced and released. The results were fantastic.

Although the songs on *Animal Lover* were woven around animal themes, this was not a half-baked concept album but a strong collection of songs that explored the human condition through either the perspective of, or interaction with, animals. The material featured a very long list of collaborators, which in large part was probably due to the length of time it took the album to come to fruition. Molly Harvey, one of the core vocalists on songs like *Inner Space* and *What Have My Chickens Done Now?*

has fond memories of the project, "*Animal Lover* was really fun to work on, on so many different kinds of songs. My life was in transition then – I was beginning to move to Atlanta but living in LA for that summer, so I can remember listening to the initial instrumental tracks on the beach in LA, and then hearing it in Atlanta, more than I remember recording it in San Francisco." Despite some unsettling information on the press release, which talked about the mating sounds of whales and humans being thrown into the mix, the album had a strong emotional impact.

The Residents were now around sixty years old, and in an interview around the release Hardy Fox revealingly spoke about another element to the recordings, "Age brings an increased awareness of death. When you're young, you don't really think about it, even though the risk is just as great. As you get older, you slowly begin to realise that death isn't just something that happens to other people, so there's a certain sadness in coming to terms with it. And accepting it."

The album hangs together as a cohesive whole despite Fox openly discussing the almost disparate way it was recorded, "With *Animal Lover* the members of the band all worked separately on the songs, without even being told what type of music the others were writing. Then they came together afterwards and put the record together. It was also thought of sorta like a film, with the stories being different scenes from the film." That Randy, the singing Resident, was not central to all of the songs or was outshone in some cases by Molly Harvey, and that some tracks, like *Mr. Bee's Bumble*, were instrumentals, did not detract from a memorable album. This was a collection of strong songs that anyone could listen to and enjoy.

"My personal favourite, although I love them all," Robert Schilling told me, "was *Animal Lover*. I think the effort there was great and the result was amazing. It connected with a lot of people. It was psychedelic and it had all of these elements, as if the whole history of music was condensed. It also did not sound like any of the other albums they did, which is another great thing that they do. They change and do something else and so don't get stuck in a style."

How well *Animal Lover* sold is a moot point. Whilst it connected to the Residential core as one of their best albums, there was, by this point, the issue of file sharing and illegal downloads to contend with, which was affecting artists from Metallica to The Residents. But there was no doubting the commitment of Mute to working with The Residents, and Schilling threw himself into his work with the passion and drive of a true believer, overseeing the reissue and repackaging of classic albums like *Third Reich And Roll*, *Duck Stab/Buster & Glen* and *Eskimo*, and ensuring that the remastering and repackaging was perfect.

Schilling's commitment to quality control was taken to such an extreme that he spent time ensuring the printers found the exact red to match the original cover of *Duck Stab/Buster & Glen*. At one point even Homer Flynn was telling him that it was fine, that the original colours had not been perfect, but he later told Schilling that Mute's packaging of that album was the best ever. With *The Third Reich And Roll* there was a different problem. "We released the uncensored *The Third Reich And Roll* (cover)," Schilling recalls, "We did the record and sent it to Germany and were told that they could not sell it. They sent the albums back because on the front they had the swastika. Obviously I was very upset, but I did understand. So we decided to put a slipcase outside the album so you couldn't see the cover. But we put a sign on there like a parental advisory sticker, like a joke, and on the sign it said, "Avoid if you are a bigot, a narrow-minded bastard or have no sense of humour.""

At this time, the music business was going through seismic changes, and the World Wide Web was undermining existing business models that had worked so well for so long. The quote at the head of this chapter is not from a Resident but the brother of Shawn Fanning, one of the founders of Napster, who turned the music industry on its head between 1999 and 2001 when their development of peer-to-peer file sharing software allowed people to share music for free online. Although the San Francisco based company was eventually closed down, this did not end the problem, and from that moment onwards music was freely shared online and available to listen to or download for free, killing physical back catalogue sales and eroding the sales of new releases.

Record labels large and small, from Mute's parent EMI to Mute itself, saw sales decrease and inventory rise, which led to cost cutting, redundancies and label collapses and impacted upon forward planning. As a consequence, Mute's plans to reissue The *Gingerbread Man* were put on hold. "I have always had a good feeling about that album," Homer Flynn told me, "When Mute was doing all of those great reissues in those hard backed books, *Gingerbread Man* was set to be released and I did all of the artwork for a book that ultimately never got released. Mute were going through all of those changes, and ultimately decided not to do those little books anymore as they were too expensive. The next thing that came out on Mute was *Bunny Boy*, and that came out as a standard package - it was never done as a book."

Despite their strong connection with their fans, The Residents were victims of file sharing, and so much of their music began appearing online that it was near impossible to police without incurring massive legal bills. One interesting result of this digital Wild West was that the *Baby Sex* and *Warner Brothers* albums were uploaded to various sites and fans could now hear them. For The Residents this was particularly galling - not only were they not receiving any money from this file sharing between their own fans, but these were recordings they'd worked hard to keep out of the public domain. True, they had released portions and parts in the past, but these downloads were full albums taken from copies of the master tapes given out in the early days when trying to get radio play. The Residents' response was to issue *WB RMX* in 2003, on which they retooled and remixed portions of the original Warner Brothers demo tape. This album might have been bought by Residents fans, but those fans still wanted to hear the original tapes in their original form.

Despite the fact that they were, like many bands, the victims of file-sharing, The Residents had a very firm grasp of their position in the music business, and of the advantages and disadvantages of the internet. Robert Schilling made a very valid point when I spoke to him, "I remember Iggy Pop did a talk recently about this dilemma that artists have. If they started in the '80s, or, like The Residents, much earlier, things have changed so much that if you think like you thought in the '80s you have no chance. You have to have an open mind and be prepared to think outside the box, and I think that they (The Residents) have been at the forefront of thinking outside the box. That is why they will always be fresh."

Like Iggy, The Residents had made a conscious decision after the collapse of the immersive CD-ROM industry to tour, which, if managed properly, not only promoted the band but also produced a decent revenue stream. After all, you could not illegally download a T-shirt. But unlike Iggy, who trots the globe primarily singing old Stooges numbers, The Residents' live shows were inventive theatrical pieces hung upon the sturdy frame of newly hatched, studio constructed LPs. Thus each project not only produced new music releases but a touring show and all manner of ancillary fauna, from comics to DVDs. The Residents were no longer growing solitary flowers but abundant gardens.

One garden The Residents thought would grow was that of podcasts, and in 2005 they began to record an ongoing series of short stories that people could buy through Warner Music's Cordless netlabel. The idea combined a very old and orthodox method of communication - the short story - with a modern, digital one, and, taken on their own merits, *The River Of Crime* series (which ran to five fifteen minute episodes) was excellent, and shared a kinship with *God In Three Persons* in that the music was subservient to the dialogue. This is not to denigrate the music of *The River Of Crime*, which was flexible and supportive, but as the central core was the story itself the music was relegated to a support role.

Although The Residents were prepared to devote time and energy to recording more stories, the chair was kicked out from under them by Apple. As Homer Flynn relates, "This was a point when podcasts were just starting to become popular, so we were seeing the potential of a paid podcast being a new medium to explore. The problem was that all of this technology was controlled by Apple and iTunes, who had absolutely no interest in paid podcasts. As far as they were concerned, podcasts existed primarily for selling more iPods, so ultimately the paid podcast got absolutely no support at all from Apple. The only way you could buy one was like buying it like a track off an album, and it all kind of got buried in the huge gigantic haystack of iTunes music. It was really hard to market it."

The River Of Crime series did, however, feed directly into a future album project, 2007's The Voice Of Midnight, an album based on E.T.A. Hoffman's fabled Sandman story. The role of the main protagonist was taken by actor Corey Rosen, who had taken part in the River Of Crime series, and the singing Resident took a more withdrawn vocal role, although he wrote all of the dialogue. Once again the music served the narrative, and this was another album that polarised opinion among fans. For some, once played a couple of times and absorbed, the album didn't really lend itself to repeated plays as it was a long story rather than a musical album. Carla Fabrizio, who was involved with both projects on some level, shares some interesting insights, "I honestly don't remember much about working on River Of Crime, but I thought it was a neat idea to do a podcast. Narrative in the forefront is not unusual for them, but it *is* often challenging for the listeners, sometimes me included. I have to be in the right mood. I remember enjoying being Ophelia on Voice Of Midnight, another word-heavy concept album."

At one point The Voice Of Midnight was seen as a project that, like Freak Show before it, would lend itself to becoming a show in its own right. "I think that they were very hopeful when they did it that it could become musical theatre," muses Homer Flynn, "and once again those contacts, the people in the musical theatre world, are still developing, but when The Voice Of Midnight was done those contacts were not there to make it happen. But it still might."

Prior to The Voice Of Midnight, the previous album out of the box was 2006's Tweedles, a very dark album about a sexual predator, or at best a character obsessed with sex who suffers from an inability to emotionally connect with his multitude of lovers. Using a first person narrative, the character was well drawn and Tweedles was a very mature, bold album that dealt with a taboo area. "It is dark," agrees Homer Flynn, "but I don't think it's any darker than God In Three Persons. The main character is not as likeable as Mr. X. It's interesting, because the character of Mr. X is, in some respects, more despicable in terms of what he does, but somehow he comes across as sympathetic, whereas the *Tweedles* character is never really sympathetic. It was a good project. Part of the idea was to work out how to do an album around this character who was not sympathetic, and in a lot of ways I feel that pointed towards the potential of music theatre. There has always been talk of doing *Tweedles* as a theatrical piece."

Unlike *Animal Lover, The Voice of Midnight* and *Tweedles*, The Residents' next project, *Bunny Boy*, was seen as the perfect show to take out into the road. The project was, in many respects, one of the most multi-faceted and satisfying of all The Residents' works as it combined so many elements. At the core was the music that became *The Bunny Boy* album in 2008, but this was a project where the Residential energy cells went into overdrive.

The press release issued by Mute for the album was, in some respects, a throw back to the days of N. Sendada and the *Eskimo* tapes publicity japes. Check out this hyperbole:

"Not long ago, an unsolicited DVD arrived at The Residents' studio. Since the location of the group's private inner sanctum is a closely guarded secret, the appearance of the disc was definitely regarded as a little strange. Other than the occasional piece of junk mail, nothing ever arrived at The Residents' intimate workspace without an invitation. But the envelope containing the disc bore a familiar return address, so, after first ignoring it for a few weeks, The Residents finally opened the package and put the disc, crudely-labelled 'Postcards From Patmos' into a DVD player."

The DVD was from a former colleague named Bunny, who was convinced that his brother had disappeared to the Greek island of Patmos and was seeking The Residents' help in finding him. This led to The Residents recording a series of songs based on the original DVD, as well as resolving to help Bunny to try to find his lost brother.

The mention in Mute's press release of The Residents' workspace affords a good opportunity to detail how their approach to recording changed with advances in digital technology. "In terms of them all working together in a studio, probably *Wormwood* was the last time that happened," states Homer Flynn, "The last several albums have been done in various locations. The general kind of working situation is that they all have home studios at this point, so tracks will get created and then everybody creates their own additions to those backing tracks and then they all get blended together again at the end."

With one Resident composing most of the music, the days of a dedicated studio space were in the past once most of it could be created and edited on a computer or laptop. The key factor, as Flynn indicates, was that The Master Resident was open to input from collaborators. As Nolan Cook communicated to me, "I'm going to spare you the technical mumbo jumbo about how it works, but yes, modern advances have afforded us the luxury of working together remotely. And this organisation has always been, and ever will be, in vigorous pursuit of advancing technology. I will say, though, that the years we spent getting together to record the old fashioned way was key to our ability now to successfully collaborate without being in the same room, or city for that matter."

As for *Bunny Boy,* one collaborator told me that, "While we were working on the stage show we received demos from The Residents, and were invited to create our own parts for them. I found this an unusual way to work, whereas the other musicians were used to it, so they were quick to figure out what they were doing and send recordings of their parts back to the band, who incorporated much of it into the product. I only did that with a couple of accordion parts, which were used, but I think they were tickled to include a wheezy old folk instrument amid all those electronic sounds!"

As Molly Harvey had moved to Atlanta, she was no longer in the picture, so the main collaborators outside of the magic circle were Nolan Cook and Carla Fabrizio. "In some ways they aren't collaborative and in other ways they are," states Fabrizio, "And you never know which way things are going to roll. I think that's what makes it so fun. If they don't get anything out of how you might be contributing they're probably not going to repeat it. But on the flip side, even if it happens only once that doesn't necessarily mean they didn't get something out of it. They just have so many ideas and need to move on to the next one."

As for how the collaboration progressed with the advances of digital technology and computer based home studios, she was very much in accord with Nolan Cook, "There has always been some working at home. You'd have to draw a line between work and non-work to be able to tell for sure. My feeling is that they're always working on something, whether it's at home or away from home. My work with them has always been a combination."

Molly Harvey would have liked to have been involved, but as a singer distance was a problem. "I miss working with them tremendously," she says, "I naively assumed we'd simply continue working together, since our tour manager is Dutch I figured that them splurging for a plane ticket for me to come out to SF would be no problem. I was able to do a couple of things with them, but it's a little like out of sight out of mind. Their reputation aside, I have never found that perfect chemistry with other artists since."

Bunny Boy was conceived to exploit the full gamut of multimedia. After the album was released the tour began, and included a unique element of fan interaction. The band not only posted short films of Bunny on YouTube, but also set up a dedicated password activated email address for fans to send suggestions and comment on the plot to as the tour progressed. Back in 1992, Homer Flynn had stated that the Mole Show had shown why stressed musicians "took drugs in terrific loads," and allowing fans to interact with the lead singer of The Residents could have been another path to pharmaceutical refreshment.

"In terms of interacting with fans, that was Randy" Flynn wryly recalls today, "And it nearly drove him crazy trying to keep up. I don't think anyone anticipated the thousands and thousands of emails that were going to come in. Some of the interactions Randy got into with the fans were very long streams of email that have never really come to the surface. Personally I have always felt that there was a really good book that could come out of them. Some fans sent him artwork, some really interesting artwork, and although some of it got posted and some of it got used, a lot of it has never seen the light of day. There was much more in that project if there had been the correct support for it."

Flynn is correct in stating that there is probably a fascinating book in the Randy-fan exchanges, as many of them were very personal. One such fan was Dawin Laskowski, whose correspondence with the lead singer included asking if any more items would be sold on eBay – a request which received the following reply:

"DER DAWD WEL IM SORRY YOU DIDN'T GET ANYTHIN ON THE EBAY THIS MUCT BE A BIG DIASOINTMENT AND ALL IM SORY BUT I WONT BE SELING ANYTHIN ELSE BECAUASE I ALREADY SOLD THE REST AT A GRUDGE SALE WHICH ONLY MADE 15 DOLARS AND 72 SENSE"

Laskowski also discussed his personal reaction to seeing The Residents perform in Munich, where some members of the audience disrupted the show by shouting...

"DER DAWID WELL THE MOONICH SHOW WAS PRETTY WERD AND ALL SOMEONE TOLD ME HAT THE BAVARANS ARE THE TEXANS OF GERMANY SO I THINK MAYBE THEY WERE ALL FIENDS OF GEORG BUSH OR SOMETHING BUT WHO KNOWS I WAS GALD TO LEAVE THERE FROM BUNNY."

Bunny Boy did eventually generate one book - a comic book. Adam Weller became a fan of the band when he was seventeen years old, and by the time of the *Bunny Boy* album and tour was hardcore. "The Bunny Boy internet series was special because it allowed the viewer to interact," he recalls today. "One was able to regularly communicate with

Bunny, offer suggestions and try to steer the direction of the show. The challenge of helping to solve questions and mysteries was too great to ignore." Weller not only helped to provide some suggestions and solve some puzzles but also, at the end of the series, "My name was included in the credits."

Weller was a comic book artist, and conceived of a book about Bunny, "The comic book was born simply from a need to keep the character alive for a bit longer. I suddenly missed Bunny when it was all over, knowing there would be no more erratic emailing. Anybody who followed the show may relate to the fact that Bunny's voice and mannerisms lingered in the subconscious, so this was probably the best way I knew of exorcising him."

Weller approached The Cryptic Corporation, who were agreeable to the project, especially as Weller offered to cover the cost of producing the comic himself. That he was based in England and they were in America was no issue as the collaboration – mostly with Randy, who helped knock the script into shape - took place over the internet. The finished result was fantastic, and was sold direct to fans as well as being made available on the *Talking Light* tour. "I went to the merchandise stand and saw my comic there and customers buying it," recalls Weller, "That gave me a warm glow, the journey from idea to completion."

As for Mute, *Bunny Boy* was the last new album they issued as the deal ran its course. "Initially the deal was worldwide," states Homer Flynn, "But we were not happy with the job Mute was doing in the States, so we wound up leaving them with the UK and Europe and working the States on our own." With regards how things worked out financially during the Mute years, "I think they did well," Robert Schilling told me, "Obviously they came to Mute at a period when the internet began to grow, and as you know music sales went down. I think they could have done better, but the reasons were nothing to do with them or to do with us either. It was just the situation. But at the same time it reached the right people and we did some very courageous things. "

By the late 2000s there had had been a massive decrease in the sale of physical product, and the eventual closing down of Ralph America and Euro Ralph mail-order operation was part and parcel of this process. As Guido Randizio stated, "Starting in 2004 it became harsh out there." So harsh that the business models of both Euro Ralph and Ralph America were no longer sustainable. "Closing Ralph America was a difficult decision," states Lorrie Murray, "but ultimately there were just too many mouths to feed between The Residents and me and Dren and not enough revenue. Dren left in early 2009 and I ran it until August 15th 2010. Trying to stop the illegal download sites became almost a full time job, and the recession certainly hit us hard. I think for some folks the lack of funds and the need to get Residents product amplified the temptation to get it off one of those sites. The final nail in the coffin was the *Bunny Boy* Comic book. As soon as it went up for sale someone bought it, scanned all of the pages and offered hi-res PDF files for free. There was no putting the toothpaste back in the tube at that point."

Thus, whilst The Residents own website now had a stranglehold upon information about the band and their massive back catalogue tail, those new to them might not buy their music but just find it for free online. This still frustrates Homer Flynn today, "Everything is on YouTube. There are hundreds and hundreds of Residents tracks on there and there is no royalty stream coming from that at all." The need to generate income from another source other than dwindling physical sales and legal downloads through iTunes and other sites was imperative. Also, according to Flynn, The Residents' reputation and decades of creativity alone did not guarantee a pension pot.

"The fact that they have never had any major commercial success has made them feel that they don't have any laurels that they can rest on," he reveals, "They don't really have a series of greatest hits that they can go out and tour forever and make an income off. Consequently, they have to keep creating the future to keep themselves interested, to keep the fans interested and to keep doing it."

Of course, The Residents were never short ideas, especially when it came to stirring up interest in the band. The next step in their story was to be very courageous, and the most exciting one in years.

Randy, Chuck And Bob

"Back in the old days we all used to live together. We had this really cool artists' space in San Francisco and everybody had their own bedroom and it was all decorated weird, abstract, artistic and cool. It was just like the Beatles in hell. But now, Chuck lives on a Goddamn chicken farm. It's true! He lives on a Goddamn chicken farm! He's just like an old married man living with his fucking husband on a chicken farm. I used to be the one who got all the chicks!" - Randy Rose.

"There is a different fan base now. The Residents' fans are not all old or ageing guys, there are now women and young people, because their music, over the forty year period and all the genres they've looked at and the things they have made, can appeal to a new fan. A sixteen year old can spend the next fifty years buying all the stuff!" - Brian Poole.

Considering that The Residents had originally intended the eyeballs to be just another image change to promote the *Eskimo* album before they moved onto something new, it's remarkable that, over the years, the eyeballs probably helped to sell more Residents items that there are letters in this book. The orbs proved so popular that new models that were easier to function inside for photo shoots and live work were developed to replace the originals, and the eyeball imagery was used on everything that could be merchandised, from T-shirts to earrings. The *Eskimo* image also became the stock imagery used whenever something was written about the band in print or online.

But, by 2010 the eyeball, tuxedo and top hat combination were thirty years old, and, like the logo of a long established multinational company, was outmoded and no longer reflected what The Residents were creating in the digital age. Their solution was to reinvent themselves in a totally new, original and almost shocking fashion - abandoning the eyeballs, The Residents stepped out of their branded shadow to reveal themselves to their fans as a power trio of Randy, Chuck and Bob. Oh, and there *had* been a fourth Resident named Carlos, but he'd recently left the band after a dispute with Randy, the lead singer and front man. It seems there was in-band friction behind the dressing room door, or fictional friction at least...

The unveiling of Randy, Chuck and Bob certainly got fans interested, and totally refreshed The Residents' image in the modern world of social media, where *Facebook, Twitter, Tumblr* and other bite-sized sites are the main windows into culture. The eyeball, tuxedos and top hats were gone, and crucially, in Randy, The Residents now had a spokesman.

Although garrulous onstage or online, he was canny enough not to give face-to-face interviews to journalists, but more than happy to post his thoughts online and answer the odd question. It still feels equally strange and thrilling to read online, "Well, *Rest Aria* was written by my buddy Chuck so I don't really don't know too much about it. But as I recall, Chuck tried to gather up a bunch of people to play it but it didn't really work, so he played most of the parts himself. He never talked about that stuff much so I don't know what inspired him, but he sure used to practice it a lot."

Of course, there was also a very practical purpose behind this image change - slimming down to three members was part of a new touring strategy. As Hein Fokker explains, "From *Bunny Boy* onwards, they reinvented themselves by being Randy, Chuck and Bob. Three people on stage, and the idea was if they wanted to do this and make it financially feasible we had to have a show that could fly. We are travelling with six people, so we can take six boxes and everything has to be in those. They designed a show that could fly anywhere and it is still like that, it's still Randy, Chuck and Bob, and we have done three tours, *Talking Light, WOW* and now *Shadowland*. Of course, there is some local production, but that is minimal. The show is small, and has the minimum hauling around of cases but *maximum* expression on stage."

The first tour of what is now seen as the Randy, Chuck and Bob era was the *Talking Light* outing, which embraced over fifty dates, starting with a warm up show in Santa Cruz on the 23rd January 2010 and ending in San Francisco on the 16th April 2011. Sandwiched between those dates were four distinct tranches of shows across North America and Europe. "As Frank Zappa said in *200 Motels*," laughs Fokker, "touring drives you crazy. He is completely right, and that is why tours a month and a half long are too long. At this point, two weeks is max because you are working with older people. Even myself, I would go for a month no problem, but when people get tired they make mistakes."

He continues, "With The Residents' shows, when there is just one fuck up in the audio or one computer not starting which makes the show dead, its very bad because you are naked on stage and the people watching suddenly have nothing. With a normal rock and roll band that can be fun and they can make a joke out of it, but not with The Residents, it is too theatrical, and that happens when people are touring for too long."

The *Talking Light* tour saw Randy clad in a bald wig with a frizz of grey hair and a bathrobe, and looking like an ancient monument, although on stage he moved with energy and vitality. Meanwhile, both Chuck (on laptop) and Bob (on guitar) not only sported masks to conceal their identities but had dreadlocks, making it look like Randy had hooked up with two digital rastas. Chuck began to use software called Ableton Live, which is an amazing tool, not only in the studio but also for generating the basis of live shows on a laptop. Now Chuck could prepare what was to be broadcast live in the comfort of his home studio and then cue each track when the band played live for Bob and Randy to augment with guitar and vocals. "But (sometimes) he has a keyboard," adds Hein Fokker, "So throughout the whole show he is filling in on his keyboard and can make changes if he wants to. But basically the show has been conceived at home, and that takes a long time. I think it is totally brilliant what he is doing."

On later tours, Chuck began adding some colour by playing an electronic Wave drum, and, although some collaborators could not be there in person, they could be there musically. "I haven't toured with them since they became the power trio," states Carla Fabrizio, "But I still feel connected, and I've contributed bits of music here and there. Both the *Wonder of Weird* and *Shadowland* shows have my presence if you listen for it."

As with every tour, *Talking Light* included a theatrical presentation. There were three circular video screens behind and above the performers, stools for Chuck and Bob and an armchair and fireplace for Randy, who would appear on stage last as Chuck generated opening music from and old Coca-Cola advert. Initially, the plan was for the show to be based around ghost stories told through the medium of TV, but, as Hardy Fox told a journalist from *Pollstar* in November 2011, "The TV aspect has shrunk down to almost nothing at this point. Originally, that was going to be a big aspect of the show. But it's really taken a different angle. This show is concerned with the universal experience of death. Not so much the negative aspects of death, but the overall." Musically, the set list was not all doom and gloom, and rotated and evolved during the touring process to incorporate a number of ghost stories related by Randy as well as tracks from The Residents' back catalogue, including *Semolina, Lizard Lady, Six More Miles, The Unseen Sister* and *Demons Dance Alone*.

Importantly, the tour was a financial success, even if the hotels had to be of a certain standard due to the age of some of the Residential limbs. "We cannot stay in dumps, we have good transportation and all things are more expensive because of that," states autumnal chicken Hein Fokker. As well as selling the usual merchandise hand over fist, the *Talking Light* project also generated a number of ancillary CDs, DVDs and downloads that the band sold through their own website, Amazon or other digital outlets. For example, *Lonely Teenager* was an album reflecting songs performed or rejected for the tour, including some music Chuck had generated for the set which was then augmented and retooled with the addition of vocals and guitar. Tracks like *Six More Miles*, *Boxes Of Armageddon* and *My Window* are fantastic, and with the addition of a 2009 rehearsal version of *The Unseen Sister*, *Lonely Teenager* really was an excellent album which not only reflected the prism of *Talking Light* but also stood on its own two feet as compelling music.

"There is always music that is done for intermission, walk-in and exit, and a lot of times that is just marketed straight out," states Homer Flynn on this project, "I think that music got developed more for *Talking Light* as most of the music was back catalogue, but then there were the *Talking Light* stories, and all of that music was improvised, so I think there might be some of that in there too." *Lonely Teenager* was certainly better than *The Ughs!* which had earlier presented the core music from *The Voice Of Midnight*.

"I think that what happened was that when the project was over it was not so much that they were dissatisfied with *The Voice Of Midnight*," states Flynn, "but that so much of the emphasis went towards the story. I think that when they went back and listened to those backing tracks they felt that something had been lost, and they felt that there was a lot of stuff there that could stand on its own without all of the vocals and the story stuff. In a way, *The Ughs!* is almost like a remix of *The Voice Of Midnight* that eliminated a lot of the vocal tracks." The album is sonically interesting, especially *The Lonely Lotus,* which flowers beautifully with the addition of what sounds like a string quartet in which, I imagine, Carla Fabrizio had a hand. But the worst thing about *The Ughs*! was the artwork – it was packaged in, to my mind, The Residents' worst ever cover. Ugh!

If the appearance of Randy, Chuck and Bob shook up the perception of who The Residents were and what they looked like, The Cryptic Corporation still made sure that their extensive back catalogue was available for new and old fans. Indeed, in May 2011 fans were able to get their hands on some of the original artwork that graced many of the band's earlier releases, when graphic designer Homer Flynn displayed some paintings at the Johannsson Projects gallery in Oakland

California, along with a vast selection of Residents related material. Drawings, illustrations, photos and other art was shown, from the cover of *The Beatles Play The Residents And The Residents Play The Beatles* to the original sketch for the *Not Available* LP cover, which was actually done by Hardy Fox, who also designed most of the artwork for the Mole series of albums and the Mole Show.

Better still for hardcore fans, some of the artwork and photos were available to buy, including the original cover art for *The Third Reich And Roll* for $70,000, Beatles head masks at $1000 each (or four for $3000), and an original photo of The Residents' Sycamore Street recording studio for $1000. Did Flynn find it hard selling such iconic stuff? "I didn't have a problem letting it go. I have been caretaker of this stuff for so long at this point and a whole lot of it has been sitting in boxes and filing cabinets. I'm happy for it to get into the hands of people who want it and will take care of it."

The selling of Residential history led to some wonderful commercial subversion when, in December 2012, Randy was featured in a short video clip dressed as Santa Claus and offering the Ultimate Boxed Set, which was "so huge it takes a refrigerator to hold it all." On offer was a first edition of every single, LP, CD, video and DVD, as well as "a genuine eyeball mask in every refrigerator." There were only ten sets on offer for the "low bargain basement price of $100,000." The UBS went on sale on 25th December 2012, and one was sold to the Museum Of Modern Art in New York whilst another went to a devoted fan who arranged to pay in installments. And the 'special item', valued at $5 million really did exist…

Of course, many Residents fans do not have such deep pockets, but they *are* part of a small, select group of fans with a museum dedicated to their idols. The museum was established in Germany by Andreas Mathews as a means of displaying his enormous collection of Residents related material, which extends to over ten thousand individual items, ranging from "One of the four original performance eyeballs from the *Wormwood* Show" to numerous records and test pressings. As he got into the Residents in 1978, after hearing *Third Reich And Roll*, Andreas has had plenty of time to amass his collection and take trips to America to buy items, as well as to trade with other fans, and even The Cryptic Corporation, directly.

"I know some collectors who collect only the first ten years," he told me, "Some only the music, others are downright obsessed with everything, especially the rare limited editions. I simply collect everything! From the smallest scraps of paper. The goal is, of course, to establish the most complete Residents and Ralph Records collection."

This is, as you might imagine, something of a tall order as The Residents have generated such a vast amount of collectable items.

The Residents' fan base also includes many other individuals around the world with massive collections, from the legendary Kim Andrews – who has to have four of everything - to Paulie and a multitude of others. But for Mathews, "The museum is my normal habitat, and every day I am surrounded by it, imbibing their music, their art, artifacts of their existence, things from many different countries. It is like a cosmopolitan art cocoon in which I swim. For me it's just a daily pleasure to be surrounded by all this. I once read that collectors are happy people and for me that's definitely true."

Mathews was delirious when The Residents once came to view his museum when on tour. "That definitely was the most surreal day of my life as a collector," he fondly recalls, "Can you imagine your 'star' suddenly standing on your doorstep? It is the Wonder of Weird!!"

Exhibitions, sales and museums aside, though, just prior to the unveiling of the UBS in 2012 came the surprising release of *Coochie Brake*, which, rather than feature Randy on lead vocals, showcased the recently departed Carlos, who sang the entire LP in Spanish! This departure was not due to internal band conflict, but to Randy spreading his wings. "Randy had a solo show that he was doing called *Sam's Enchanted Evening*," states Homer Flynn, "So that was really taking up lots of his time over a period of a year. The rest of the group were kind of anxious to do another album, and Randy was not available. He was the one who made the suggestion that they bring in Carlos instead, and he wrote all of the lyrics for it, but he just did not have time to participate in the way that he wanted to, so that is how that evolved."

The fact that the LP was sung in Spanish was a real curveball, but one with a logical pitcher. "Because Carlos is Mexican, Randy wrote the lyrics in English and then translated them into Spanish via Google translate," states Flynn, "Then Carlos kind of fine tuned them a bit so they did not sound too clinky." So, despite looking like the sort of old man who could not start a computer, Randy was deploying his advanced technological skills to harness Google to write lyrics. As for who Carlos really was, now that really *is* a mystery for Sherlock Holmes and Columbo.

Coochie Brake is a very worthy album, with real depth and nuance. The music generated by Chuck is again inspired – a rich gumbo of sound - and the contribution of Nolan Cook's guitar adds some bite and flair. Tracks like *Theatre Of Shadows*, *Tied To A Cactus*, *Rot Of Ages* and *Dead Man On The Floor* captivate with repeat plays, but not everybody liked it. As Homer Flynn states, "There was definitely some feedback. There were certainly some fans who were not happy. Randy's voice is kind of the most consistent line through the whole forty years, so if you do anything like that you are going to get negative feedback from people who don't like change or something different. Then again, there are people who love things that change and are different. There was some negative feedback on *The Voice Of Midnight* too as the guy who did the lead voice on that was very different from Randy, and there were some people who were not happy about him doing it. Personally, I thought he did a great job. But you are always going to get that kind of stuff."

But fans of Randy now had the opportunity to see him in the flesh on a regular basis. *Sam's Enchanted Evening* was performed between October 2nd and November 26th 2011 at The Marsh, Berkeley, and at the Abrons Art Centre in New York between 24th and 27th March 2012. The premise behind the show was the life story of Sam, told through monologue and song. "None of the songs are original," a Cryptic spokesman related to a journalist at the time, "they're partly telling (Sam's story) with the songs that he considered to be important in his life, so they're doing things like *Ode To Billy Joe*, *Sixteen Tons* or *Livin' La Vida Loca*."

"Like many Residents projects, either recorded or performed, it evolved over time," states Carla Fabrizio, "I'd heard the original arrangements early on and really liked them, but the project was set aside for a while. I got to arrange all the percussion parts for a performance with a string trio, keyboard and accordion at Berkeley Art Museum. Then, when it moved to The Marsh Theatre, it was a simplified accompaniment, and I played cello on the balcony."

Randy was accompanied on stage by Joshua Raoul Brody. "I loved that show and I loved working on it," he recalls, "It was a huge honour to be one of the few musicians to work on a Residents project under his own name." Although the music was selected and arranged in demo form by Randy, "I took the demos and transcribed them, first for a string orchestra, which was the original plan for the show, then for a string quartet (with an accordion taking the place of the viola) augmented by piano and percussion – that was the version that went up at the Berkeley Art Museum (on 10th June 2010). Then finally (I did it) for solo piano, augmented on one night by cello, played by Carla Fabrizio. The show was directed in Berkeley by my friend Jim Cave, who has also worked with composer Erling Wold and other new music theater pieces, and it was re-directed in New York by Travis Chamberlain. I had no major input into the staging, although I'd pipe up with an opinion or two from time to time."

Brody greatly enjoyed the experience of working on a theatrical rather than a concert piece, and found that things could grow organically. "The thing I came to appreciate about doing the same show over and over is that it doesn't have to get boring," he told me, "There's an excitement about digging deeper into the material and discovering new stuff buried there, even when you yourself created the dirt in which its buried. There's something about mastering the material and getting to a place with it where you can try out different things without losing the original intent."

Homer Flynn believes that *Sam's Enchanted Evening* was an important milestone in The Residents' career as it finally allowed them to present a performance with theatre at its core, "It is purely musical theatre as opposed to a concert, but it certainly is a performance. I think it was very satisfying. There has always been a certain segment, more of a pull towards musical theatre and away from concerts. What The Residents have always done is very theatrical, but always presented in concert or rock venues as opposed to theatres. Even if it is in a theatre it's marketed to a rock crowd, so the audience will come and has that expectation. To go purely into a theatre and get away from the expectation of a rock show or some kind of concert situation was something they had wanted to do for a long time. In that regard it was really satisfying."

The producer and director of the New York show wanted to take the show to the next level, but the project had to be abandoned. "The music that was in it, the rights to be able to do that music in a theatrical context are so expensive that it was financially prohibitive to take it further," states Flynn, "Small shows are kind of under the radar, but to take it off-Broadway – which was certainly talked about – would have cost too much money to finance."

Sam's Enchanted Evening also revealed how The Residents' working processes in the Randy, Chuck and Bob era were to be different from the previous incarnation of The Residents, which had always tried to present a four-piece band. If Randy was happy to do his own thing, so was Chuck, who began to generate a number of tracks and albums, including some under the umbrella A Charles Bobuck Contraption. "In a lot of ways it is a parallel situation," muses Flynn, "What it amounts to is that Chuck – Charles Bobuck – has more creative energy and has been prolific in creating more music than can fit into The Residents format. So there have always been things like the *Brumalia* series that Chuck has done that got labeled as Residents. With the surfacing of Randy, Chuck and Bob, that gave an opportunity for Randy to have a voice, but also an opportunity for Chuck to have his own voice separately singled out. I think, in a lot of ways, it is a natural evolution of things."

What Flynn describes here is the fact that, as The Residents career progressed, Chuck became more and more productive, until his output outstripped the actual release of Residents albums. In many respects, this had been evident as far back as the Mole Show, where Chuck had specifically recorded music to be played during the intermission, and the same applied to many subsequent tours.

The *12 Days Of Brumalia* project saw Chuck post a new track on The Residents' website every day for twelve days, and one final track on the thirteenth day titled *The Feast Of Epiphany*. Although initially designed as download only releases, these were later compiled onto a 'Residents' CD in 2004. This inventive set was just one example of Chuck's abundant musical creation, which now found full flower as Charles Bobuck, and even saw a dedicated Charles Bobuck Contraption website. Whilst Chuck never spoke publically about his music, he was more than happy to write about it on his website and Facebook page, which suddenly gave old and new believers a direct line into his thoughts on his creative processes. "I didn't intend to record an album or make this website," he wrote when issuing *Codgers On The Moon* in 2012. "When I am not working on a specific project, I usually spend my time trying different musical ideas on the computer. I'm not the kind of composer that sits at a piano or strums a guitar. I don't have melody lines running through my brain. My fascination is directed towards listening to the way layers interact rhythmically and harmonically."

The establishment of the Charles Bobuck site unleashed a torrent of music that was rich, varied and, at times, extremely personal. *Roman De La Rose (2014)* was a touching musical exploration of his decade long relationship with his husband, and, whilst the album was instrumental, Chuck shared some personal insights online that ranged from their meeting, their life together and one extremely touching moment, "...I kissed him in public for the first time. It took ten years because we are same gendered and sensitive to our surroundings, unlike different gendered couples. A kiss like that is a kiss that different gendered people never get to know, it is an act of rebellion driven by passions from a decade of oppression."

Randy and Chuck's exploration of their own muses did not stop The Residents' creative momentum or their famed collaborative processes, which led them to work with dancer and choreographer Grace Ellen Barkey, who was part of a dance company in Belgium called Needcompany. "*Third Reich And Roll*," I loved that so much," Barkey told me, "and it is still my most favourite piece. I grew up with it. As a choreographer, when you hear that music you think "Wow! I love the energy". That one is close to my heart." It should be stressed that Barkey did not buy the LP upon release in 1976 but many years later, and when she had the idea to set a dance piece in a mushroom world, she wondered if it would be possible to collaborate with the band.

"I contacted them and they offered to make the music. We did it together. I started giving them the idea of the show and they started writing things. As soon as they wrote things they would send them to me and we would have a conversation about it, so it was not like they made music and I made my piece around it. It was more we were having a conversation about what I wanted to tell, and they made compositions for me and we would talk about it." This game of musical and choreographic tennis evolved over two years between 2011 and 2013, and "At the end they had eleven pieces or something that were completely ready, so after two years of talking together I really succeeded in having all of the music that they wrote in the show."

"The people there were huge Residents fans," states Homer Flynn on the collaboration, "They had this new project that they were working on and asked The Residents if they would be interested in doing the music for it. They were, and ultimately the great thing about it was that they really gave The Residents a lot of freedom in creating the music. They let The Residents do what they wanted to do and that led to a really good situation."

Mush-Room was visually exciting, from the paper mushrooms that were suspended as part of the set to the costumes that the performers wore. As with the 13th Anniversary Show, there was even the deployment of hand-held lighting, although Barkey is keen to stress that this was incidental rather than a homage to the band, "I was not thinking of that when I was diving into this mushroom world, and I was not so much aware of what they did on stage, but it may have unconsciously been in the performance. In my piece the performers are masked, but it is all-intuitive, and for me holding the light is another gesture coming out of what I was doing in that moment. There is this mushroom group and this one human, and this human is invading space and changing space with smoke, tape and light, and that is why they are holding the light. It was logic coming out of creating this piece rather than the memory of what the Residents did on stage."

Homer Flynn and Hardy Fox both saw the performance, and Flynn recalls that it was a very positive experience, "I enjoyed it, but also felt blissfully removed from any responsibility. It was very easy to watch and Grace is a delight." *Mush-Room* was performed in a number of European venues, as well as at a single show in South Korea, and The Residents later issued a CD of the music.

That was a big success," states Hein Fokker, "Lately, they have got back together to see if there is a double bill or a mixed bill, or to prepare a new production with them. That should be good as it's in the theatrical field, and they have contacts at a different level. That could be a nice alternative to rock touring. I think those people in Brussels are really honoured that The Residents asked them to do something together again. That would be good for them as it would mean staying in good hotels, having nice travel arrangements and days in between. You should do that when you are seventy, don't you think?"

In 2014 Fokker made the arrangements for a short European tour. "There was an offer from an arts centre in Nantes for the Residents to come and perform," states Homer Flynn, "The offer was good enough that they put a brand new show together." This show became *Shadowland*, and as well as the date in Nantes on 10th May 2014 it was also performed at five other European venues, and in Tel Aviv in Israel. "There are excerpts of earlier shows worked in there," says Hein Fokker, who managed the dates, "But everything is different in the Randy, Chuck and Bob era. It's a new start. The Residents 2.0".

Whilst the set list saw a prowl through a number of retooled classics like *Weightlifting Lulu, Benny, Mickey Macaroni, Hard And Tenderly, Constantinople, Judas Saves* and *Betty's Body*, the setting was, as always spectacular. Perhaps the most arresting sight was Randy not only wearing an anatomical body stocking but also, audaciously, a pair of silver pants over the top of them! "Randy, keeps himself trim!" laughed Brian Poole, who attended the show in Nantes, "The storytelling era was not, for me, as exciting as some of the other stuff. I like music. I like singing. That's why I enjoyed *Shadowland* immensely, the stories were implicit in it and there was a lot of music and singing. The collision of the back catalogue tracks and all that sort of thing was great."

One of the most interesting collisions with The Residents' back catalogue took place on 16th October 2014, when *Eskimo* was presented at The San Francisco Exploratorium and broadcast through its Kanbar Forum's ninety-nine speaker system, accompanied by visuals from the *Eskimo* DVD released in 2002. Such was the demand for the 7pm show that another had to be added at 9pm.

"We were able to take the original sixteen track tapes and transfer them onto a digital format," states Homer Flynn, "and it was played with a live soloist playing along. I was heavily involved in putting all this stuff together, and it really caused me to go back and revisit the album in a way that I had not done for a long time, and I felt that it had held up really well." Flynn asked Peter Whitehead to be the soloist - Whitehead not only played a wide variety of acoustic instruments but some that he also constructed himself. Flynn had seen him perform four years previously, and when this project got off the ground thought he would be perfect.

"I think that Homer chose me to collaborate because my instruments are from a sort of imaginary world," Whitehead told me, "which mirrors the world of the Eskimos as portrayed in the album.

My instruments make unusual sounds and work well for creating atmospheres, which is what the *Eskimo* album is about. It is not a lot of tunes with melodies. The album is mysterious."

As for what Flynn wanted for the performance, he gave Whitehead the *Eskimo* DVD and some indications as to where he thought it might be apt for him to play. Whitehead went away and worked out a musical approach, then played along to the DVD with Flynn listening, using a variety of instruments including a ball flute, thirteen string dulcimer, eight string lyre, glass pan pipes, sixteen inch steel drum, toy whistles and a slide whistle. "Then we discussed what worked and what might be modified or left out," recalls Whitehead, "Mostly Homer agreed with my ideas, which surprised me. Since it's such a classic album I thought he might be more protective and controlling about what a new person might add to it, but he was very open."

As for the two performances, Whitehead recalls, "I had a good time playing live, but unfortunately we only did two shows back to back. By then I was just beginning to refine what I was doing and wished I could have done many more nights – there's no substitute for playing to an audience for real fine-tuning. It was a perfect context in which to use instruments that are unique and have their own particular sound. The album felt to me like a world imagined – a culture that had its rituals and ways of making music with its own unique instruments. I never did find out what The Residents used to make the sounds on the album."

The Theory Of Obscurity

"I ran into Norman at the grocery store the other day. Searching for a line of communication, he asked if I had any shows coming up and I told him about the two, The Rio in Santa Cruz and SXSW. He feigned interest until I mentioned that they were going to be my last two on-stage participations. He looked at me quizzically. I explained that I was not personally performing shows anymore after those two. My health has been too unpredictable to drag my carcass around on a tour bus. I would stay busy doing what I did best, composing." - Charles Bobuck Facebook post

"OBSCURITY IS ITS OWN REWARD" - Placard deployed by headless faux-Resident at SXSW, March 2015

According to Don Hardy, he found himself making the first comprehensive documentary about The Residents not as the result of divine inspiration but due to "dumb luck". A former NBC news cameraman, he'd been making independent documentaries since 2006 with his KTF Films partner Dana Nachman, and, although *Witch Hunt* (2008), *Love Hate Love* (2011) and *The Human Experiment* (2013) had been issue-based films, had always hoped to do something about music. One day, over a few beers with two former NBC colleagues, he found out that not only was one a Residents fan but the other had actually taken some photos and worked with the band. "I watched the two of them talking about them," Hardy recalls, "and Josh (Keppels) knew that they were gearing up for their 40th Anniversary tour. I thought, this would make a great documentary, so I asked, "Has anyone ever done one?""

The answer was no. This intrigued Hardy and, after an introduction through Keppels, a couple of weeks later he sat down with Homer Flynn. After the Cryptic official had watched some of Hardy's work, "We just hit it off, and before you knew it he basically said, "Yes let's give it a try, let's work out the details and everything later," as time was of the essence as the tour was starting relatively soon."

Hardy attended the *Wonder Of Weird* rehearsals and then went out with The Residents on the first handful of dates of the tour across

America. As for how he paid for the filming, "It was self-financed. Credit cards. The good old fashioned way." Hardy not only filmed the band performing live but also backstage as The Cryptic Corporation had given him full access to Randy, Chuck and Bob. Crucially, Hardy was not a fan of the band and so was able to approach The Residents' history and fans from a measured perspective, without any preconceptions or predilection for a particular period in their career. As he told me, "I was learning about the band as we started to make it, learning about their impact, and I guess trying to figure out what it meant to me. I knew early on that it was not going to be a complete history – it was not going to be your book – it was not going to be everything they had done. It was more of a way into The Residents for people who maybe don't know them, and I thought the best way to do that was through the people they've inspired."

Armed with footage of the *Wonder Of Weird* show, Hardy set about interviewing as many people as he could get in front of a camera. This certainly impressed Homer Flynn, who helped by providing some contact details. "I don't know how many people he interviewed - maybe forty or fifty, maybe more than that," relates Flynn, "He went back and found people from the very early days. There is a guy called Roland Sheehan, who still lives back in Louisiana and was there when The Residents were barely forming. He was a friend of theirs and to have this guy show up – Don went back to Louisiana to find and interview him - makes a nice presence in setting the stage for the film."

As for the important players, "The four founding members of The Cryptic Corporation were a huge part of the story," states Hardy "and once we got those it started to fall into place." Peggy Honeydew, Brian Poole, Matt Groening, Gary Panter, Jerry Casale (Devo), Jerry Harrison (Talking Heads), Chris Cutler, Les Claypool (Primus), Graeme Whifler, Penn Jillette and many more followed. There was also no attempt at sensation or mystery, or to unmask the band – *The Theory Of Obscurity* was to be a straightforward documentary.

As his company credit card could not take all of the strain, Don Hardy also launched a campaign on Indiegogo, "We were really fortunate that, because of The Residents' strong fanbase, we were able to do a crowdfunding campaign that was very successful. It gave us the push that we needed. We'll never get paid back for the time we put into it, but we were able to finish it in the right way and transfer their archival material to HD (High Definition digital). We were able to take care of all of that stuff and get it ready to finish the film."

The Indiegogo campaign offered fans a number of "pretty sweet perks" that ranged from the Secret Stash's "exclusive access to our Secret Stash of online extras" for $75 to The Top Banana package, which, amongst a mind-blowing number of extras, offered an Executive Producer credit. Over a hundred and sixty people claimed the Secret Stash, but the Top Banana remained unpeeled. Still, it was a great campaign which was 161% over-subscribed and raised $40,230.

One of the most interesting rewards on offer was The Starmaker, wherein for $1000 you could "Show off your acting chops with a boffo role in an upcoming episode of the *In My Room/Randyland* series featuring Randy, the Lead singer of The Residents." Five people took up the opportunity to appear in the show....

Hey, back up there one moment.
Randyland?

Once The Cryptic Corporation allowed Hardy access to The Residents, Randy was very quick to drag the film-maker into an interesting side project, which began as *In My Room* and then expanded into the broader *Randyland* concept, a series of short films wherein Randy talked about whatever was on his mind. And Randy had a *lot* on his mind. "We talked it through," laughs Hardy, "about how much he thought he had to say, and that's where we landed at a hundred and forty three episodes!" These wonderful forays gave fans a unique insight not only into Randy's home, basement and attic, but also his experiences with alien abduction, his fictional home in Los Angeles, his aborted career as a porn star and his life-partner, Maurice the cat.

"Randy's job is to be a loose cannon," understates Flynn on the *Randyland* concept, which was posted regularly online before and after the crowd funding campaign. "You never know what is going to come out of him, and that makes it kind of interesting and gives a personality to play with. Randy is looking for new adventures now. I hear he is getting very interested and obsessed with Bigfoot, so that may play a part..." Well, Randy was indeed soon talking about Bigfoot and preparing to hunt Bigfoot. I wouldn't be surprised to find out in a few years time that Bigfoot is probably N. Senada!

The *Randyland* films showed just how much trust The Residents had in Hardy, and he greatly appreciated this fact, "They were hugely supportive. Every film that we make has to be a collaboration and a partnership really. I've done a few of them now and you never know how co-operative people will be. They say, "Yeah, yeah, yeah, we'll be there," but with the Cryptics they opened up the vaults for us. They really just welcomed us and believed we were going to treat the material in the right way, and we had that level of trust because they respected the way we jumped into it. It wasn't about signing a contract, sorting out the money and waiting to do it only when the financing was ready. It was "OK, let's go for it.""

Randy displayed the same attitude when *Randyland* was filmed, and each episode really was all about going for it. "So there's me there with a camera," states Hardy, "Randy is there, and sometimes we have a second or third camera. The fun is showing the strings and showing that it doesn't have to be a crew of ten people sitting around. You can just do it because it's a cool idea and hope people will dig it. Generally what happens is that we will shoot it in one day, or a couple of episodes in one day, and I will edit it the next day or two. That seems to impress people right away, that I'm doing the post-production myself. Trimming here, adding the music and titles and putting it out so quickly, which probably stems from my background in the news business, where you get it out quickly and don't think about making it perfect."

When it came to *The Theory Of Obscurity*, Hardy spent a lot of time editing and perfecting, and ended up with a fantastic documentary which laid out a path through the rich foliage of The Residents' history. Crucially, he simply told their story through interviews, archive photos and the richness of their own films. The completed film was first shown to many of the people who had been interviewed in the Bay area, and received a positive response. Homer Flynn was in the audience, "It is sort of a combination of exhilarating and exhausting," he recalls, "because when you see the documentary you certainly get the effect of forty years, and at some point it makes you feel, "OK, That's enough!" But at the same time to have it all condensed into an hour and a half is pretty thrilling. I think Don has done a great job of being able to condense it into that hour and a half."

Charles Bobuck saw the film at a special showing where he lived, and posted a reaction on his Facebook page. Although a lot of it was tongue in cheek, this comment summed up his feelings, "The people who didn't immediately run out when it was over seemed to have a warm glow about them. Even Roman. He asked if we could rent tuxedos and attend the Oscars next year. He pantomimed small-talking with George Clooney." One wonders if that small talk would occur with eyeballs on the heads of the tuxedos.

Of course, what those who had appeared in the film thought about it was incidental to the real purpose, which was to try to get as many people around the world to see it as possible. It's very hard for a documentary to get a general cinematic release, and most go straight to DVD or online, so Hardy had to work very hard on the festival circuit to get the film shown in an effort to attract a distributor. One of his holy grails was to get the film shown at the 2015 South By South West festival in Austin, Texas, and he lucked in.

"I was fortunate enough to speak to the head of the festival in September or October 2014," he says, "I said that I have this film about this avant-garde band from San Francisco called The Residents and her ears pricked up immediately, "I know The Residents! I lived in San Francisco in the late '70s and early '80s. Send me the film I would love to take a look at it." That was exciting. It was where we always wanted to go and we were so fortunate to be where there is a great showcase for independent film."

Better still, to make even a bigger splash The Residents agreed to play at SXSW to help promote the film. On Saturday 14th March the film was shown at the Violet Crown Cinema, and on 18th March at the Austin Convention Centre there was a panel discussion involving Homer Flynn and Don Hardy. In the meantime, The Residents reactivated the *Shadowlands* show, and after a warm-up date in Santa Cruz on 12th March the band flew out to Texas to play the Paramount Theatre on the night of 20th March.

The film showing generated a generous amount of media attention - from *Rolling Stone* labeling it a "must see" to extensive coverage online - which really created interest in both the film and the band. Everything bodes well for the documentary, and the attention has also steered traffic towards The Residents' website, which was something they were prepared for. "It (the website) has recently been revamped," Flynn told me, "With the film about to come out we are expecting a lot more traffic and the site was getting a little bit dated - it was set up for fans who already had long time knowledge of The Residents and involvement with them. Now those people can get to the parts that they want, but there is a more general interface at the front end for people who have heard about The Residents but don't know much about them and are looking for more general information."

Throughout 2015 the film was shown across America and Europe on the festival circuit, and there were even dedicated screenings as far away as Australia. It received a very positive reaction, as Carla Fabrizio pertly states, "It is a safe and friendly introduction to a potentially challenging enigma. I think The Residents leave more room for questions and interpretation than your average person is comfortable with. The film helps set that up nicely, and prepares viewers in case they want to delve in a little more deeply."

Whilst the SXSW show went well it was also a bittersweet moment for fans and The Residents themselves - Chuck had announced prior to the shows through his Facebook page that these two concerts would be his last appearances on stage. This was not due to whim or any showdown with Randy, but for age-related reasons (he was seventy years old). If SXSW was his last show, it was a poignant moment indeed.

"He's been doing it since 1981, 1982... way back" stated Randy when making the announcement from the stage, "I just wanna give him one more hug – hard and tenderly." And he did.

"It was very emotional," Flynn later told me, "a very sentimental, emotional moment. The audience responded to it. Randy made this announcement and went over and hugged Chuck. It was a very nice moment."

The retirement of Chuck was, in some respects, not unexpected. As Hein Fokker told me, "In the last few years, Chuck is not interested in playing live. Only with hard work can we convince him to stay on the scene. I dig that. For the last couple of tours there has always been problems with his health." Saying that, Chuck had no intention of closing his laptop, as he was quick to explain online, "Some people thought that I was going away entirely, but that is far from the case. I am merely realigning my priorities. I am far more interested in developing new projects, especially new musical projects. Despite the concept album format having lost favor, I am still enamored with the idea. I see no reason not to return to what I love to do. Touring will continue without me, but you probably won't notice much difference. I'm still writing arrangements and working on the production. And with masks, who can tell anyway."

Nolan Cook's sentiment probably summed up the feelings of many Residents fans, as well as those who might or might have not been behind those masks for all of those years, "We will certainly miss Charles on tour, but he has put in his time, circling the globe for decades, and he feels more comfortable in his home base doing what he truly loves - designing systems and creating music. And that is something that is not likely to change anytime soon."

But Homer Flynn imagines that, in the future, Chuck could return. "Personally, I have a hard time imagining that he will never appear again," he says, "Although he may limit it to extremely short tours or local shows in the San Francisco or Bay area. I expect he will show up again at some point. But for now he seems happy with his decision, and I know that he has been really conflicted over this for a long time. He will admit he was never all that comfortable as a performer. He is a studio guy, for him the most fun is putting the show together, and once he gets to the point of performing it and doing the same thing night after night, well it loses an amount of interest for him. The problem, though, is that he has always enjoyed the camaraderie, he has always enjoyed being with other people, and so that is where the conflict is. He seems to be dealing with it OK at this point."

Epilogue

For me, the fact that The Residents remained anonymous gave them an advantage over other bands, in that they were invisible and unknowable beneath their masks and disguises... Who even knows if it has always been the full array of Residents on stage?

Forward planning was always something that The Cryptic Corporation were past masters at, and one wonders whether they ever discussed succession planning or The Residents creating the world's first musical franchise?

"There has certainly been talk of putting The Residents out on a tour that does not include any of the originals at all, and by the same token that could apply to the recordings as well," Homer Flynn told me. "But at this point The Residents are too entrenched, and still too creative, to be looking for people to take their place. So it is all charging ahead."

Indeed, even without Chuck, The Residents charged ahead in the summer of 2015 with a shows in Poland, South America and Paris, with Rico (aka Eric Drew Feldman) taking the place of Chuck onstage, although Chuck had laid down and arranged the music for the performances. So now, on stage at least, it's Randy, Rico and Bob!

This new live line-up certainly did not dampen the enthusiasm of fans who attended these concerts, or quell the online speculation as to how Rico would fit into the Residents' mythology.

As for the future, despite Randy and Chuck being in their seventies, there is certainly no lack of creativity. With more music in the works, the real possibility of *God In Three Persons* hitting the stage and a number of other collaborations bearing fruit, The Residents continue to engagement with fans old and new, either in concert or through their website and social media. *The Theory Of Obscurity* documentary will continue to attract attention and new fans, and the curious across the world will have the opportunity to immerse themselves in something that very few bands have ever created; an alternative reality full of myths, legends and interactive experiences, all powered by a truly magical soundtrack that began with *Santa Dog* in 1972 and continues with music that is still being composed, created and released today.

The Author Recommends

Earlier editions of this book contained what were, for their time, comprehensive discographies of all Residents and Residents-related releases. However, in the two decades since then the internet has spawned countless sites that not only offer a comprehensive and up to date listing of Residents releases but can be updated and nuanced twenty-four hours a day.

Therefore, in this edition I have decided not to offer a discography. Not only would its length run to twenty or more pages, but it would become quickly redundant. Instead, I think it more instructive to serve up a list of releases that, in my opinion, somebody new to The Residents should explore.

This takes two forms – firstly, a list of fifteen essential albums (which does not include compilations or live releases) and then a proposed, mythical twenty track compilation of songs which, in my opinion, best reflect the diverse sonic output of The Residents since 1972.

ESSENTIAL ALBUMS:

Meet The Residents	1974
The Third Reich And Roll	1976
Fingerprince	1977
Not Available	1978
Duck Stab/Buster And Glen	1978
Eskimo	1979
The Mark Of The Mole	1981
God In Three Persons	1988
Freak Show	1990
Gingerbread Man	1994
Wormwood	1998
Demons Dance Alone	2002
Animal Lover	2005
The River Of Crime	2006
Lonely Teenager	2011

PLAYLIST:

A kind of *ITunes* hit-list for the curious, which gives a flavor of this particular eyeball brand of musical chewing gum. Please note that *Not Available, Third Reich And Roll* and *Eskimo* are not represented - those albums MUST be played in their entirety to achieved the desired effect. The same also applies to the seminal *Six Things To A Cycle*, which is one of life's best ways to spend a quarter of an hour.

Please also note that this list isn't chronological, and does not represent my personal top twenty, but is intended for educational purposes for the curious. I look forward to seeing hardcore fans' own entry-level compilations flamed in my direction on Facebook. Bring it on!

Track:	*Source:*
Hunters Prelude	Hunters TV series soundtrack
Mr. Wonderful	Demons Dance Alone
Moisture	The Commercial Album
The Lonely Lotus	The Ughs!
Rest Aria	Meet The Residents
I Hate Heaven	Single
From The Plains To Mexico	Cube-E live in Holland
Tourniquet Of Roses	Fingerprince
Broccoli And Saxophone	Whatever Happened To Vileness Fats
The Sold-Out Artist	Gingerbread Man
What Have My Chicken's Done Now	Animal Lover
Constantinople	Duck Stab EP
March De La Winnie	Fingerprince
Serenade For Missy	The Tunes Of Two Cities
Make Me Moo	Demons Dance Alone
Skratz	Meet The Residents
Boxes Of Armageddon	Lonely Teenager
Almost Perfect	Tweedles
Whoopy Snorp	Blorp Essette
Fire	Santa Dog single

A Plugged In State Of Mind: The History of Electronic Music
Dave Henderson

All The Young Dudes: Mott The Hoople & Ian Hunter
Campbell Devine

Arguments Yard – 35 Years Of Ranting Verse And Thrash Mandola
Atilla The Stockbroker

Best Seat In The House: A Cock Sparrer Story
Steve Bruce

Bittersweet: The Clifford T Ward Story
David Cartwright

Block Buster! – The True Story of The Sweet
Dave Thompson

Burning Britain: A History Of UK Punk 1980 To 1984
Ian Glasper

Celebration Day: A Led Zeppelin Encyclopedia
Malcolm Dome and Jerry Ewing

Children of the Revolution: The Glam Rock Encyclopedia
Dave Thompson

Death To Trad Rock: The Post-Punk fanzine scene 1982-87
John Robb

Deathrow: The Chronicles Of Psychobilly
Alan Wilson

Embryo:- A Pink Floyd Chronology 1966-1971
Nick Hodges And Ian Priston

Fucked By Rock (Revised and Expanded)
Mark Manning (aka Zodiac Mindwarp)

Goodnight Jim Bob: On The Road With Carter USM
Jim Bob

Good Times Bad Times - The Rolling Stones 1960-69
Terry Rawlings and Keith Badman

Hells Bent On Rockin: A History Of Psychobilly
Craig Brackenbridge

Independence Days - The Story Of UK Independent Record Labels
Alex Ogg

Indie Hits 1980 – 1989
Barry Lazell

Irish Folk, Trad And Blues: A Secret History
Colin Harper and Trevor Hodgett

Johnny Thunders: In Cold Blood
Nina Antonia

Please visit **www.cherryredbooks.co.uk** for further info and mail order

Here at Cherry Red Books we're always interested to hear of interesting titles looking for a publisher. Whether it's a new manuscript or an out of print or deleted title, please feel free to get in touch if you have something you think we should know about.

books@cherryred.co.uk

www.cherryredbooks.co.uk
www.cherryred.co.uk

CHERRY RED BOOKS
A division of Cherry Red Records Ltd,
Power Road Studios
114 Power Road
London
W4 5PY